LITHUANIA

Westview Series on the Post-Soviet Republics

Alexander J. Motyl, Series Editor

Lithuania: The Rebel Nation, V. Stanley Vardys and Judith B. Sedaitis

Belarus: At a Crossroads in History, Jan Zaprudnik

Estonia: Return to Independence, Rein Taagepera

FORTHCOMING

Central Asian States: Discovering Independence, Gregory Gleason

Latvia: Independence Renewed, Janis J. Penikis

Siberia: Worlds Apart, Victor L. Mote

The Transcaucasian Borderland Republics: Armenia, Azerbaijan, and Georgia, Henry Huttenbach

Published in cooperation with
The Harriman Institute, Columbia University

LITHUANIA

The Rebel Nation

V. STANLEY VARDYS
AND JUDITH B. SEDAITIS

WestviewPress

A Division of HarperCollinsPublishers

To Mrs. V. Stanley (Anna) Vardys, for her unending support,
and Geri Rowden, for her editorial assistance and
unending patience. To Professor Vytautas Kavolis (1930–1996),
whose gentle spirit and critical scholarship inspired
all who knew him.

Westview Series on the Post-Soviet Republics

Published in 1997 in the United States of America by Westview Press, 5500 Central Avenue,
Boulder, Colorado 80301-2877, and in the United Kingdom by Westview Press, 12 Hid's
Copse Road, Cumnor Hill, Oxford OX2 9JJ

Library of Congress Cataloging-in-Publication Data
Vardys, Vytas Stanley, 1924–
    Lithuania : the rebel nation / V. Stanley Vardys and Judith
Sedaitis.
        p. cm.—(Westview series on post-Soviet republics)
    Includes bibliographical references and index.
    ISBN 0-8133-8308-0 (hc).—ISBN 0-8133-1839-4 (pbk.)
    1. Lithuania—History. I. Sedaitis, Judith B. II. Title.
III. Series: Westview series on the post-Soviet republics.
DK505.54.V37 1997
947'.5—dc20
                                                                96-42556
                                                                CIP

The paper used in this publication meets the requirements of the American National Standard for Permanence of Paper for Printed Library Materials Z39.48-1984.

10   9   8   7   6   5   4   3   2   1

▪ Contents ▪

· Tables and Illustrations ·

Maps

· Preface ·

Professor Vardys and I were fortunate to have access to the early publications and documents of the Lithuanian Movement for Perestroika—the independence movement known as Sąjūdis—and documents, some still in mimeographed form, of the Lithuanian government and parliament. Lithuanian press and periodicals of the period were also of help, not to speak of diverse Western sources. As a visiting scholar at the Hoover Institution on War, Revolution and Peace at Stanford in 1990, Professor Vardys gained valuable data on the period from some diplomatic archives deposited at Hoover. A research fellowship at the Kennan Institute for Advanced Russian Studies in Washington, D.C., gave him an opportunity to study documents at the National Archives that yielded important data and deepened his understanding of Nazi policies and Lithuanian responses during the Nazi occupation, 1941–1944. Finally, we greatly profited from Professor Vardys's interviews and conversations with Lithuanian political and government leaders, parliament members, academics, churchmen, artists, and people in small towns and villages throughout Lithuania during a trip to the Baltic states in June and July 1991.

After Professor Vardys's untimely death, I was able to complete the manuscript during my tenure as a research associate at the Center for International Security and Arms Control at Stanford University. I am grateful for the time and support received there and at the Harriman Institute at Columbia University, where Professors Alexander Motyl and Mark von Hagen were especially attuned to the important role the "national minorities" would ultimately play in shaping the fate of the Soviet empire.

Most of all, this book stands as a monument to the fine scholarship of V. Stanley (Stasys) Vardys and of the great love he bore for his native land, Lithuania.

Judith Sedaitis

The post-Soviet republics

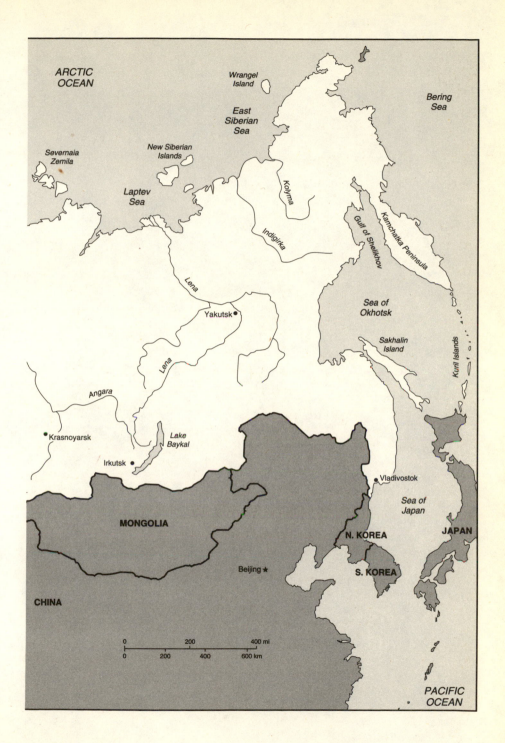

ARCTIC
OCEAN

Wrangel
Island

East
Siberian
Sea

Bering
Sea

Severnaia
Zemila

New Siberian
Islands

Kolyma

Laptev
Sea

Indigirka

Gulf of Shelikhov

Kamchatka Peninsula

Lena

Sea of
Okhotsk

Yakutsk

Lena

Kuril Islands

Sakhalin
Island

Angara

Krasnoyarsk

Lake
Baykal

Irkutsk

Vladivostok

Sea of
Japan

MONGOLIA

N. KOREA

JAPAN

Beijing ★

S. KOREA

CHINA

| 0 | 200 | 400 mi |
| 0 | 200 | 400 | 600 km |

PACIFIC
OCEAN

ONE

At the European Crossroads: Lithuania's Historical Roots

Lithuania is the largest of the three Baltic states and, like Latvia and Estonia, it has been strongly influenced by geography. Geopolitically, Lithuania's position is not enviable (see Map 1.1). As an extension of the Eastern European plain, Lithuania lies at the southern Baltic crossroads between Western Europe and Russia, which in the past has been trampled upon by European and Russian conquerors. The German Teutonic Knights of the Middle Ages, the Swedes and Russians of the seventeenth and eighteenth centuries, the French in 1812, and the Germans twice in the twentieth century, in 1915–1918 and again in 1941–1944, devastated Lithuania's infrastructure and inhibited its economic and cultural development. Lithuania's own armed insurrections against the Russian occupant in 1831, 1863, 1941, and 1944–1953 added to the devastation and instability of its realm. The Russians were the final conquerors. After signing a Treaty of Amity and Commerce with the British in 1766, Tsarina Catherine II allied herself with Prussia and Austria to devour Poland. Lithuania was reduced to the state of a "northwestern" province in the Russian empire." The Tsars ruled Lithuania until 1915. After a brief interlude of Lithuanian independence, the country was reoccupied by Russia, this time under the Soviet banner, and held captive until 1991.

Czeslaw Milosz, the Nobel laureate of Lithuanian-Polish descent, quite artfully characterized the tenacious Lithuanian people by emphasizing the history of their ancient language and religion. Lithuanian culture is rife with pagan images and lore rooted in an animistic religion that these forest dwellers were loath to relinquish. The Lithuanian nation adopted Christianity only in 1385, becoming the last Western state to do so after more than a century of often fierce battle against Rome and the Teutonic Knights, a German militaristic and religious order. Similarly, the Lithuanian language is also the least changed among modern, spoken languages and is often studied by linguists as a template for the original

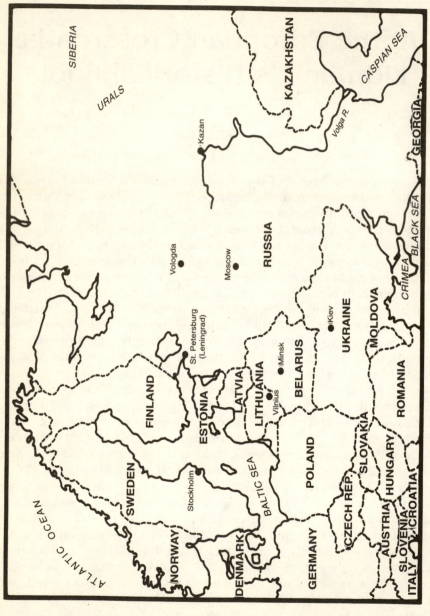

MAP 1.1 Lithuania's geopolitical location, 1990s

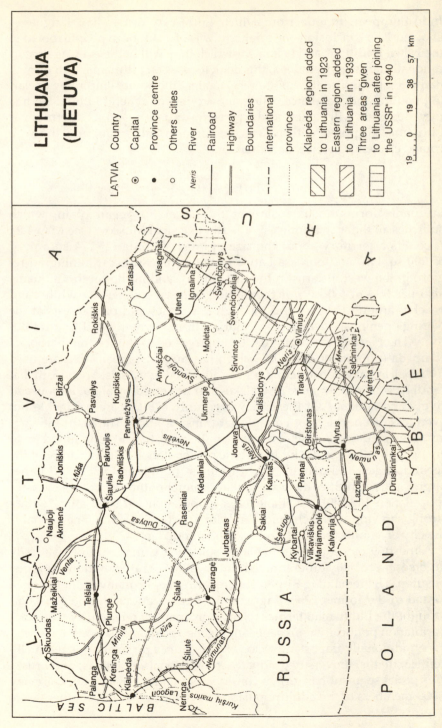

MAP 1.2 Lithuania

Indo-European tongue from which European and Indian languages evolved. The conclusion one might draw is of a stubborn people rooted in their own traditions and beliefs for which they will battle even against irrationally large odds. Indeed, this book focuses on Lithuania as that small nation that was also the first to rebel against the Soviet empire by declaring political independence. After an overview of general Lithuanian history, this book will center on the perestroika period and its aftermath as Lithuania grappled with reform, national mobilization, and the welcomed challenges of new state building.

THE LAND

Lithuania forms an extension of the Great European plain, which stretches all the way from west of Berlin to east of Moscow (see Map 1.2). It covers a territory about the size of West Virginia (25,174 sq. mi. or 65,200 sq. km) and borders Latvia in the north, Russia (Kaliningrad region) in the west, Belarus in the east, and Poland in the south. Lithuania also has 99 km (60 mi.) of the Baltic Sea coast covered by white sand beaches around Palanga and the high rise dunes and pine forests at the Neringa peninsula, which draw tourists from Germany and Central Europe. The Neringa strip guards the approaches to the ice-free harbor of Klaipėda (population 206,000), which has huge dry docks that are used for repairing and constructing oceangoing fishing vessels. The mostly flat republic is dotted by some 2,900 lakes and traversed by about a thousand rivers and streams. Of these, however, only 628 km are navigable but even less can be used for commercial transportation. The main Lithuanian river, Nemunas, which originates in Belarus, has been dammed up to create a huge lake and a hydroelectric power station in the vicinity of the second largest Lithuanian city of Kaunas (population 435,000).[1] Other large Lithuanian cities include Šiauliai, a center of the electronics industry (population 149,000), and Panevėžys (population 132,000), a city with a strong showing in the chemical and auto parts industries. The capital is the city of Vilnius (population 600,000), founded in 1323.

Almost 69 percent of Lithuania's population is made up of politically diverse and socially differentiated city dwellers of rather nationalistic disposition. The remaining 31 percent are farm people, many of them accustomed to the former Soviet agricultural organizations that in the 1970s brought the Lithuanian farmer relative prosperity and security. The rural population politically represents homogeneous and conservative views.

A traditionally important sector of Lithuania's population is its intelligentsia, that is, university graduates, professionals, scientists, and artists. This social segment has grown considerably under Soviet rule. For every 1,000 members of the adult population over the age of fifteen, there were

108 university graduates in Lithuania in 1989, as compared to 115 for Latvia and 117 for Estonia.[2] In social origins and attitudes, this group differs considerably from their predecessors of the independence period. In 1918–1940 Lithuania's intellectuals represented the first generation of university graduates to leave the family farm and as such were shaped by religious and traditional views. In contrast, the postwar intelligentsia is more urban and shaped by Soviet-style secularization and modernization.

Lithuania's agricultural land for the most part is very fertile and is suited for diverse crops as well as for various forms of farming, such as dairy, cattle, or animal husbandry. Lithuania's natural resources, however, are rather modest. The republic has limestone, clay, quartz sand, gypsum, sand, dolomite, chalk, mineral water, and iron ore. Limestone, clays, and sands are very suitable for making good quality cement, which Lithuania does, for construction materials, glass, and ceramics. Oil, first discovered in Lithuania in the 1950s, promises supplies of 15–20 percent of the country's annual needs for some twenty years, though recent optimistic estimates of probable oil finds under the Baltic Sea shelf may augment this expectation. Western Lithuania has thermal energy resources that, if exploited, can help with home heating for some hundreds of thousands of people. In the past, Lithuania was covered by thick and vast forests. These have been severely cut by various invaders, primarily Russians and Germans, and forest land has been reduced to 28 percent of the territory. The country's well-developed furniture and paper industries have to import wood from Siberia and Karelia.

THE PEOPLE

The Lithuanian people are not Slavs but belong to the Baltic family of nations. Their forebears moved to the Baltic area in approximately 2000 B.C.,[3] possibly from the Eurasian steppes. Confronting the sea, they had no means of crossing it to Scandinavia but spread along the Baltic coast and on the East European plain, all the way from the Mazurian lakes in the south to the boundaries of today's Estonia in the north. The Balts, or Aestii, as Roman historian Tacitus referred to them when they traded in amber with ancient Rome, once inhabited much of Pomerania and parts of Belarus and Russia, but the demographic as well as political pressures of the Germans and Slavs continuously pushed them to the Baltic littoral. Only the Lithuanians and the Latvians entered modern history. The other Baltic peoples, the Jotvings and Prussians, were conquered by Teutonic Knights in the eleventh and twelfth centuries and were absorbed, destroyed, or assimilated by the Germans. The Couronians, Semigallians, and others were assimilated either by the Lithuanians, the Latvians, or the Slavic peoples of Belarus and Poland. This history has led to modern territorial claims and counterclaims between the Lithuanians and the Germans, Poles, and Byelorussians. A note of nostalgia for the city of Vilnius can still be detected in the voices of some current Polish and Byelorussian intellectuals and politicians.[4] The Baltic-speaking Lithuanians and Latvians today occupy only one-sixth of the territory their linguistic forebears did before the Slavic and Germanic expansion during the second millennium.

Lithuania is the larger of the two surviving nations. In 1989, 3,067,390 Lithuanians lived in the Soviet Union; of these, about 100,000 lived outside of Lithuania in the Kaliningrad region, Latvia, Russia, Belarus, Ukraine, Uzbekistan, Azerbaijan, and the former deportation region of the Komi republic.[5] Some 30,000–40,000 Lithuanians are compactly clustered in the Suwalki-Sejny (Suvalkai-Seinai in Lithuanian) district of Poland. About two-thirds of a million people of ethnic Lithuanian ancestry are found in Western countries, mostly in the United States and Canada, but also in Latin America, Australia, and Western Europe.

Lithuanians speak an ancient tongue related to Sanskrit and often required in academic study of linguistics in universities around the world as the closest living example of the Eurasian proto-language. The languages of Lithuania and Latvia separated over 1,000 years ago and, though still very similar, are not as close as are the Estonian and Finnish tongues.

The Lithuanians were also the last nation in Europe to convert to Christianity. Before 1387, Lithuanians were pagans. Their religion could be characterized as belief in spiritualized, animized natural phenomena and in reincarnation.[6] They venerated holy groves, water, fire, trees, and fields and used animal sacrifices. Belief in the life-sustaining spirituality of nature carried over into Christian times as pagan practices and animistic images were incorporated into Christian ritual.

The growth of the ethnic Lithuanian population has historically been slow. At the height of Lithuanian power, when the medieval empire was ruled by Grand Duke Vytautas (approximately 1350–1430), the estimated population of ethnic Lithuanians was about 590,000.[7] Three hundred and fifty years later, at the time Lithuania was taken over by Catherine II of Russia, this number had increased by less than a million, to 1,540,000. It reached 2 million in 1923, soon after Lithuania had embarked on its short-lived era of independence, and 3 million seventy years later. Although the population growth of Lithuania has been greater than that of Western Europe, Latvia, or Estonia, it has been considerably slower than that of the Slavic neighbors—Byelorussians, Russians, and especially the Poles.

Once a large state—at the end of the fourteenth century it stretched from the Baltic to the Black Sea—it was reduced to a territory of 65,200 sq. km after World War II. Although the vastness of the medieval empire is still a source of nostalgic pride for Lithuanian nationalists of modern times, the region was never inhabited by a majority of Lithuanians. In comparison to the Slavic groups, which made up the largest part of the empire, the ethnic Lithuanian group was small. Nevertheless, it produced the rulers of the realm, who wisely co-opted Slavic natives to the ruling class and perhaps not so wisely themselves assimilated with their subjects.

Just before Lithuania declared independence in 1990, ethnic Lithuanians constituted 79.6 percent of the republic's population of 3,761,400 (see Table 1.1).[8] Russians are now Lithuania's largest ethnic minority. In 1989 they constituted 9.4 percent of the population. The Poles constituted 7 percent; Byelorussians 1.7 percent; Ukrainians 1.2 percent; Jews 0.3 percent; Latvians, Tartars, Gypsies, Germans, and Estonians 0.1 percent each; and there were even a few ancient Karaites left.

About two-thirds of the Russian minority had migrated to Lithuania or were descendants of immigrants under Soviet rule. A smaller percentage had escaped to Lithuania in the nineteenth century in search of religious freedom. Some had fled the Communist revolution of 1917. While the percentage of Russians grew, that of the Poles declined. A portion of the Poles are descendants of inhabitants in the Grand Duchy of Lithuania, others are heirs to immigrants from Poland between the two world wars when the city and province of Vilnius were ruled by Warsaw, and still another group represents assimilated Lithuanians. The majority of the Byelorussians are descendants of old residents, though some are assimilated Lithuanians or immigrants of the Soviet period.

BIRTH OF A NATION

The Pagan State

The Lithuanians appear as a nation in the pages of historical writings when the Grand Duke Mindaugas integrated the Lithuanian tribes into a single state around 1230.[9] Until then, the attention of the Lithuanian ruling families was not concentrated on unification of linguistically related groups but on expansion into Slavic territories south and east of Lithuania.

The pagan Lithuanian state, ethnically composed of minority Lithuanians and a majority of Russians as well as Byelorussians, put pagans, Russian Orthodox Christians, Moslems, and a sprinkling of Latin Catholics and Jews into close proximity. It was known for its unusual, for the times, religious tolerance and for the adaptability of power to local conditions. As was typical for medieval states in that region, the language used in official documents and affairs of state was different from the one that prevailed as the local spoken language. The former, from the end of the fourteenth century on, was old church Slavonic, also known as Byelorussian.[10]

TABLE 1.1   Statistical Profile of Lithuania's Population, 1990–1992

Demographic Characteristics (1992)
Total	3,761,000
Urban[a]	68.8
Rural (percent)	31.2
Men (percent)	47.0
Women (percent)	53.0
Young people (0–15) (percent)	23.9
Working adults (percent)	56.6
Pensioners (65–) (percent)	19.5
Birthrate (1991)	15.0
Net population increase	4.1
Child mortality under one year (per 1,000 births)	14.3
Marriages (per 1,000 population)	9.5
Divorce (per 1,000 population)	4.1
Average size family (1989)	3.2

Employment Characteristics (1992)
Total	1,860,000
Industry (percent)	30.0
Agriculture and forestry (percent)	18.9
Construction (percent)	11.3
Education, culture, and art (percent)	10.0
Health, social care (percent)	5.9
Other fields (percent)	23.9
Unemployed (thousands) (1991 figures)[b]	9.6

Quality of Life (1990–1991)
Average life expectancy	71.3
Men 66.3	
Women 76.1	
Child mortality under one year (per 1,000 births)	14.3
University students (per 10,000 population)	124.0
Doctors (per 10,000 population)	46.0
Paramedical personnel (per 10,000 population)	127.0
Hospital beds (per 10,000 population)	124.0
Telephones in apartments (per 100 population)	16.7
Circulation of newspapers (copies per 1,000 population)	1,547.0
Radio sets (per 100 families)	107.0
TV sets (per 100 families)	115.0
Refrigerators (per 100 families)	91.0
Washing machines (per 100 families)	77.0
Private cars (per 100 families)	36.0

[a] Percentage
[b] Unemployment has been steadily and severely increasing since 1991.
SOURCE: Compiled from data published by Lithuania's Bureau of Statistics and the Government Committee on Statistics of the USSR.

Lithuanian King Mindaugas, who reigned in the thirteenth century. (Sculptor: V. Košuba. Courtesy of *Lietuvos Istorija*.)

Encroaching Western Europeans seeking to Christianize and rule the pagan population hastened unification. Western merchants and missionaries first landed in Livland (Livonia in Latin, today's Latvia) during the twelfth century and quickly conquered the Livs and the other Finno-Ugrian tribes. Latvia's Christianization began in 1186 from Ikšķilė (Üxküll) by Bishop Meinhard. The city of Riga was founded in 1201 by another bishop, Albert, and the next year the Order of the Brothers of the Sword was established militarily to protect missionary activities. The order's expansion into Lithuania was thwarted, however, with its serious defeat by Lithuanian princes in the battle of Saule in 1236.

The disintegrating order was rescued by another German military-missionary organization, the Knights of the Cross, which had invaded Prussian territory to aid Konrad, the Polish prince of Mazovia, in his effort to Christianize the pagan Prussians and expand his rule into their lands. The Knights secured permission from Emperor Frederick II von Hohenstaufen to conquer not only Semigallia—a part of Latvia—but also Curlandia and

Lithuania. After the Prussians murdered a missionary bishop, the Knights, with the consent of Pope Gregory IX, established a secular state in the conquered territory. In 1237, they absorbed their compatriots in Livonia. After subduing the resistant Prussians, they colonized the conquered areas with Western settlers—Germans, Saxons, and others—in order to bridge the territorial gap between the Prussian possessions and Livonia. To completely unite their dominions, they had to acquire Samogitia, a western Lithuanian province inhabited by a fiercely independent Lithuanian tribe. The Knights of the Cross succeeded in wresting away a strip of Baltic littoral to connect Prussia and Curlandia and in 1251 founded the city of Memel (today's Klaipėda), but they could not conquer Samogitia. Every time Lithuanian rulers would award the province to the Knights in exchange for peace, the Samogitians would revolt. A long military conflict between Lithuania and the Knights followed that lasted almost two hundred years.

Grand Duke Mindaugas attempted to reduce the danger of the order to Lithuania by becoming a Christian with the help of the Bishop of Riga in Livonia. In 1250 or 1251, Mindaugas was baptized with his family, relatives, and many nobles by Father Christian, a priest of the Livonian order, who shortly afterward was appointed first bishop of an independent Lithuanian diocese. In 1253, Mindaugas was also crowned king of Lithuania, the first and only in Lithuanian history.[11] However, Mindaugas's attempt to accommodate the Western world was scorned by his princes. Confronted with domestic difficulties and disappointed in small gains from the westerners, he dropped the unsuccessful idea after building a Christian cathedral in Vilnius. Modern excavations in Vilnius show remnants of a pagan temple on top of those of Mindaugas's Christian cathedral. In 1263 Mindaugas was assassinated by his nobles and the country openly reverted to paganism. Lithuania's foreign policy was redirected from pursuing ties with the West to expansionism and collaboration with the Orthodox Christian Slavs in the East.

However, the country now faced a serious threat from the Knights of the Cross. A large investment of resources and energy was required to defend against them. The Knights were capable of recruiting dedicated monastic soldiers in Western Europe for the glorious objective of converting the last pagan nation in Europe. They also were able to secure supplies and technology, and they attracted colonists to Prussia. They presented an enormous challenge to the Lithuanians.

A string of talented Lithuanian rulers emerged after the seven-year succession struggle following Mindaugas's death. They responded to the threat with a dual policy. First, they expanded to Russian lands and drew strength from them for defense purposes, and second, they attempted to diplomatically split and neutralize the forces of the order in the Baltic region. Grand Duke Vytenis (?–1315?) forged an alliance with the Bishop of Riga to forestall battle with the Prussian order. Grand Duke Gediminas (c. 1275–1341), the most distinguished ruler of that century, manipulated the politics of Christianization and sought to attract to Lithuania Western merchants, artisans, and men of letters. It was in response to this invitation to resettle that the historical Jewish community in Vilnius began to first establish itself. By the end of the fourteenth century, a large community emerged in response to royal Lithuanian charters that granted Jews important business, housing, and religious rights unusual in Europe at that time. By then, a two-pronged strategy of rule had emerged. This plan focused on defense against the Knights, on the one hand, and expansion and alliances with the East, on the other. Two pagan brothers, Kęstutis (c. 1300–1382) and Algirdas (c. 1296–1377), ably bore these burdens, Algirdas carrying the banners of state to the gates of Moscow. Lithuania by that time was larger than the Muscovy principalities and rivaled them for the leadership of Russian lands.

Algirdas died in 1377. His son Jogaila (Jagiello in Polish, c. 1351–1434) had different ideas about Lithuania's relations with the German order, the expansion to Russia, and the Christianization of Lithuania. Jogaila's brothers, in addition, did not want to bow to him as successor to Algirdas and joined with Moscow's ruler, Dimitri Donskoi, against Jogaila in Russian principalities that they governed. To relieve pressures confronting him in Russia, Jogaila sought to pacify the Teutonic order. At first he concluded an armistice, to which his Uncle Kęstutis agreed. In 1380, however, he signed a secret treaty with the German order that was directed against Kęstutis. Historians speculate whether Jogaila's objective was the takeover of land that his mother Julia coveted for her numerous sons or an opening to the West. It probably was both.

Kęstutis liked neither the shift of policy nor the direct personal challenge. He removed Jogaila from Vilnius and banished him to rule Vitebsk as his father Algirdas had done when he was young. Kęstutis himself became Grand Duke (1381–1382). However, he could not continue to defend effectively against the Teutonic Knights. Nor could he protect himself against Jogaila's manipulations in the eastern provinces.

Algirdas's successors were divided not only on their policy toward the West but also on the question of relations with Moscow. Dimitri Donskoi became the leader in the struggle against the Mongols. To contain Dimitri's influence on lands ruled by Lithuania, Jogaila sealed a pact with the Mongol Khan Mamay. However, some of Jogaila's brothers opposed this alliance. Moscow's conflict with the Mongols came to a head at the historical battle of Kulikovo in 1380, in which two of Jogaila's brothers, Andrei and Dimitri, fought on Moscow's side. For an unknown reason Jogaila and his men, who were to help Mamay, arrived too late. Dimitri Donskoi won the battle that liberated Russian principalities from Mongol domination. His victory was a crushing defeat not only for the Mongols but also for the Lithuanian authority in Russia.

Christianity and Union with Poland

Jogaila was able to regain supremacy in Vilnius when his uncle Kęstutis was killed while under arrest. Kęstutis's son (Jogaila's cousin), Vytautas, fled to the German order. Thus the Teutonic Knights won the alliance of an important player in the domestic affairs of Lithuania.

Jogaila's mother, Julia, a Russian Orthodox princess, tried to save Jogaila's position through a treaty with Dimitri Donskoi pledging that Jogaila would marry Dimitri's daughter Sophia and accept Orthodox Christianity. A choice had to be made. Jogaila and Lithuania were at a crossroads. Returning to power in 1382, Jogaila knew not only that Lithuania's position was badly weakened in the east but also that the Teutonic order had greatly enhanced its hold over Lithuania in the west. With whom should he ally?

It appears that although appropriate documents were drawn, neither Jogaila nor Dimitri were much interested in Julia's plan. An attractive alternative opened when the nobles of Poland offered Jogaila the crown of Christian Poland. The Poles hoped in this way to gain additional strength against the common Teutonic enemy and also to prevent Austria's Wilhelm von Habsburg from becoming king of Poland through a marriage to Jadwiga, the twelve-year-old daughter of Louis d'Anjou who had recently been crowned queen of Poland.

In 1385 Jogaila accepted the Polish offer. For the crown, however, he paid a price possibly higher than he would have paid to Moscow had he agreed to his mother's plan, and certainly a much higher price than acceptance of Christianity had cost Mindaugas a century and a half earlier. At the castle of Kriavo, where just three years earlier Jogaila's uncle Kęstutis had perished under mysterious circumstances, Jogaila and the Poles signed a document requiring Jogaila, in addition to becoming a Latin Christian and Christianizing Lithuania, to "adjoin" Lithuania eternally to Poland. Jogaila also had to pledge to regain for Poland all lands the Poles had lost in recent years. The vague provision of *"terras suas Litvaniae et Russiae coronae regni Poloniae perpetuo applicare"*[12] let future Polish leaders make claims that the Lithuanian state would regret.

Following the agreement, in 1386 Jogaila became a Christian. In 1387, he began the Christianization of Lithuania. As in the affairs of the state, so in church administration, Jogaila's Lithuanians fared worse than those of Mindaugas generations before. Lithuania did not become an independent church province under Rome as usually was the case with Christianizing nations but was subjected to the jurisdiction of the Polish church province of Gniezno. Church organization thus was polonized from the very beginning. Jogaila's cousin Vytautas made peace with the new Polish king and eventually gained the title of Grand Duke of Lithuania under him. Twenty-five years later, in 1412, he introduced the new faith in Samogitia.

Lithuania's late Christianization in Latin rite under a dynastic union with Poland became an intellectual and historical issue fiercely debated by the Lithuanian intelligentsia to justify ideological divisions and even partisan commitments in Lithuanian society. Anti-Catholic and Socialist partisans blamed Lithuania's Christianization under Jogaila for Lithuania's national decline. Juozas Jurginis, the dean of Soviet Lithuanian historians, wrote,

> The Catholic church ruined the state founded by the Lithuanians and renown [ed] in Europe for its resistance to aggression [by the Teutonic Knights] as well as for its political system and culture by pushing the expansion to the East which was sponsored by feudal lords of Western Europe and of Poland and also by confronting the Eastern rite church. Lithuania's Catholic feudal lords who supported this expansion became polonized. From then on the Lithuanian nation was represented by peasants who formed the foundation for bourgeois ideology by resisting social oppression.[13]

An opposite view held that it was Lithuania's tardiness in accepting Latin Christianity that was responsible for the nation's cultural lag, political decline, and subsequent polonization. According to Zenonas Ivinskis, a prominent scholar of Lithuanian history, the failure of the first attempt to Christianize under Mindaugas was to blame for this condition. Had Mindaugas been successful, "the fruits of Christian culture of the West would have reached Lithuania much sooner. This would have better saved and protected the national Lithuanian culture."[14]

Jogaila's Polish crown nevertheless brought for Lithuania some diplomatic and territorial if not strategic gains. The two cousins, Jogaila and Vytautas, militarily crushed the Teutonic Knights at the battle of Tannenberg (Grunwald, Žalgiris) in 1410. After more fighting, this time by Jogaila alone, Poland gained control of some of the Germanic territory and absorbed the surviving missionary order. The littoral strip of the Baltic with the city of Memel remained German.

Grand Duke Vytautas, a rival of Jogaila's in Lithuania's stormy succession struggles of the 1380s, continued to press for his supremacy in Lithuania and for Lithuania's diplomatic emancipation from a dynastic union with Poland. Emperor Sigismund of Luxemburg agreed to support him and sent a crown, but his effort was stopped by Poland. The coronation of Vytautas as king of Lithuania was opposed by Polish noblemen

The Grand Duke Vytautas. (Portrait by J. Mateika.
Courtesy of *Lietuvos Istorija*.)

and by the Catholic Church hierarchy. The Poles persuaded Pope Martin
V that a crown for Lithuania would weaken the Catholic Church in rela-
tion to the Russian Orthodox Church. The Pope forbade Vytautas to seek
the crown, but the Grand Duke persisted. He died, however, only days
before a rescheduled coronation on October 30, 1430. The Polish argument used against Vytautas's independence became a political principle
insisted upon by Poland as well as by the Roman curia: Poland spoke for
Lithuania. The view sank so deeply into the consciousness of Polish and
Lithuanian elites that even at the end of the nineteenth century Samogit-
ian Bishop Mečislovas Paliulionis opposed Lithuanian national awakening on grounds that support for a separate Lithuanian entity would
weaken the Catholic faith as well as the struggle against "Moskal" (a
derogatory word for the Russians) and the Orthodoxy.[15]

Native Culture and Religion

Jogaila's agreements at Kriavo did not abolish the Lithuanian state but merely established a dynastic union with Poland. The Lithuanian administrative system, the code of law known as "Lithuanian statute," functioned separately, and the Grand Duke was also elected separately each time there was a succession to the Polish crown. However, Polish nobles wanted additional rights in Lithuania and pushed for the abolition of the confederation. This happened in 1569, at the meeting in Lublin under the last Jagellonian sovereign Zygmunt II August (Sigismundus Secundus) against the strong and emotional protestation of the nobles of Lithuania. Henceforth, the king's final edict said, the kingdom of Poland and the Grand Duchy of Lithuania would become one indivisible homogeneous body united into a single nation and a single state. The Polish model of government dominated by local diets of landed nobility replaced Lithuanian law and administration. Local traditions and linguistic peculiarities, however, refused to die.

Local self-government and native culture received a strong boost from a new force from Western Europe: the Reformation. The Protestant sweep from Western Europe in the sixteenth century coincided with the domestic Polish-Lithuanian struggles that culminated in the signing of the Lublin Union. Waves of religious reform zeal spilled over into Lithuania. In the first wave, the Reformation came as Lutheranism, in the second as Calvinism, supported by families of major noblemen, such as the Radvilas (Radziwiłł). Lutheranism had the greater impact on the beginnings of Lithuanian cultural development. Lutheran advantage lay in the help from the newly formed state of Prussia. In 1525, the last grand master of the Teutonic order, Albrecht of Hohenzollern, accepted Lutheranism and converted Prussia into a secular duchy. To strengthen the position of his new state, Albrecht eagerly promoted Lutheranism among his Polish-Lithuanian neighbors and welcomed to his realm immigrant or refugee Lithuanian Protestants, mostly learned clergymen.[16]

One of these clergymen, Martynas Mažvydas, in 1547 published a Lutheran catechism in Lithuanian. This was the first book published in Lithuanian and was aimed not only at the large Lithuanian population under Albrecht's rule but especially at Lithuanians in the Grand Duchy of Lithuania. Other works followed the catechism, all printed in Gothic characters, including the translation of Sunday gospels (1579) and of the entire New Testament (1701). In 1544 Duke Albrecht established a university in Königsberg that trained Lithuanians for pastoral work. Over the next three centuries, the formerly anti-Lithuanian Teutonic Prussia became the main source of native Lithuanian literature and a haven from russification policies from the East. Until the middle of the nineteenth century, Prussia supported many unassimilated Lithuanian inhabitants and Lutheran parishes. The classic author of Lithuanian literature of the eighteenth century (Kristijonas Donelaitis, the author of *Metai* [The Seasons] also was born and worked there.

This concerted effort by Protestants to reach the Lithuanian masses in their native idiom finally galvanized Catholic response. The bishops of Vilnius, especially Merkelis Giedraitis (c. 1536–1609) and the Jesuits, led the campaign against Protestant influence. In 1570 the Jesuits established an academy in Vilnius. Elevated to the status of a university in 1579, this institution became a leading center of learning in the region, a competitor to Poland's Cracow, and the oldest university in northeastern Europe. In 1585, Canon Mikalojus Daukša was already admonishing Lithuania's nobles that only barbarians throw away their native language. However, the fact that he made this appeal in Polish indicated how far the nobility had been polonized and how large a cleavage had grown between them and Lithuanian-speaking peasants who served their large estates.

The partitions of Poland at the end of the eighteenth century and the annexation of Lithuania by Catherine II of Russia in 1795 brought about paradoxical changes. On the one hand, the Tsars destroyed Polish sovereignty and whatever remained of provincial self-government in Lithuania. On the other hand, the Russians' concerted oppression and tactics of division helped to bring about a gradual national emancipation of autochthonous Lithuanian society.

National Awakening

The political factor that most profoundly affected, and even defined, the process of Lithuanian cultural and political emancipation was the Polish conflict with Moscow. Polish patriots refused to accept Tsarist rule. The University of Vilnius became a hotbed of romantic Polish nationalism. Two insurrections against Moscow rocked the country, in 1831 and again in 1863, in which Lithuanian peasants and clergymen collaborated with the Polish, Lithuanian, and Byelorussian gentry. Both rebellions were brutally repressed, but they inspired a new Tsarist policy that offered the Lithuanian intelligentsia political alternatives that they previously did not dare discuss. The new Tsarist policy aimed at liquidating *Pol'skoe delo*, "the Polish question," in the region.[17] It was to be solved by suppressing Polish influence, recognizing Lithuanians as a separate culture, then splitting them away from the Poles and assimilating them into the Russian nationality and Orthodoxy. The Russians identified Polishness with Catholicism and therefore adopted not only a strongly anti-Polish but also a sharply anti-Catholic policy in Lithuania. The University of Vilnius was closed down after the insurrection of 1931, the Vilnius theological academy was transferred to St. Petersburg for easier supervision, and the center of

Uniate culture, a blend of Latin and Orthodox Catholicism, was extinguished. In 1839 the Tsar forced the merger of the Uniate and Russian Orthodox churches. After the 1863 rebellion, Catholic monasteries and churches, considered "nests of Latin propaganda and sources of insurrection," were also closed down. Church closure in Kražiai, in 1896, led to a massacre and an international scandal.

Above all, St. Petersburg sought to redirect Lithuania's cultural development. In 1864, the Tsar forbade Lithuanian language schools and Lithuanian (not Polish) book printing in Latin characters. Cyrillic characters were to be used in the hope that the change would produce the miracle of assimilation, bringing Lithuanians into Russian culture just as the Prussian use of Gothic print was to have helped the germanization of Lithuanians. Finally, to promote the cleavage between the estate owners and the peasants, the first presumed to be Polish, the second Lithuanian, Tsarist governors obtained favors for the peasants at the expense of estates by giving them more liberal terms in the great land reform of 1861 than Russia's peasants received. Not all Russian administrators in Lithuania were persuaded that such policies would achieve the desired results, however, and they were right.

The Tsar's attacks on the Catholic Church also failed. At the time the church had been reinvigorated by the influx of sons of ordinary peasants into the priesthood and into positions of clerical leadership. The opening of these doors brought in much new talent and strengthened the church's identification with the Lithuanian-speaking peasantry as never before in its history. The most active official on this score was the Bishop of Samogitia, Motiejus Valančius (1801–1875), who clandestinely resisted the Russian attack on Catholicism and the Lithuanian language. Himself a classic Lithuanian writer, Valančius promoted historical research and theological and literary writing by his clergy and had their works printed in German-ruled East Prussia. From there, books and periodicals were smuggled into Lithuania. He also organized a network of secret schools at farm homes where children learned Lithuanian in Latin print. Largely as a result of these secret activities, the literacy rate in the Kovno (Kaunas) guberniia, which covered most of ethnic Lithuania in 1897, was 54 percent, compared to St. Petersburg's 44 percent.[18]

The Polish side, too, suffered a defeat. The political culture of the Grand Duchy in its last decades was characterized by the idea of Polish imperial nationality, which stressed the Polish language, Polish culture, and Polish political traditions and claimed for the Lithuanian element only provincial loyalties. Expressed in a Latin sentence, *gente Lituanus, natione Polonus* ("Lithuanian people, Polish nation"), this concept now ran into deep difficulty. Bishop Valančius worked to preserve the Catholic faith in the Lithuanian, not in the Polish, idiom. Politically, he did not consider a separate Lithuanian existence apart from Russia yet possible, but at the same time, he did not advocate a union with Poland. Some of his contemporaries went further. Rev. Antanas Mackevičius, a Lithuanian leader in the revolt of 1863, insisted, on the one hand, that many of his clerical colleagues hated everything Polish and loathed the gentry because of their socially oppressive behavior. On the other hand, he said, they were willing to sacrifice everything for Lithuania. Nevertheless, he participated in a Polish rebellion against the Russians. The insurrection, he said, made the people conscious of the choice they had either to unite with Poland or to stand with Russia.[19] Such views indicated obvious cracks in the fabric of Polish imperial culture.

The political consciousness of the Lithuanians was further sharpened by the new, secular intelligentsia, which was not of nobility but of free peasant background. This intelligentsia initially came from the southwestern region of Užnemunė, which, in the 1795 division of Poland and Lithuania, was incorporated into Prussia, where there initially was no suppression of Lithuanian culture and religion. Servitude in the region was abolished in 1807, when Napoleon founded the Warsaw Kingdom after the victory against Prussia, an entire half century earlier than in the rest of Lithuania. Although the liberated peasants did not receive land from the Russian regime, their economic condition improved when the regime was integrated into Russia during the final partition of 1815 by the Congress of Vienna. The land reform of Russia in 1861 was generous to the entire Polish Kingdom to which the province belonged, and the peasants received enough free land to achieve a measure of prosperity and to eventually send their sons to schools and universities. Generally, the Tsarist regime was not as heavy-handed in this province as elsewhere. The sale of land was not restricted, and russification was not pushed as intensely. Neither the Catholic Church nor Lithuanian schools were persecuted as severely as elsewhere, although the printing of Lithuanian books and periodicals was forbidden. Several schools that taught Lithuanian as a subject of instruction operated in the region itself. New intellectuals and professionals, such as the physician Jonas Basanavičius (1851–1927), the patriarch of Lithuanian national awakening, returned to Lithuania to help the emancipation of their people. They published the first periodicals of national awakening, such as *Aušra* (The Dawn) in 1883 and *Varpas* (The Bell) in 1887. These periodicals, printed in East Prussia as in the times of Valančius and then secretly smuggled into Lithuania, preserved the history, tradition, identity, and language of the endogenous peasants despite Polish and Russian domination.

Struggle for Independence

Reform and modernization for this largely agricultural people also led to the emergence of a Lithuanian political consciousness in the 1880s. The new endogenous intelligentsia was educated in Russian universities, where the sons of the strongly religious Catholic farmers became atheists or agnostics as well as Socialists or revolutionary radicals. Publication of *Aušra*, the first journal of national awakening, stopped because the clergy refused to accept antireligious and pro-Socialist commentaries by the firebrand successor to Dr. Basanavičius in the editor's chair. Industrialization came late to Lithuania. By the 1880s the three Lithuanian guberniias, Vilnius, Kaunas, and Suvalkai (Wilno, Kovno, and Suwalki), had more than 400 small industrial enterprises with more than 3,000 workers.[20] Although this was much below Estonian or Latvian levels, it spawned clusters of an industrial proletariat that together with the landless labor force supported the birth of an independent Lithuanian Socialist party in 1896.[21] Lithuanian Christian Democrats started underground publications such as *Apžvalga* (Survey, 1890–1896) and *Tėvynės sargas* (Guardian of Homeland, 1896–1904), although the party program was first drafted only in 1904.[22] The Jewish Bund began activities in Vilnius but did not participate in Lithuanian politics. Polish Social Democrats, with whom Lithuanian Socialists were first associated, also actively moved on the political stage.

At the time of the 1905 Russian revolution, which followed the restoration of the freedom to publish works in Latin characters in Lithuania (1904), there already existed a number of political groups. There were two separate wings in Lithuanian politics, the pro-Socialist Left and the pro-Catholic Right. There also existed the incipient "center," a moderate nationalist group attempting to eschew ideological extremes and focus on common national tradition.

Since the Lithuanian farm proletariat was neither as large nor as radical as its counterparts in Latvia and Estonia and the city proletariat was also small, the revolution of 1905 transpired much more peacefully in Lithuania than in Latvia and Estonia and exhibited more national than social concerns. It culminated in the first national congress (The Great Diet of Vilnius), which was made up of all Lithuanian political groups, local government representatives, and social organizations and met in Vilnius in 1905 to review and coordinate Lithuanian demands to the Tsar.

The massive conference of 2,000 participants, known for its stormy sessions, declared that "the most vicious enemy of the Lithuanian people was the current government of the Tsar."[23] It adopted a heretofore unheard of demand by a nationality of the Russian empire, namely, a demand of national autonomy within ethnic boundaries in federal ties with the neighboring lands of Russia. It further proposed the election of a free parliament by all inhabitants without regard to religion, nationality, or sex. After a very stormy debate on whether autonomy should be sought by revolutionary violence or by peaceful means, congressional delegates agreed on a nonviolent approach. Lithuanians were asked to refuse payment of taxes, to reject service in the military, to keep children from attending Russian schools, to close down state monopoly stores selling vodka, and to organize strikes. The congress finally demanded that Lithuanian be the language of local government and that schools be "converted to national schools." After returning home, the delegates put the adopted resolutions into practice but were quickly suppressed by the Russian administration and army. Large numbers of revolutionaries were imprisoned, sent to exile in Siberia, or forced to flee the country.

If the revolution of 1905 pointed to the instability of the old imperial order, the outbreak of World War I signaled its breakdown. In 1915 German forces occupied Lithuania and some 300,000 Lithuanians—farmers, professionals, and students—fled to the Russian interior together with the retreating imperial army. In Russia, they organized schools as well as political organizations. At the start of the February revolution against the Tsar, representatives of the main political parties secretly met in St. Petersburg and declared that the objective of all Lithuanians must be the freedom to decide the nation's fate. They advocated political means for achieving this goal and established a Lithuanian National Council, which then proclaimed essentially the same national goals as had the Vilnius congress: Lithuania must be an autonomous self-governing country. A Provisional Committee for Governing Lithuania was established with functions similar to those of a government-in-exile. Russia's Provisional Government of Prince Lvov feigned support for Lithuanian autonomy but never took concrete action. The Soviet of Workers and Soldiers also procrastinated while giving lip service to the principle of self-determination. To make Lithuanian views better heard, Lithuanian groups organized a congress of representatives of Lithuanian refugees. On May 27, 1917, 320 elected representatives met in St. Petersburg. Of these, the largest group (90 representatives) belonged to the Socialist Populist party. Forty-one were Christian Democrats; 39 were Social Democrats, 32 were Catholic nationalists, 30 were left-of-center, liberal, Santara party members, and 20 belonged to the Nation's Progress party.[24] Lithuanian Bolsheviks also elected several representatives but after attending the first session of the congress withdrew from participation.

At first, it looked as if the St. Petersburg congress would repeat the demands of the Great Diet of Vilnius in 1905, but the ensuing decade had radically changed the political landscape. Russia was in the throes of real revolution, the Tsar was gone, leftist parties were on the ascendancy, and political reforms raised the possibility of a democratic Russia. Lithuanian leftist parties supported the soldiers' and workers' councils and the revolutionary parties. The Lithuanian Right, in contrast, was uneasy about the revolution and about Russia. These differences led to stormy exchanges on the floor and in the final outcome of the St. Petersburg meeting.

By a small margin, the congress adopted a resolution demanding full independence for Lithuania. This was an upgraded demand from the days of the Vilnius congress in 1905. It was proposed by Christian Democrats and other groups on the political center and right and opposed by representatives of leftist parties, led by the Socialist group. They did not want to sever from Russia, and they marched out of the meeting. Political consensus in Vilnius appeared to dissipate.

Efforts to seek political consensus continued, however. At the end of 1917, a Lithuanian Supreme Council was founded on the basis of diverse party coalition. A conference of coalition parties reconfirmed the decision of the Vilnius conference of 1905, but in April 1918 Lenin's Bolshevik government closed down the council and arrested its members.

Shortly thereafter, Lithuania fell to German occupation. Germany's Imperial government in September 1917 allowed the formation of a Lithuanian Council (Lietuvos Taryba) elected by a conference of representatives of local governments and political groups in Vilnius. From the inception of the conference, however, the Germans pressured the Lithuanians to adopt a resolution that would provide for Lithuania's alliance with Germany.[25] The conference cautiously obliged. It demanded independence, favored a democratic government and a freely elected parliament, and stated that if Germany would recognize independent Lithuania, Lithuania would establish closer relations with Germany. The nature of these relations would be decided by the parliament. The council that was elected by the conference was not formed on the basis of partisan coalition but included leaders of main political parties as well as independents. Antanas Smetona (1874–1944), a lawyer and future president of Lithuania, became chairman of the presidium of the council. After the Vilnius conference, the council conducted negotiations with the Germans.

The Germans did not rush to recognize Lithuania as the Vilnius conference had proposed. Instead, they demanded, as a condition for recognition, that Lithuania enter into a "perpetual" alliance with Germany providing for common military, transportation, customs, currency, and of course foreign policy. In December, the council agreed, despite opposition from the Socialist and Democratic party representatives. At the same time, Lithuanians learned that the king of Saxony had claimed Lithuania as his share of the war booty. Instead of having a Protestant king, the Lithuanians accepted a proposal made by the leader of the Catholic Center party—Matthias Erzberger—to invite Duke Wilhelm von Urach to ascend the Lithuanian throne. Eventually, the Kaiser's government promised recognition in order to negotiate a separate peace with the Bolsheviks at Brest Litovsk in early 1918. After achieving its objectives at Brest Litovsk, however, Berlin reneged on the promise.

Tired of cynical German manipulations that caused considerable divisiveness and political difficulties in the council, the Lithuanians united. On February 16, 1918, the council proclaimed the restoration of an independent,

Antanas Smetona, president of the Lithuanian Republic (April 4, 1919– April 19, 1920; December 19, 1926–June 15, 1940). (Courtesy of *Lietuvos Istorija*.)

democratic Lithuania with the capital in Vilnius and severed all ties that in the past had bound Lithuania to other nations.

German military authorities responded by confiscating the issue of the newspaper *Lietuvos aidas* in which the unanimously adopted declaration had been published. Nevertheless, the Brest Litovsk treaty left the entire Baltic region to the Germans, and the opposition in the Reichstag prevailed upon the military-imperialist faction to invite the Lithuanians to participate in "discussions" of Lithuania's future. After another stormy session, on March 20, 1918, the council sent representatives to Berlin. There, on March 23, the Kaiser recognized Lithuanian statehood but only on the basis of the December 11 decision, which provided for a perpetual union with Germany. Although civilian authorities in the German capital seemed accepting of some autonomy for the beleaguered Lithuanians, in Lithuania itself the German military authorities further obstructed native state administration until it was clear that they were losing the war.

A month before Berlin signed the armistice, Prince Max von Baden, the last chancellor of Imperial Germany, gave the council control over the administration of Lithuania, the local army, and the police. German troops would stay "for some time," as desired by the Lithuanians. There was, however, no more talk about an alliance with Germany.

Lithuania thus became free to organize its own government and to control its territory. This was not easy because of Soviet and Polish claims as well as attempts by some German military elements to preserve Berlin's influence in the Baltic region.[26] A war of independence had to be fought. After taking Vilnius in December 1918, the Red Army succeeded, in 1919, in penetrating almost two-thirds of Lithuanian territory. Lenin established a Lithuanian-Byelorussian Soviet republic for the administration of Lithuania, but the Lithuanian Communist party was too weak to gain hold of the country. Communist policies in opposition to private farm ownership repelled the largely rural Lithuanian people. The Red Army was driven out. In late summer 1919, Lenin recognized de facto independent Lithuania, and on July 9, 1920, he signed a treaty of peace denouncing "forever" Russian claims to Lithuania.

Polish claims were advanced by Josef Piłsudski, who wanted to reestablish the Poland of the eighteenth and earlier centuries. Diplomatic conflict led to war and a struggle over the city and region of Vilnius. Poland took over Vilnius but failed to subvert the Lithuanian government. Relations with Poland were not normalized until 1938. Finally, the newly organized and inexperienced Lithuanian army had to subdue the military forces of Colonel Bermondt-Avalov, a Russian adventurer who cooperated with the German Baltikum army under General Rüdiger von der Goltz, who sought to keep the Baltic region under German influence.

International recognition of Lithuania was delayed because of its conflict with Poland and demands by the League of Nations for a charter protecting national minorities. However, recognition gradually came. The United States—concerned with the territorial integrity of the "indivisible" Russian empire—was the last big power to recognize Lithuania's independence, as again would be the case seventy years later. Once recognition was granted in 1922, it would last throughout fifty years of Soviet occupation.

GEOPOLITICS AND INDEPENDENCE

Lithuania's birth as an independent nation was conditioned by three historical factors: the two revolutions of Russia in 1917, the German occupation, and the actions of the Western Allies. In this environment a crucial role was played by the Lithuanians themselves.

The Russian revolutions of 1917 signified the disintegration of the Tsarist regime. In February the war-weary masses spilled into the streets of Petrograd and swept away the centuries-old rule of Russia's royal autocracy. Everyone, without regard to nationality, breathed more freely. A constitutional democratic government, which was expected to succeed the Tsar, was similarly expected to protect individual rights. Such government, it was thought, would also find a more liberal political arrangement for the peaceful coexistence of national minorities that the Tsars had severely suppressed. The Provisional Government, however, while supporting general freedoms, repressed national freedom for border nationalities except Poland and Estonia, which kept administrative autonomy. Prime Minister Kerensky even threatened to train his artillery on Finland in case the Finns decided to leave the empire. Such a policy did not restrain the emancipation of non-Russian nations, however. Of importance at the time was not Kerensky's wishes but his inability to solidify the Russian government and troops. This inability fatally weakened the central government's power to control events.

The Bolshevik coup d'état—in history books known as the October revolution—frightened the non-Russians and intensified their desire to flee the empire. Soviet scholars have generally extolled the October revolution as an event that liberated national minorities from the Tsarist "prison of nations." The immense importance of October should not be denied; its influence, however, was manifested not in liberation of the non-Russians but in the ultimate destabilization of the empire. Lenin's social and ideological radicalism alienated large segments of non-Russian peoples from any alliance with the new Moscow and further encouraged centrifugal forces even among those political groups that otherwise shared with Communist revolutionaries certain socio-reformist policies or ideological views. After the October revolution, most of those Lithuanians who either stood solely for autonomy or wanted to delay independence radically changed their minds in light of the results of the October coup d'état. Lenin's revolution turned a great majority of Lithuanian Social Democrats against an alliance with revolutionary Russia.

World War I of course was a major catalyst for the Russian revolutions and brought the Germans to Lithuania. The entire Lithuanian territory was under German occupation, which eventually provided the local political elite with some direct experience in state building and daily administration. At first completely opposed to any thought of Lithuanian independence, the Germans changed their mind at least partly in response to the idea of self-determination that then swept over Europe, promoted by President Woodrow Wilson, even as their main motive was to exploit Lithuania's independence, primarily to gain the upper hand in the Brest Litovsk conference. Though largely symbolic, German support for independence eventually increased because it would stem Poland's expansionism. Poland sought to reclaim boundaries of the old Rzeczpospolita to which Lithuania once belonged.

The Western Allies were notable for their absence in Lithuania. President Wilson's famous Fourteen Points did not list Lithuania among the nations to be restored to statehood. The British had some interest in the former Baltic provinces, that is, the newly born states of Estonia and Latvia, and had dispatched their navy to Riga and Tallinn to support Latvian and Estonian endeavors to disentangle themselves from Bolshevik Russia and from the machinations of the Germans. The French had brainstormed a concept of a security organization to protect Western Europe from the Bolsheviks. This was the *cordon sanitaire*, a string of nations along Russian borders. It was to include Estonia and Latvia but not necessarily Lithuania, since the latter was expected to be absorbed or federated with Warsaw. Poland was expected to function as the main link in the safety chain. Direct Allied interest in Lithuania therefore was of negligent proportions. Lithuanians, however, were helped by the Allied fear of Communist Russian expansion into Europe. To thwart it, Germany was forbidden to withdraw military forces from the occupied Baltic region until the region organized itself for defense. Thus, Germany helped Lithuania establish the mechanisms of an independent state during World War I and after its defeat aided Lithuanian resistance to the Bolshevik armies.

The two giants, the Russian and Germanic empires, whose alliance had spelled the doom of the old Polish-Lithuanian commonwealth at the end of the eighteenth century, lay prostrate in the aftermath of World War I. In this environment, Lithuania was able to emerge as an independent nation-state.

NOTES

1. Except as otherwise indicated, statistical data for this section were taken from *Lietuva skaičiais/Lithuania in Figures 1991* (Vilnius: Lithuanian Department of Statistics, 1992).

2. Gosudarstvennyi komitet SSSR po statistike, *Narodnoe khoziaistvo SSSR v 1990g* (Moscow: Finansy i statistika, 1991), p. 210.

3. Marija Gimbutas, *The Balts* (New York: Frederick A. Praeger, 1962), p. 43. The boundaries of the Lithuanian-speaking population are also discussed by Dr. Petras Jonikas in *Lietuvių kalba ir tauta amžių būvyje* (Chicago: Institute of Lithuanian Studies Press, 1987), esp. pp. 34ff. In this volume, *The Lithuanian Language and Nation Through the Ages*, Jonikas surveys and analyzes the history of the Lithuanian language in its social context. See also R. Rimantienė, *Pirmieji Lietuvos gyventojai* (Vilnius: Mintis, 1972). Literature on the early settlements of the Balts is reviewed by Henryk Paszkiewicz in *The Rise of Moscow's Power* (Boulder and New York: East European Monographs, Columbia University Press, 1983), pp. 401–408.

4. See, for example, Vladzimir Kananovich in *Literatura i mastactva* (Minsk), April 24, 1992. "There is no other city in the world of equal importance to Belarus

as is Vilnius," writes Kananovich. In the same publication of September 24, 1992, V. Bogush complains that in 1939 not all of Western Belarus was joined to the Byelorussian republic because Stalin had donated Vilnius to Lithuania.

5. Lithuanian and comparative population data are drawn from Ann Sheehy, "The Ethnographic Developments and the Soviet Federal System," in *Soviet Federalism and Economic Decentralization,* ed. Alastair McAuley (New York: St. Martin's Press, 1991), pp. 56–88.

6. Gimbutas, *The Balts,* pp. 179ff.

7. Kazys Pakštas, "Lietuvių tautos plotai ir gyventojai," *Lietuvių enciklopedija,* vol. 11 (Boston: LEL, 1968), p. 449.

8. Population data for 1992 are taken from *Lithuania in Figures 1991,* p. 7.

9. In Western languages, comprehensive works on the history of Lithuania are rare. Mention may be made of Thomas G. Chase, *The Story of Lithuania* (New York: Stratford House, 1946), and Constantine R. Jurgela, *History of the Lithuanian Nation* (New York: Lithuanian Cultural Institute, 1948). Henryk Paszkiewicz covers medieval Lithuanian history up to the union with Poland in *Origins of Russia* (New York: Philosophical Library, 1954), pp. 183–254; Oscar Halecki writes about Lithuania's place in Central-Eastern Europe in *Borderlands of Western Civilization* (New York: The Ronalds Press Company, 1952), pp. 79–125, 164–172. In German, a short but valuable survey of medieval Lithuania is found in Manfred Hellmann, *Grundzüge der Geschichte Litauens und des litauischen Volkes* (Darmstadt: Wissenschaftliche Buchgesellschaft, 1966).

10. See Adolfas Šapoka, ed., *Lietuvos istorija,* 3rd printing (Germany: Patria, 1950), p. 154.

11. See Zenonas Ivinskis, "Mindaugas und seine Krone," *Zeitschrift für Ostforschung* 3 (1954): 360–386; also Manfred Hellmann, "Der deutsche Orden und die Königskrönung des Mindaugas," in *Grundzüge der Geschichte Litauens und des litauischen Volkes,* pp. 387–396.

12. Document cited by Zenonas Ivinskis, *Lietuvos istorija iki Vytauto Didžiojo mirties* (Roma: Lietuvių Katalikų Mokslo Akademija, 1978), p. 285. The origins of the Lithuanian state according to Marxist methodology are discussed by a well-known Russian historian, V. T. Pashuto, in his *Obrazovanie Litovskogo gosudarstva* (Moscow, 1959). In 1971, a revised volume of this study was published in Lithuanian. See V. Pašuta, *Lietuvos valstybės susidarymas* (Vilnius, 1971).

13. Juozas Jurginis, *Lietuvos krikštas* (Vilnius: Mokslas, 1987), p. 320.

14. Zenonas Ivinskis, *Lietuvos istorija,* p. 195.

15. See Zenonas Ivinskis, *Rinktiniai raštai,* vol. 4, *Krikščionybė Lietuvoje* (Roma: Lietuvių Katalikų Mokslo Akademija, 1987), p. 167.

16. See Antanas Musteikis, *The Reformation in Lithuania* (Boulder and New York: East European Monographs, Columbia University Press, 1988), pp. 41ff. On Lithuanians in East Prussia, see P. I. Kushner, *Etnicheskie territorii i etnicheskie granitsy* (Moscow: Academy of Sciences, 1951), and Martin Brakas, ed., *Lithuania Minor* (New York: Lithuanian Research Institute, 1976).

17. For more detail see V. Stanley Vardys, *The Catholic Church: Dissent and Nationality in Soviet Lithuania* (Boulder and New York: East European Quarterly, Columbia University Press, 1978), pp. 4–17.

18. I. M. Bogdanov, *Gramotnost' i obrazovanie v dorevoliutsionnoi Rossii i v SSSR* (Moscow: Statistika, 1964), pp. 59, 61.

19. Text in J. Žiugžda, editor-in-chief, *Lietuvos TSR istorijos šaltiniai*, vol. 2, *1861–1917* (Vilnius: Mintis, 1965), p. 83. On Bishop Valančius, see Antanas Alekna, *Žemaičių vyskupas Motiejus Valančius*, 2nd ed. (Chicago: Lituanistikos Institutas, 1975).

20. M. Meškauskienė, *Ekonominė Lietuvos padėtis pirmojo pasaulinio karo išvakarėse (1900–1913 m.)* (Vilnius: VPMLL, 1963), pp. 15–17.

21. See Leonas Sabaliūnas, *Lithuanian Social Democracy in Perspective, 1893–1914* (Durham: Duke University Press, 1990).

22. For a historical survey see Algirdas Kasulaitis, *Lithuanian Christian Democracy* (Chicago, 1976).

23. Žiugžda, *Lietuvos TSR istorijos šaltiniai*, vol. 2, p. 390. See also Pranas Čepėnas, *Naujųjų laikų Lietuvos istorija*, vol. 1 (Chicago: Dr. K. Griniaus Fondas, 1976), pp. 340ff.

24. Čepėnas, *Naujųjų laikų Lietuvos istorija*, vol. 2 (Chicago: Dr. K. Griniaus Fondas, 1976), p. 66.

25. For a detailed description and the text of the declaration of independence, see Simas Sužiedelis, "Lietuvos taryba," *Lietuvių enciklopedija*, vol. 16 (Boston: LEL, 1958), pp. 155–164; also Čepėnas, *Naujųjų laikų Lietuvos istorija*, vol. 2, pp. 184–234; *Lietuvos TSR istorijos šaltiniai*, vol. 3 (1958), pp. 90–99.

26. On Lithuania's early international difficulties and armed struggle for independence, see Alfred E. Senn, *The Emergence of Modern Lithuania* (New York: Columbia University Press, 1959); Stanley W. Page, *The Formation of the Baltic States* (Cambridge: Harvard University Press, 1959); and Alfred E. Senn, *The Great Powers: Lithuania and the Vilna Question* (Leiden: E. J. Brill, 1966). On early relations with the United States, see Albert N. Tarulis, *American-Baltic Relations, 1918–1922: The Struggle over Recognition* (Washington: The Catholic University of America Press, 1965). On diplomatic relations and military conflict with Soviet Russia, see another volume by Albert N. Tarulis, *Soviet Policy Toward the Baltic States, 1918–1940* (Notre Dame, Ind.: Notre Dame University Press, 1959).

· TWO ·

A Taste of Independence, 1918–1940

Among the Baltic nations Lithuania was the least developed in 1918 but could draw on its older, more documented national history to face the challenge of creating its own independent nation-state. The Lithuanian struggle for statehood drew inspiration from its "illustrious past"[1] of medieval glory and, in 1905, Lithuanians were the first among Tsarist Russia's nationalities, after the already autonomous Finns, to demand autonomy for their land. Yet when the time came for the organization of the state and its recognition by world powers, the Lithuanians were severely hindered by key aspects of their history, in particular by claims to territory by both Poland and Germany.

PROBLEMS OF HERITAGE: FOREIGN AND DOMESTIC

Lithuania had to fight off the claims to political union by its historical Polish partner. Poland still hoped to reestablish its medieval greatness in a single nation named "Rzeczpospolita"—a Polish-Lithuanian Commonwealth that would unite Lithuanian, Ukrainian, and Byelorussian provinces. Josef Piłsudski, the founder of modern Poland, fought for this goal; his life, and even his death, stands as a symbol of this idea. A native of eastern Lithuania, he willed his body to be buried in Kraków. Piłsudski ultimately failed to restore Poland within its historical boundaries, but he succeeded in slowing Lithuania's de jure recognition by the League of Nations and in October 1920 also occupied and annexed the historical Lithuanian capital of Vilnius (Wilno, Vilna).[2]

The Poles claimed the city not solely on historical but also on demographic grounds. In 1916 German statistics showed that, after the Russians fled the city before the advancing German armies, the Poles constituted 50.1 percent of its population. The Lithuanian percentage was very low (2.1 percent in 1916), as it had been for several generations, but constituted an overwhelming majority in many rural areas. The city's population until that time was not predominantly Polish, however. The Russian imperial census of 1897 showed that Vilnius's population was 40 percent Jewish, 30.9 percent Polish, and 20 percent Russian. Over the centuries, Vilnius had been an international city, sometimes predominantly Polish, sometimes Jewish, sometimes strongly Russian, and since World War II, predominantly Lithuanian (over 50 percent). Founded by the Lithuanian Grand Duke Gediminas by 1323, it had served as the capital of the medieval Lithuanian state and later as a cultural center that drew not just Poles and Lithuanians but neighboring Byelorussians and the Uniate Ukrainians as well. In addition, Vilnius was an important seat of Jewish learning and the headquarters of the famous gaons. It was known as Lithuanian Jerusalem.

Polish annexation substantially hurt the conduct of Lithuania's international relations. It cast a pall on the legitimacy and diplomatic authority of the new Lithuanian state. At the same time, it made the Lithuanians inhibited and inflexible on any international initiatives that might lend recognition to the Polish annexation or endanger the legality of Lithuania's claims to Vilnius. Furthermore, the conflict with Poland poisoned Lithuania's domestic development by enormously strengthening domestic Lithuanian nationalists, upsetting the fragile social balance on which its democracy rested. Finally, it directly fueled an intensive and largely successful effort to undermine the vitality of Polish linguistic and cultural influence.

A further international burden that fostered the growth of domestic nationalism and international difficulties was the Lithuanian annexation of the Klaipėda-Memel territory in 1923 (see Map 1.2).[3] This province was a strip of land on the Baltic sea coast that was wrested away from the Lithuanian tribes by the Teutonic Knights in the thirteenth and fourteenth centuries. They founded the city of Klaipėda there in 1252 in order to secure safe passage and communication between German conquerors in East Prussia and Riga. After the defeat of the German Reich in World War I, the Western Allies detached the city and the territory from Germany on grounds that an overwhelming majority of the original population was still Lithuanian, which was statistically true, and that the new state of Lithuania, for economic reasons, would need an outlet to the sea. However, the Versailles Allies did not return the detached province to Lithuania. Instead, the territory was administered by the Allied-appointed French commissioner and military. The French and the Poles wanted Lithuania to accept the Klaipėda territory in lieu of the lost province of Vilnius, but the Lithuanians would not consider it. They wanted Klaipėda without losing Vilnius and pledged autonomy for the province. The Poles then suggested the creation of a Klaipėda Freistaat.

Concerned with this development, the Lithuanians decided to take over the territory. They had a precedent for this course of action. Poland's Piłsudski had engaged an "independent" Polish general, Lucjan Żeligowski, to break an early armistice with Lithuania and occupy Vilnius. After creating an artificial political entity, "Litwa Środkowa" (Middle Lithuania), for this special purpose, Piłsudski was able to legitimize his conquest. On February 3, 1922, the Council of the League of Nations set boundaries between Poland and Lithuania, leaving Vilnius to Poland.

On January 9, 1923, Klaipėda's Lithuanians rose to seize power from the French administration. They were helped by supporters from Lithuania, mostly members of the Riflemen's Association, who crossed the border and by January 15 captured the city. The timing for insurrection was well chosen. On January 10, French and Belgian troops had marched into Germany's Ruhr province, thus drawing European attention away from events in Lithuania and occupying Western forces in action in Germany's south. The insurrectionists were further helped by the Western suspicion that Soviet Russia was helping the Lithuanians, and the Western powers did not desire military conflict with the Soviets. In actuality, the Soviets were not involved militarily, although they supported Lithuania diplomatically. French army units offered only sporadic resistance. The German police did not resist. The insurrection was well organized by Lithuanian military and paramilitary units in civilian dress as well as individual volunteers. After losing Vilnius, the Kaunas government chose to use the same tactic used by the Poles: establish possession and negotiate later. Negotiations indeed began with the conference of Versailles ambassadors, and a year later, on May 8, 1924, sovereignty over the territory was transferred to Lithuania under a provision of broad autonomy for the province. On March 25, 1923, the same group had "retaliated" against Lithuania for the Klaipėda insurrection by formally allocating the Vilnius territory to Poland.

Before the ink dried on the international agreement establishing Klaipėda's autonomy under Lithuanian sovereignty, disagreements over what it meant in political life arose. These led, in 1931, to the International Court in the Hague and created many irritations in relations with the Weimar republic. After Hitler won power in Berlin, Nazi and Nazi-front organizations in Klaipėda took over the leadership of the German population and promoted Anschluss. After almost 500 years of German rule, Klaipėda's Germans had never reconciled themselves to becoming Lithuanian citizens. In 1934, the Lithuanians responded by charging the Nazi leadership with conspiracy against the state and tried them in a public court in Kaunas. Many defendants were found guilty and received prison sentences. Little Lithuania was the only European country to try Nazis for subversion against the state. Hitler was furious. Germany broke a trade agreement, causing great hardship to Lithuanian farmers whose products Germany now refused.

Although international difficulties with Poland and Germany intensified domestic nationalism, the early determination to undermine Polish cultural influences helped revive native language, literature, and especially education. However unfortunate and painful the political and diplomatic quarrel with Poland now appears, it encouraged the development of the Lithuanian national and cultural identity as no other influence of earlier times had done and served the Lithuanians well under the later Russian rule.

In its nation-building efforts Lithuania had to begin with a very small native leadership elite insufficient to staff the positions of state administration. This dearth of personnel, inherited from the Tsarist past, when educational opportunities were few, created many new openings and careers for young Lithuanians as well as for minorities and foreigners. In 1923, when 83.9 percent of the country's population was ethnic Lithuanian, Lithuanians constituted only 63 percent of state employees.[4] The largest minority group representation was Jewish (20.4 percent), more than double this group's population percentage. Even the thoroughly distrusted Poles were represented, as were foreigners (3.2 and 3.3 percent, respectively). This composition was to change later, at a time when Lithuania educated its ethnic cadres and Lithuanian nationalism enabled them to escape many democratic restraints. Thus, on the one hand, the early Lithuanian state and society exhibited rather international characteristics. On the other hand, appointments of semi-educated personnel—or unfit but politically selected officials—made administration inefficient and, very soon, corrupt. By 1926, corruption in office became the main electoral issue contaminating the ruling Christian Democratic alliance, which was unseated for this reason.

Most important, the political culture and institutions of the new state were developing in a peasant population with little experience in democracy and multiculturalism and with a rather low level of general education and literacy. In 1923, the Lithuanian census registered 44.1 percent illiterates,[5] reflecting a society not prepared for the trials of modernization and democracy that lay ahead.

DEMOCRACY: MULTIPARTY ASSEMBLY MODEL

The Allied victory in World War I ushered in the first wave of democratization in the twentieth century. More important than the circumstance of Western victory over Central powers, however, was the political philosophy of the leaders of the newly emergent nations. The Lithuanians, educated not only in Russia but in Western Europe as well, were men of

The old Kaunas city square, at the confluence of two rivers. (Photo by A. Sutkus. Used by permission.)

democratic and egalitarian convictions, influenced by the revolutionary climate of the times. Thus, like the Estonians and the Latvians, the Lithuanians chose a democratic system, and influenced by the example of Weimar Germany, they followed a model of governance that elevated the legislature over the executive. With Polish forces in Vilnius, the founders of the first Lithuania Republic moved the capital to Kaunas.

In the political process Lithuania's first modern statesmen provided for a multiparty system operating under an unadulterated system of proportional representation. There were three elections during the period of Lithuania's first independence. In the first election to the Seimas (parliament) in 1920, the Christian Democrats won the majority, as they did again in 1922. This system tended to make access to the political process very easy, but it also made government very weak and prey to instability. In 1923, for example, twelve parties put up candidates for the election to the Seimas, of which ten were elected.[6]

The system encouraged proliferation of political parties and divisions but at the same time limited opportunities for establishing working political coalitions in support of an effective executive. As in the other Baltic countries, a multiparty system was needed to accommodate the deep ideological divisions of society, but very quickly this very system became the main source of political turmoil undermining the democratic process it sought to create. In 1926, a right-wing group overthrew the elected government and governed by dictatorship until the end of the republic.

Lithuanian politics were heavily influenced by Catholic parties in the parliament and by the historically strong Catholic Church in society. Lithuania's Catholic Church was a mixture of tradition and modernity.[7] An overwhelming majority of its leadership and clergy came from generally prosperous farming families and kept close ties with the village population. It had emancipated itself from Polish domination and supported Lithuanian independence. The leading bishop of the time, Pranciškus Karevičius (1861–1945), even lobbied the German Imperial government in support of Lithuanian statehood. Four of twenty members of the Lithuanian Council (Lietuvos taryba) who in 1918 signed the declaration of Lithuanian independence were Catholic priests. The church similarly supported the establishment of a democratic system and almost belligerently opposed the rise of authoritarian rule in the 1930s. The bishops denounced censorship and closure of political parties, fought for freedom of Catholic organizations, and helped to contain the extremism of the nationalist regime. The church, furthermore, supported social reforms. It approved the then radical land reform of 1922 and provided leadership, both clerical and secular, for its planning, adoption, and execution.

Although the Catholic Church supported democracy, it steered clear of liberalism to enforce the power of religion in public life. Catholic-oriented political parties, aided by a Jewish minority in parliament, defeated attempts by Social Democrats and Populists to separate church from state. The Catholic Church demanded and gained control of marriage laws. Lithuania was one of the very few European countries without civil marriage and divorce. Only marriages sanctioned by religious authorities were recognized. The church further won compulsory religious education in state-supported schools. Individual exceptions were possible but very difficult and complicated to obtain. The church also claimed financial support from the state and received the lion's share, with the Jews following as a very distant second.[8]

Since most Social Democrats and Populists were ideologically either antireligious or anticlerical, disagreements of a purely ideological nature spoiled the continuously needed practical consensus on policy making. Like France some generations ago, Lithuania of the 1920s was plagued by the misfortune of ideological politics. The adoption of the constitution of 1922 well illustrates the point. Afterward hailed by all as a great democratic achievement, it was approved in parliament only by the votes of the Christian Democratic majority and six out of seven of the Jewish minority deputies with a lonely dissident from Populist ranks. The Social Democrats and Populists abstained. In light of their failure to achieve a formal separation of church from state, the Socialists even left the assembly hall.

Catholic-oriented political parties were independent of the church, as conflicts of Christian Democratic governments with the Vatican conspicuously demonstrated, but politically they could not afford to alienate the powerful institution. Many Catholic clergymen not only ran as candidates for office but, what is more important, actively participated in party activities and electoral campaigns, using the pulpit for partisan propaganda to support Christian Democratic candidates.

The dominance of the Catholic Church meant that Lithuanian politics were less oriented toward representation of single economic interests or classes than were the politics of the other two Baltic states. Loyalty to the Catholic Church and commitment to the Catholic view of the world and society provided the arch spanning over conflicting class and occupational interests. This commonality helped to unite economically and socially diverse groups into the Christian Democratic bloc. This bloc consisted of the Christian Democratic party, the Farmers Alliance, and the Labor Federation, which represented, respectively, professional and financial, agricultural, and workers' interests. On economic and social issues, it overlapped with the social democratic program of the Populists (*Valstiečiai liaudininkai*). This overlapping of Christian Democrats with the Populists created possibilities for parliamentary agreement and coalitions on many political and economic issues. The period of their parliamentary cooperation provided the greatest political stability and creativity of the democratic period. The collapse of this coalition, primarily on questions of religion, enormously weakened the democratic consensus in the country and allowed for the rise of the radical Right.

The conservative Right belonged to two small groups that in 1924 merged into the Alliance of Lithuanian Nationalists. This alliance gained power by virtue of a military coup d'état in 1926. Politically and economically, it was the most conservative of all the political groupings of the preauthoritarian era. At the other end of the political spectrum, Lithuania's "Left" in public life was represented by the Social Democratic party. The Socialists and Communists could draw on only very small constituencies of urban workers. In the 1920s, over 70 percent of the population lived in rural areas. Thus, the most popular Socialist party, the Social Democrats, won only 15 out of 85 seats (17 percent) at the very peak of its success in 1926.[9]

THE ERA OF AUTHORITARIAN RULE

Lithuanian democracy suffered a jolt in December 1926 when on President Kazys Grinius's birthday of December 17, nationalist army officers staged a coup d'état and deposed the ruling Populist–Social Democratic coalition.[10] Elected only seven months before, the coalition could muster a parliamentary majority only with the help of representatives of ethnic minority parties, primarily Polish and German. Yet this politically weak government took on politically very strong forces, namely the military and the Catholic Church. The government, especially its Social Democratic coalition partner, threatened to reduce the size of the army. Socialists generally opposed the principle of a standing professional army. They also spoke of cutting the salaries of clergymen, eliminating religious education in schools, and reducing the size of the church's land holdings. The Social Democrats were obviously hostile to the church, but in 1926 they gained a good reason for questioning certain agreements with the church's leadership. On April 4, the Vatican unilaterally announced the creation of a Lithuanian church province. The establishment of such a province was welcome—for the first time in the 600-year history of Christianity, the Lithuanian church was constitutionally freed from subordination to ecclesiastic Polish authorities. But the terms of the new arrangement were problematic. The Pope excluded from the church province the city and territory of Vilnius, which implied recognition of the Polish annexation of the historic Lithuanian capital. The Papal bull *Lituanorum gente* became a domestic election issue that hurt the Christian Democratic government. The leftist coalition picked up the issue for further political mileage after the election by rejecting the Papal reform as unilaterally imposed and by refusing to recognize its legality.

In the countryside, the political atmosphere was charged by other circumstances as well. There occurred a noticeable increase in Communist activities. The lifting of civil rights restrictions by the new government allowed more freedom for Communist propaganda and other activities but troubled the generally conservative farm population, the military, and many educated groups.

Ultimately, the reasons for the internal revolt are not clear. Inspiration for it may have come from the example of Josef Piłsudski, who marched his legions to Warsaw in May to discipline the government and establish an authoritarian regime in Poland. The Lithuanian and generally Baltic tilt toward the Soviet Union may have given cause for such reasoning. On September 28 Lithuania had signed a nonaggression treaty with the Soviet Union. Even though the treaty had been negotiated and prepared by the outgoing Christian Democratic government, Lithuanian conspirators claimed they needed to save the nation by stopping its "polonization" and "Bolshevization."[11]

Some military leaders became panicky over incipient terrorist activity, attributed to leftists, in a district adjacent to Klaipėda province. Thus, the coup expressed imprudent and insecure nationalism, exaggerated fear of the Communists, and opposition to the new government's cultural concessions to the Polish minority (at the time, Polish authorities in the Vilnius region were closing down Lithuanian schools). Finally, the Christian Democrats who had lost the May elections proved to be poor losers. Many Christian Democrats supported the coup, and their leaders cooperated with the military in the removal of the democratically elected president, Kazys Grinius, and the installation of a new government. Germany's minister to Lithuania, Hans Ludwig Mohrat, at first considered the coup an expression of the general incompetence of Lithuanian statecraft,[12] but he changed his mind after talking to the new prime minister, Professor Augustinas Voldemaras, an enigmatic but persuasive right-wing leader.

The beneficiary of the coup was the small Alliance of Nationalists (Tautininkų sąjunga) and its leaders, Antanas Smetona (1874–1944) and Augustinas Voldemaras (1883–1942). Smetona was elected to the presidency by a rump parliament that consisted largely of the Christian Democratic bloc. The other parties boycotted the election. Smetona promised to respect the constitution and formed a cabinet with the cooperation of two members of the Christian Democratic wing.

At first, Smetona ruled solely with the support of the military. He called its leaders "heroes of Lithuania." To be sure of the military's continued loyalty, however, he replaced the commanders who had brought him to power. In addition, he quickly built up the rightist Nationalist party, which in 1926 could elect only three representatives to the parliament.

Generally, he exercised a personal rather than a party or class dictatorship, displaying considerable political ability to balance military and social forces in such a way as to control top positions and enforce his will. His rule was conservative and nationalist in character but restrained by the pluralistic social organization of the country, which he in some ways fostered but in other ways contained.

Various attempts to depose him failed. After almost ten years of dictatorial rule, however, his power began to decline. In 1935, Smetona had to confront a considerable economic upheaval in southwest Lithuania (Suvalkija), the most prosperous Lithuanian province. Hamstrung by cheap prices and unable to pay their creditors, farmers in Suvalkija staged economic boycotts to drive up the prices of milk and other products. The boycott soon gained political overtones because outlawed democratic political parties and the Communist underground participated. It led to violence and confrontation, which Smetona ruthlessly suppressed. But from then on his base of power began to collapse. The Populists and Christian Democrats formed an alliance against him and demanded the formation of a coalition cabinet. Smetona responded with the election of a rubber-stamp parliament and a new, authoritarian state constitution that was summarily adopted in 1938. In the end, only outside, international forces could dislodge Smetona's authoritarian regime. In 1938, Marshall Rydz-Śmigły forced Lithuania to accept diplomatic relations with Poland through an ultimatum requiring the mending of political fences. The result was the removal of the prime minister, Juozas Tūbelis, who was also Smetona's brother-in-law, and his replacement by Rev. Vladas Mironas, who was perceived to have influence in the Catholic Church.

Smetona suffered another blow in early 1939. Hitler demanded the surrender of the city and territory of Klaipėda to Germany. Under pressure, Lithuania submitted to Berlin, and on March 22 Hitler annexed the area. This loss finally led Smetona to make concessions both to Christian Democrats and Populists. A "generals" cabinet was formed that included representatives of these outlawed but still existing political parties. Smetona's hold over the government was broken, and despite attempts by the president's younger political followers, the liberalizing trend could not be stopped. Lithuania gradually was turning away from the authoritarian regime toward a more democratic system.

By 1940, Smetona's power was eroded. Army leaders no longer completely obeyed him. During the crisis of June 1940, confronted with a Soviet ultimatum threatening invasion, Smetona found only three supporters in the cabinet for his demand for armed resistance to Soviet invasion. Though Smetona had constitutional powers to override the cabinet, he felt powerless and left the country. He died in a Cleveland fire in the United States in 1944.

LITHUANIAN COMMUNISM

Although the Communist party was proscribed during the first republic, it came to play a historical role in its demise. The Communist party in Lithuania evolved from the Bolshevik-Leninist faction of the Lithuanian Social Democrats, a separate branch of the Bolshevik party created by Lenin to support Moscow's efforts to regain Lithuania for the Soviet revolution. On the wings of the Red Army, in the last days of 1918 and the first seven months of 1919, the Communist party attempted to introduce Soviet administration under the name of the Lithuanian-Byelorussian Socialist Republic. After the German defeat of Soviet forces, the party was practically destroyed. Its elite retreated to Moscow. Its leaders, among them Vincas Mickevičius-Kapsukas and Zigmas Aleksa-Angarietis, blamed their own agrarian policy of opposition to private farming for the Soviet defeat.[13] For a couple of years afterward, the party languished, and the clandestine party conference in 1920 was attended by only 13 delegates. However, in 1922, under an assumed name of "Workers Alliance," it succeeded in winning 5 seats (5 percent) in the first parliament. Running under non-Communist labels, underground Communists also won seats in some municipal elections, even during the latter authoritarian era. In the mid-1920s the party's membership increased to 872. Its agitation and strike activity peaked during the second half of 1926 under the new government coalition composed of Populists, Socialists, and ethnic minorities.

Communist support came primarily from segments of the farm and city working class, but also from intellectuals, writers, and artists. The party's recruiting efforts were relatively more successful among sections of very small Russian and very sizable Jewish minorities.[14] It gained Jewish membership especially in the early 1930s, when many in the Jewish community became uneasy about Hitler's rising influence in Europe and when domestic nationalist policies were perceived as impeding economic opportunities and career advancement. According to the data of the Lithuanian Bureau for Internal Security, 52 percent of the Communist membership was Jewish in 1937.[15] In 1941, half a year after the country's occupation by the Red Army and the admission of large numbers of ethnic Lithuanians to party ranks, according to Soviet data, 47 percent of the total membership consisted of minorities, among them 25 percent Russians and a lesser percentage Jewish.[16]

The total number of Communists gradually rose in the mid-1930s. According to Zigmas Aleksa-Angarietis, a Lithuanian Communist leader in Moscow eventually killed by Stalin, Lithuania had 1,500 party members in 1935.[17] In June 1940, the month of occupation, Party Secretary Antanas Sniečkus listed 1,500 members, but Communist party historians later inflated the membership to 1,780 and even 2,200.[18] Even the amplified numbers, however, reflect a membership of only .01 percent of the population.

MINORITIES IN POLITICS AND SOCIETY

The authoritarian evolution of Lithuania's nascent political system affected ethnic and religious minority groups. In 1938, including the Klaipėda region, Lithuanians constituted 80.6 percent of the total population. The rest consisted of Jews (7.2 percent), Germans (4.1 percent), Poles (3.0 percent), Russians (2.3 percent), Byelorussians (0.2 percent), and others (2.6 percent).[19] The Jews, Germans, and Poles actively participated in political life through their own political parties. For four years, between 1918 and 1922, the Lithuanian government included a person of Byelorussian nationality as minister for Byelorussian affairs, and for six years, from 1918 to 1924, there was a Jewish minister for Jewish affairs. The Byelorussian appointment reflected the view that in 1918 Lithuania expected to have a sizable Byelorussian population in the Vilnius territory—an expectation that did not materialize. The Ministry of Jewish Affairs reflected a similar expectation concerning Vilnius Jews, but it also indicated recognition of the importance of the Jewish population in Lithuanian politics and life generally. At the Paris Versailles peace conference, the Lithuanian delegation pledged the Jews full national and cultural autonomy, and in 1920 the Jewish community was recognized as a legal institution with the right to legislate binding ordinances. The project was terminated, however, in 1924. Its failure has been blamed partly on the conflict between the secular and religious, or Yiddish and Hebrew, wings of the Jewish community. The Lithuanian government, however, was willing to accept religious self-government and linguistic as well as educational minority rights but not separate legislative jurisdiction.[20]

Economic opportunities for minorities diminished under the authoritarian regime because of its restructuring of foreign trade and its domestic marketing policies. Political activities were also proscribed. Educational and cultural activities, however, were for the most part not affected. The Germans, autonomous and concentrated as they were on the Baltic coast, dominated Klaipėda's political, educational, cultural, and social life. The Jews maintained a good number of both grade schools and high schools as well as publications, a theological seminary, and cultural and sports activities plus the largest network for Hebrew education outside of Palestine.[21] The Poles also had publications and schools, but the Russians and others were much less articulate and effective as a community. The Russian Orthodox Church nevertheless received financial support from the state.

ECONOMIC DEVELOPMENT, 1920–1930

Since Lithuania economically and politically had to start from scratch, its young leaders had to organize the country's finances and currency and had to work out basic economic relationships to create a productive system. Unlike Estonia and Latvia, Lithuania did not have great difficulties with industrial readjustment. Since Lithuanian industry under the Tsars was very underdeveloped, separation from the Russian hinterland did not create economic havoc or additional strain. As it developed, Lithuania's economic system was of a mixed character, basically capitalist but with a very strong cooperative movement and increasingly large direct state ownership and state participation in economic, especially industrial, activities.

The Lithuanian agricultural system was determined by the reforms of 1922.[22] These were economic as well as sociopolitical necessities. Until that time, 40 percent of the land was in the hands of very few owners, and it was inefficiently managed by landlords, many of whom did not live on land they owned. The new country's economic and social problems could not be resolved without more equitable distribution of land, the basis of prosperity in Lithuania at that time. Politically, the redistribution of land that occurred in 1922 helped to recruit loyalties for the new state and strengthened the hand of democratic parties against the Communists. The agricultural reforms, executed by Minister of Agriculture and Christian Democratic leader Rev. Mykolas Krupavičius (1885–1970), helped to transfer land title from the Polish and Russian nobility to the Lithuanians, primarily landless peasants. Finally, the reforms established the medium-sized farm (20–50 ha, or 44–110 acres) as the mainstay of Lithuanian agriculture. This arrangement differed considerably from the old landholding pattern and changed the political geography by giving birth to new, more middle-class, economic and political interests. Fears expressed by some agricultural specialists that the smaller size of the average farm would ruin productivity eventually did not materialize, though the new system required time for adjustment.

Successful land reform was crucial for a country virtually without industries. In 1911, there were only 7,000 workers engaged in industry in Lithuanian provinces, one-third of them in metal and machine-tool production, the rest in small enterprises, the most important of which was the processing of leather. This number grew to about 20,000 in 1929, and after the depression increased to about 34,000 (without the Klaipėda area), mainly in food processing and related industries. Thus, Lithuania's industrialization between the two world wars was relatively slow and meant a slow growth for the cities. In 1939, industrial workers constituted a mere 8 percent of the work force. Between 1913 and 1940, the urban population increased only from 13 to 27 percent, while the total population, through normal increase and the territorial addition of Vilnius, grew from 2,100,000 in 1923 to 2,925,000 (2,880,000, according to Soviet sources) in 1939.

The country's industrial development was hampered by shortages of natural and financial resources and by the lack of technological know-how. Domestic capital was scarce and had to be sought from abroad. Foreign capital, however, did not find agricultural Lithuania a very attractive investment. Some foreign money was attracted only through monopolistic concessions that proved to be very expensive economically and highly unpopular politically. During the depression, foreign capital was not available at all. Prime Minister Tūbelis, furthermore, preferred an autarchic economy to foreign debt. The result was that foreign investment and foreign debt were both moderate but that the state itself entered into the economy as prime investor. Under Smetona, the state held up to 62 percent of capital in common stock companies.[23] Cooperatives were also encouraged. The idea of consumer cooperatives had found fertile soil in Lithuania before World War I. In 1923–1926, the democratic state very actively promoted producers' and marketing cooperatives, especially in dairy and meat industries. In the late 1920s, the country's agricultural policy moved from grain exports to specialize in dairy and meat production and promoted further cooperatives and state companies in those industries. The chosen course proved to be successful; thirty years later, already under Khrushchev's rule, Soviet Lithuania returned to the same specialization in agriculture. In the 1930s, Lithuania earned much foreign exchange exporting dairy and meat products to industrial countries.

Its main trading partner was Germany, but this trade slumped in the mid-1930s as a result of political difficulties between the two countries. Hitler curtailed imports from Lithuania as punishment for Lithuanian policies in the Klaipėda-Memel district, especially for court sentences imposed on Nazi or pro-Nazi conspirators accused of an attempt to overthrow Lithuanian sovereignty. During this period, England became the main importer of Lithuanian products, but Germany regained this position after the outbreak of World War II.

The trajectory and pace of Lithuania's economic development were reflected in its budget. Government income and expenditures consistently grew in the 1920s under relative boom conditions that followed the stabilization of European, and especially German, economies.[24] But the budget stagnated after 1932 and in 1937 recorded a level of revenue only slightly higher than in 1931. Conservatively managed by Smetona's prime minister, Juozas Tūbelis, the budget was in surplus even during the depression. The government was domestically and internationally criticized for such fiscal conservatism, especially after its refusal to follow the example of other European countries by devaluing Lithuanian currency. Such cautious management was safe, but it hurt exports, denied access to capital, and thus gave prominence to the role of state sponsorship.

Independent Lithuania was also criticized for its emphasis on military spending. During Smetona's rule, between 20 and 24 percent of the budget was spent by the Ministry of Defense, but only 15–16 percent was spent by the Ministry of Education.[25] During the period of independence, the armed forces counted between 22,000 and 28,000 men. Its size was a point of some contention. A large armed forces, it was said, was not really needed since a small country cannot militarily defend itself anyway. The money was therefore being wasted for the self-serving political purpose of keeping Smetona in power. In defense of Smetona and his policies, others argued that the army in Lithuania functioned not merely as a defense force but also as an important institution of education and socialization. Incomplete primary education was usually completed in uniform. The young recruits also learned crafts and trades needed in the private economy. Especially under the command of General Stasys Raštikis (1896–1985) in the 1930s, the armed forces helped to promote national and civic consciousness among the young peasant recruits. Instead of blind submission, the well-supported military was not always pro-Smetona. In fact, General Raštikis eventually lost his position because of opposition to President Smetona's national policies.

At the same time, the engagement of resources in education by the new Lithuanian state was immediate and enthusiastic. Primary education was made obligatory in 1928. A new network of secondary and special agricultural as well as technical schools grew and spread. In 1922, a university was established in Kaunas, followed by the founding of the Academy of Agriculture, the Academy of Veterinary Medicine, the Academy of Arts, the Conservatory of Music, pedagogical and commerce colleges, and the like. These pioneering efforts laid the groundwork for the rapid growth of scientific and technological personnel after World War II. In addition, large mass organizations were promoted for agricultural training. Social and religious organizations also grew in number to the hundreds of thousands. In addition to formal and outreach education, which some critics found too humanistically oriented, native literature and the arts began to develop, and some of the best-known figures in Lithuanian literature either wrote or matured during this period.

The late Lithuanian Communist party's first secretary, Petras Griškevičius, kept complaining that "the bourgeois" regime had left in 1940 some 12 percent of the population illiterate or semi-literate.[26] Comparatively few developing countries, however, ever managed to reduce illiteracy from 44 to 12 percent in seventeen years. Such progress escaped most parts of the Soviet Union itself, as well as some Eastern European Communist countries.[27]

In Gorbachev's age of glasnost', the life, politics, and achievements of independence emerged as the rightful legacy of Lithuanian citizens. Old leaders and institutions that had been denounced by the Soviets were fondly remembered and idealized. The experience of national independence had become a permanent part of Lithuania's political culture. It survived a ruthless half century of Soviet violence and manipulation and could not be eradicated from the national memory.

NOTES

1. This terminology is taken from the preamble to Lithuania's constitution of 1938. Text in V. Stanley Vardys and Catharine V. Ewing, eds., *Constitutions of Dependence and Special Sovereignties* (Dobbs Ferry: Oceana Publications, 1978).

2. For the story see Alfred Erich Senn, *The Great Powers: Lithuania and the Vilna Question* (Leiden: E. J. Brill, 1966). For an early U.S. view see F. Kellor and A. Hatvany, *Security Against War*, vol. 1 (New York: Macmillan, 1924), which discusses problems in Vilnius and Klaipėda.

For population statistics on Vilnius, see *Lietuviškoji tarybineė enciklopedija*, vol. 12 (Vilnius: 1984), p. 275. Professor Kazys Pakštas has published a most interesting historical study of Lithuania's demographic development in *Lietuvių enciklopedija*, vol. 15 (Boston: LEL, 1981), pp. 430–450. Russian statistics showing how the percentage of Lithuanian population declined in the nineteenth century are found in Čepėnas, *Naujųjų laikų Lietuvos istorija*, vol. 2 (Chicago: Dr. Kazio Griniaus Fondas, 1986), pp. 253–271.

3. See Kellor and Hatvany, *Security Against War*, and Thorsten Kalijarvi, *The Memel Statute: Its Origins, Legal Nature, and Observation to the Present Day* (London: R. Hale, 1937). A German researcher's point of view is found in Ernst-Albrecht Plieg, *Das Memelland, 1920–1939: Deutsche Autonomiebestrebungen im litauischen Gesamtstaat* (Würzburg: Holzner, 1962). For a short historical analysis by a Lithuanian historian, see Pranas Čepėnas, *Naujųjų laikų Lietuvos istorija* (Chicago: Dr. K. Griniaus Fondas, 1976), pp. 721–796. See also Rudolfas Valsenokas, *Klaipėdos problema* (Klaipėda: 1932).

4. P. Žostautaitė, article on the professional, social, and ethnic composition of state employees in Lithuania, 1919–1926, *Lietuvos TSR Akademijos darbai*, A series, no. 4(61): 106–116.

5. *Statistikos biuletenis*, no. 10 (October 1924): 29, published by the Central Bureau of Statistics of Lithuania.

6. See V. Stanley Vardys, "Democracy in the Baltic States, 1918–1934: The Stage and the Actors," *Journal of Baltic Studies* 10, no. 4 (1979): 320–336; Georg von Rauch, *Geschichte der baltischen Staaten* (Stuttgart: 1970); Royal Institute of International Affairs, *The Baltic States* (London: 1938); K. J. Čeginskas, "Litauen," *Lexikon zur Geschichte der Parteien in Europa* (Stuttgart: 1981), pp. 377–386.

7. For further information on the church's historical development, see V. Stanley Vardys, *The Catholic Church: Dissent and Nationality in Soviet Lithuania* (New York and Boulder: Columbia University Press, East European Quarterly, 1978).

8. See Finance Department of the Ministry of Finance, Republic of Lithuania, *Receipts and Expenditures of the Republic of Lithuania for the Year 1938* (Kaunas: 1938), p. 53.

9. *Lietuvos TSR istorijos šaltiniai* (Vilnius: Lietuvos Mokslų Akademija, 1961), statistical table on p. 275.

10. See Manfred Hellmann, "Der Staatsstreich von 1926 in Litauen," *Jahrbücher fur Geschichte Osteuropas* 28, no. 2 (1980): 220–242; V. Stanley Vardys, "The Rise of Authoritarian Rule in the Baltic States," in *The Baltic States in Peace and War, 1917–1945,* co-ed. Vardys. A biography of the military coup leader has been written by Petras Jurgėla and Paulius Jurkus, *Generolas Povilas Plechavicius* (Brooklyn: Karys, 1978). The most recent short biography of Antanas Smetona, the political victor of the coup, has been written by Alfonsas Eidintas in *Antanas Smetona* (Vilnius: Mintis, 1990). An earlier, more extensive biographical study was authored by Aleksandras Merkelis, *Antanas Smetona* (New York: ALTSL, 1964). Both authors discuss the coup d'état and Smetona's rule.

11. *New York Times,* December 20, 1926.

12. See Mohrat's statement in Hellmann, "Der Staatsstreich von 1926 in Litauen."

13. *Lietuvos Komunistų partijos istorijos apybraiža* (Vilnius: Party History Institute of the Lithuanian CP Central Committee, 1971), pp. 440, 488ff.

14. Cf. Alexander Shtromas, "The Soviet Ideology and the Lithuanians," *Russia,* no. 3 (1981): 25.

15. Juozas Daulius, *Komunizmas Lietuvoje* (Kaunas: 1937), p. 198.

16. *Mažoji lietuviškoji tarybinė enciklopedija,* vol. 2 (1968), p. 386. Also Shtromas, "The Soviet Ideology and the Lithuanians."

17. Aleksa Angarietis's published work cited in Daulius, *Komunizmas Lietuvoje,* p. 83.

18. Speech by Antanas Sniečkus, longtime first secretary of the Lithuanian Communist party, at the 5th Conference of the Lithuanian Communist party in 1941, cited by Shtromas, "The Soviet Ideology and the Lithuanians"; A. Pankseev et al., *Zhiznenaia sila leninskikh printsipov partiinogo stroitestva* (Tallinn: 1975), p. 67; Partijos istorijos institutas, *Lietuvos koministų partija skaičiais* (Vilnius: Mintis, 1976), p. 42.

19. *Lietuvos statistikos metraštis 1939 m.,* vol. 12 (1940), p. 16.

20. S. Gringauz, "Evreiskaya natsional'naya avtonomiia v Litve i drugikh stranakh Pribaltiki," in *Kniga o russkom evreistve,* ed. Ya. G. Frumkin et al. (New York: Soyuz russkikh evreev, 1968), esp. pp. 51–52; Norman Berdichevsky, "The Baltic Revival and Zionism," *Lituanus* 38, no. 1 (Spring 1992): esp. 75–76; also Max M. Laserson, "The Jewish Minorities in the Baltic Countries," *Jewish Social Studies* 3 (1941): 273–284.

21. *Encyclopedia Judaica,* vol. 11 (1971), p. 382.

22. Anicetas Simutis, *The Economic Reconstruction of Lithuania After 1918* (New York: Columbia University Press, 1942). A useful Soviet source on the interwar economy is K. Meškauskas, *Tarybų Lietuvos industrializavimas* (Vilnius: VPMLL, 1960).

23. *Ten Years of Lithuanian Economy,* Report of the Chamber of Commerce, Industry, and Crafts (Kaunas: Chamber of Commerce, Industry, and Crafts, 1938), pp. 139ff.

24. Ibid. A brief article on Lithuania's armed forces is found in *Encyclopedia Lituanica,* vol. 1 (Boston: EL, 1970), pp. 158–165.

25. See Receipts and Expenditures of the Republic of Lithuania for the year 1938, *Ten Years of Lithuanian Economy,* passim.

26. Speech to the Lithuanian party congress, January 29, 1981, reported by Moscow radio. See FBIS, no. 20 (1981), pp. R 1–2; also see Petras Griškevičius, *Lenino keliu didžiuoju* (Vilnius: Mintis, 1975), p. 57.

27. *Narodnoe obrazovanie, nauka i kultura v SSSR* (Moscow: Statistika, 1977), pp. 9–10. The source reports that Lithuanian illiteracy in 1939 was 23.3 percent, which contradicts Lithuanian party leader Griškevičius as well as many other Communist detractors and critics of independent Lithuania. There is no explanation given for the percentage. Since the statisticians have used as a base the equivalent Lithuanian territory (1939–1977), their calculations very likely include the Vilnius territory returned to Lithuania in October 1939. The percentage given therefore may reflect a much lower literacy level in the previously Polish-ruled province. On Eastern Europe, see, for example, a study on Yugoslavia by Othmar Nikola Haberl, "Die nationale Frage im sozialistischen Jugoslawien," in *Nationalitätenprobleme in der Sowjetunion und Osteuropa,* ed. Georg Brunner and Boris Meissner (Köln: 1982), pp. 130–131.

· THREE ·

Foreign Rule:
Invasion from the East

Lithuania lost its political independence in 1940 as a result of a geopolitical agreement between Russia and Germany to carve Eastern Europe and split it between themselves. Since the eighteenth century, alliances between Russian and German empires had spelled the doom of countries in between. So it was that Poland and Lithuania were divided up among the Russians, Prussians, and Austrians in the final partitions of 1795 and 1796. Their imperial alliances in the nineteenth century obstructed for decades Eastern Europe's political emancipation. When the imperial hold was broken by the outcome of World War I, independent Eastern European countries emerged, but not for long. In 1939, Stalin and Hitler repeated history. They concluded a pact that divided Poland, destroyed the Baltic states, and unleashed World War II.

The sequence of events is well known.[1] On August 23, Soviet and Nazi foreign ministers Vyacheslav Molotov and Joachim von Ribbentrop signed a public nonaggression pact in the Kremlin securing the freedom for Germany to attack Poland. Signed as well were secret protocols changing the map of Eastern Europe. Poland was to be partitioned between the Soviet Union and Germany. Estonia and Latvia were assigned to the Kremlin, Lithuania was left to Germany, and Soviet influence recognized in Bessarabia.

STALIN, HITLER, AND LITHUANIA

After the German attack on Poland on September 1, Lithuania and the other Baltic states declared neutrality. Lithuania also partially mobilized its reservists to cope with possible incidents along the Polish border. Several thousand Polish troops who had fled from the Germans were admitted.[2] Very many of them, including Piłsudski's wife and other refugee civilians, were helped to reach Sweden or other Western countries. On

September 9, the Lithuanian government was urged by Berlin to enter the war quickly and seize Vilnius, a course of action favored by Lithuania's ambassador in Berlin, Kazys Škirpa. But Smetona and the "generals government" refused.[3] Lithuanians had no desire to complicate relations with the Western powers by a forcible takeover of Vilnius nor to become—as would have happened—a virtual German protectorate. Lithuania, foreign minister Juozas Urbšys stated, had "some unrealized national aspirations but she seeks their realization only by peaceful measures."

After the Soviet invasion of Poland on September 17, Stalin bargained for more territory. Hitler was dependent on the Soviets for trade and war supplies and conceded Lithuania to Moscow in exchange for Lublin and parts of the Warsaw provinces in Poland that had been freshly taken by Soviet troops. The Nazis, however, continued to claim a strip of southwestern territory of Lithuania.[4] In part to appear disapproving of the partitioning of Lithuania, Stalin never relinquished the promised territory and instead compensated Germany with 7.5 million gold dollars for the loss of what von Ribbentrop had considered excellent buffalo hunting territory.

The Soviets wasted no time in consolidating control over their new acquisitions.[5] On October 10, 1939, Stalin suggested a mutual assistance pact with Lithuania that would allow the Soviets to station 20,000 troops there, including armored divisions and the air force. The Lithuanians were powerless to resist. In turn, Moscow returned to Lithuania its historical capital city of Vilnius and a small piece of the Vilnius territory that Lenin had recognized as Lithuanian in the peace treaty of July 12, 1920. Both the Soviet and the German governments, the secret protocol stated, recognized Lithuania's claim to Vilnius. Soviet Byelorussian authorities and the secret police were actively preparing for such an eventuality.[6]

After establishing Red Army garrisons, the Soviet Union initially abided by the terms of the past and did not interfere in Lithuania's domestic affairs. This restraint lasted only as long as Moscow was occupied with the winter war against Finland, however. Once the Soviets succeeded in subduing their northern neighbor, they refocused attention on the Baltic states. After months of severe propagandistic and diplomatic pressure, Lithuania was the first to receive an ultimatum, on midnight of June 14. Lithuania was accused of organizing and participating in a Baltic military alliance against the Soviet Union, holding secret meetings with Baltic foreign ministers, and sponsoring a military Baltic journal. The Lithuanians were further accused of kidnapping Soviet soldiers from bases in Lithuania. Molotov demanded that a new government be formed guaranteeing compliance with the mutual assistance pact and that an unspecified but "sufficiently large" number of fresh troops be allowed to move in as defense against Lithuanian "provocation."[7] Smetona and his government had eight hours to respond to this demand.

View of modern Vilnius from the air, with the old cathedral and bell tower in the foreground. (Photo by A. Sutkus. Used by permission.)

With Soviet garrisons inside Lithuania, the Soviet fear of the Germans establishing themselves in Lithuania militarily and diplomatically was far-fetched. Nonetheless, the Soviets insisted that President Smetona had asked Hitler for protection in February 1940 based on the interrogation of Augustinas Povilaitis, former director of Lithuanian security, who was arrested in 1940 and imprisoned in Moscow.[8] This Soviet claim has not been corroborated by any other documentary or oral evidence. Former Lithuanian foreign minister Juozas Urbšys in his memoirs denied the existence of any such agreement between Smetona and Hitler. General Stasys Raštikis, former chief of the Lithuanian army, also denied any knowledge of such an agreement or attempt to achieve one. The Soviets apparently needed the story to justify their occupation and annexation of Lithuania.

The Lithuanian government, presided over by Smetona, held a stormy night session discussing Moscow's ultimatum. Since the Soviets refused to accept any diplomatic entreaties, the question before the Lithuanians was whether to resist the Soviet intrusion by force of arms or to accept.[9]

Lithuanian military men argued that the Red Army could not be successfully resisted. Opposition ministers, though deeply worried, did not seem fully to appreciate all the implications of Soviet demands; some seem to have been blinded by their dislike and even hatred of authoritarian Smetona. Of the president's Nationalist majority, only Smetona himself and his defense minister, Kazys Musteikis, demanded defense by the use of arms. They were supported by Minister of Education Kazys Jokantas, the elderly opposition Christian Democrat, and State Controller Konstantinas Šakenis.

The die was cast. Smetona, to be sure, had constitutional authority to order defense, but he had no power to order the military. His own commander of the army, General Vincas Vitkauskas (1890–1965), chose to cooperate with the militarily superior Russian forces. Unwilling to cooperate, but unable to fight, Smetona left the capital.

The issue of surrendering without a shot fired would remain one of the gnawing questions of national debate for years to come. Why didn't the armed forces, which in recent years had annually consumed over 20 percent of the nation's meager budget, defend the country in its hour of need? Was it eventually better for the masses of civilian population that bloodshed was avoided, or did the Lithuanian meekness merely encourage future Soviet ruthlessness? Didn't failure to fire on the invaders indicate to the world a tacit acceptance of Soviet rule? Should it have been at least symbolically demonstrated that this was not the case? Failure to resist opened for Moscow enormous opportunities to justify the occupation and annexation. The tradition of resistance to foreign occupation in Lithuania was old. But so was the habit of fatalistic acceptance of imposed superior force, and similarly, the habit of passive resistance. The leadership of the 1940s chose to accept the inevitable in order to spare senseless bloodshed. But they misjudged the severity of the occupation to which Lithuania was to be delivered.

The leadership and the masses of supporters of the independence movement of the rebellious 1990s rejected the reasoning of the government of the 1940s. When under Soviet attack on January 13, 1991, the Lithuanians, unarmed as they were, confronted Soviet tanks. President Vytautas Landsbergis later explained the changed views:

> There seemed to be nothing left but to stand our ground with determination to be ready to die. But we were certain that this [Soviet] attack would strengthen our legal foundation in the future. Even brief clashes between the Red Army and the forces of sovereign Lithuania would strengthen our independence. That night I left my quarters and, together with our armed men, took an oath in the presence of a priest.[10]

Similarly, member of parliament Romualdas Ozolas articulated the lessons learned from Lithuania's earlier capitulation to Russia:

> Armed resistance is the most extreme means of self defense. . . . But what if the other side [Moscow] loses the desire or possibility of negotiating with us? Should we quietly suffocate? Excuse me, I did not rise to freedom for that. Independently of how events will unfold around me, I will be a person whose children will not be able to accuse me that again, like in the 1940s, not a single shot was fired [in defense of independence].[11]

Thus, the public's and the leadership's determination to defend national freedom seems to be radically different today from what it was fifty years ago, June 15–17, 1940, when the country was for the first time totally overrun by the Red Army.

THE SYNTHETIC REVOLUTION AND ANNEXATION

Even before completing the military occupation, Moscow set in motion the plan to legitimize its conquest. This was done by means of a synthetic revolution, a technique new in the arsenal of Communist politics of expansion. It was a model of "people's democracy," applied at greater leisure in other Eastern European countries after World War II although not for the purpose of annexation as in the Baltic states. In six weeks during the summer of 1940, Lithuania was, by manipulation, transformed from an independent state into a Soviet republic when, on July 21, 1940, Lithuania formally requested admission into the Soviet Union as its constituent part.

Officially, Soviet politicians and historiographers referred to the introduction of Moscow's rule as "Socialist revolution" led against the bourgeois government by the native Communist party. At first, the Red Army's role was recognized in such interpretations; later the "role" was changed to "help," still later to a "factor," until recognition of Soviet force and orchestration was totally left out. The youngest generation of Lithuanians were taught only that a popular revolution led by the Lithuanian Communist party occurred in 1940.

Indeed, according to the late Lithuanian Communist party leader, Petras Griškevičius, the then underground party's first secretary, Antanas Sniečkus (1903–1974), was already on June 16 directing the formation of the "people's government" from a cell in a Lithuanian prison. Sniečkus had worked in the underground in Lithuania in the 1930s and had been ordered back to Moscow, where Stalin was purging Comintern and foreign Communist leaders. Sniečkus then chose a Lithuanian prison as his base of operations.[12]

Moscow's man in Kaunas was not Sniečkus, however, but Moscow's deputy foreign commissar, Vladimir Dekanozov, who was immediately dispatched to Lithuania.[13] Dekanozov demanded establishment of "people's government" and chose its members. Justas Paleckis (1899–1980), a pro-Soviet but otherwise politically inconspicuous journalist, was selected to replace Nationalist Prime Minister Antanas Merkys (1887–1955). Thus Paleckis became both acting president and prime minister. Afterward, Merkys and foreign minister Juozas Urbšys (1896–1991) resigned. They were deported together with their families to the Soviet Union.

The choice of Paleckis and some other undistinguished ministers was insufficient to assure the Soviets of Lithuanian acceptance. Dekanozov was lucky to persuade Professor Vincas Krėvė Mickevičius (1882–1954), a distinguished and left-leaning author, to join the "people's government" as deputy prime minister. With him on board, Moscow could hope to defuse potential resistance to what lay ahead. Krėvė Mickevičius was an opponent and bitter critic of Smetona who shed no tears for his departure, but he was also a patriot committed to Lithuania's independent statehood. Dekanozov assured him that Lithuanian statehood was inviolate. The old professor consulted with resigning Prime Minister Merkys, who advised the writer to accept the inevitable.

Within two weeks, however, Mickevičius began to doubt Dekanozov and his promises. Soviet actions in Lithuania were destroying its independence; they were not mere measures for a better and more compatible reorganization of the Lithuanian system. Alarmed by what he saw, he decided that Moscow's plenipotentiaries in Kaunas and Vilnius were overstepping their powers. Against Dekanozov's wishes, he flew to Moscow to complain directly to foreign minister Vyacheslav Molotov. Annoyed by the writer's visit, in a long midnight conversation Molotov laid his cards on the table. Ever since the days of Ivan the Terrible, Molotov said, Russia had aspired to possess the Baltic region, and now again it had the opportunity to do so. In the modern world, he said, small states have no future, and the Baltic states, together with Finland, would be incorporated into the Soviet Union.[14]

The novice Lithuanian politician was shocked. After returning home, he attempted to resign from the government but was allowed only to take a temporary medical leave. He could not stop or slow down the adoption, on July 6, of a new election law setting guidelines for choosing a "People's Diet," which was to end Lithuania's independence. The law allowed only one slate of candidates. This slate was to be provided by the Communist party, in consultation with the Soviets, under the title of Union of the Working People of Lithuania. Election dates in the Baltic states were synchronized. Balloting took place on July 14–15 in Estonia and Latvia, and on July 14 in Lithuania. The Lithuanian voters were so slow in coming to electoral precincts, however, that the election had to be extended into July 15. To intimidate articulate opponents and the public, on the night of July 11, Communist authorities arrested an estimated 2,000 persons in various leadership positions of local and central government entities and public or social associations. In order to trace the noncompliant, passports were stamped at the polling places.

The Lithuanian Election Commission declared that a total of 95.51 percent of eligible voters had cast their ballots and that 99.19 percent of these had voted for the union list of Communist and nonparty candidates.[15] A British writer, Bernard Newman, has reported that through an error the Soviet news agency in London announced the final results even before the polls in Lithuania were closed.[16] In times of glasnost' fifty years later, orthodox Communists and even some former Election Commission members admitted that the electoral results were falsified and the election itself was manufactured.[17]

The Soviets claimed that a plebiscite was held in Lithuania. On July 21, the new Diet met in Kaunas and in a national drama theater hall, surrounded by more spectators than there were newly elected members, unanimously declared the establishment of Soviet power in Lithuania. In the same resolution the Diet asked the Kremlin to admit the Socialist republic of Lithuania into the Soviet Union. Shortly afterward, Paleckis and his delegation left for Moscow by special train to bring back to Lithuania "the bright sun of Stalin's constitution." In Moscow, the Supreme Soviet obliged on August 3, 1940, the date Lithuania formally became a Soviet constituent republic.

The process of legitimization, conducted for domestic and foreign consumption, thus was completed. It did not bring, however, universal recognition abroad. Nazi Germany of course acquiesced. But the United

States denounced "the devious processes whereunder the political independence and territorial integrity of three small Baltic republics—Estonia, Latvia, and Lithuania—were to be deliberately annihilated by one of their more powerful neighbors."[18] This statement, signed by Under Secretary of State Sumner Wells, was issued on July 23 and in a less articulate way was echoed by a number of Western and Latin American countries. It formed the cornerstone for the U.S. policy of nonrecognition of Soviet annexation that continued for the next half century.

After the dramatic Soviet ultimatum and the subsequent coup d'état, the formalities of the sovietization of Lithuania proceeded without incident. The Lithuanian army, already reorganized into a "people's army," on August 30 was incorporated into the Red Army as its 29th corps. The value of Lithuanian currency was reduced from 3–5 rubles to 0.9 rubles. Although this extremely unfavorable rate fueled the financial panic that had begun with the occupation, it provided a lucrative financial boon for the incoming Russian military. Communist land reform limited private landholding to 30 ha (66 acres), except for church parishes, which were restricted to 3 ha. Financial institutions were nationalized on July 23, commercial institutions on September 27, and by October 31, almost all private housing was nationalized. To make way for incoming Russian officials, "bourgeois" elements—former merchants, clergy, and land owners—were relocated from their homes to the far suburbs. By December 1, Soviet laws formally superseded all Lithuanian statutes.

At the same time that a new system was being imposed, so were policies on how to handle potential dissenters. In September, at a sumptuous dinner with the Kremlin's top leadership, Baltic government officials were instructed to deal swiftly and summarily against those who refused to cooperate with the Communist regime.[19]

Stalin's orders to clamp down on the Lithuanians were well timed. Changes connected with wholesale replacement of managerial and governmental personnel had not only stunned the country but brought about economic displacement and produced bitter, publicly uttered criticism. Protests quickly overwhelmed the new rulers. Mečislovas Gedvilas, an underground Communist with long managerial experience in the state-run Lithuanian health insurance system, discussed frankly the worsening social situation and outlined four reasons for popular discontent during the festivities celebrating the October revolution:[20] (1) Lithuanian anxieties over the future of their national identity and culture; (2) fear of religious persecution; (3) feelings of discrimination and anger by the autochthonous Lithuanian intelligentsia, who found themselves demoted or even replaced by local ethnic minorities or inexperienced Communist cadres; and (4) economic conditions. Prices rose, goods disappeared from the stores, and the standard of living plummeted. Not only farmers but also city workers loudly complained of economic shortages and difficulties much worse than under Smetona's rule. To these shortcomings Communist party leader Antanas Sniečkus added a perceived rise of "chauvinism" (read: nationalism) and anti-Semitism.

The pains the country's sovietization produced were further aggravated by the Stalinist terror. Arrests had preceded elections to the People's Diet. In the fall, secret police started to organize networks of informers, recruiting them from among the clergy, the military, educators—all walks of life. Arrests became frequent. During the first twelve months of Soviet rule, approximately 12,000 people were sent to prison for alleged political and economic crimes. Most of them never came out. State terrorism reached its apogee on the anniversary of Lithuania's occupation by the Red Army on June 14–15, 1941, when an estimated 34,000 people, including whole families and children, were packed into freight cars and deported to the "inland" of the Soviet Union.[21] Deportee lists prepared in advance covered all of Lithuania's ethnic, religious, and political groups and all the social classes. Several massacres of prisoners were perpetrated by Red Army troops and local Communist officials retreating before the advancing German armies on June 22, 1941.

THE INSURRECTION AND THE NAZI RETRENCHMENT

German attack interrupted Soviet rule for a short but politically and socially very significant three-year period in which sovietization was abated. The outbreak of World War II created historically dramatic events that gave rise both to hope and tragedy. The flight of the Red Army brought immediate relief to an overwhelming majority of the ethnic Lithuanians: Soviet deportations ceased; prisons disgorged their political captives. Yet, the Nazi conquest spelled wholesale death for Lithuania's Jewish population, by far the largest casualty of the German occupation. Less than 10 percent survived the Holocaust. As in France and Poland, organized bands of local Lithuanians willingly participated in atrocities against the Jews. Authorities who served under the Germans were also later implicated in these crimes by Soviet historians, but the evidence of their willing and active collaboration has been difficult to establish.

Several historical factors help illuminate but not condone the sometimes active, but largely passive, collaboration with the Nazi decimation of Lithuanian Jews. The cleavage of the Jewish from the non-Jewish population across Eastern Europe was historically reinforced over the ages by differences not only in religion but across cultures, classes, and occupations as well. The Jewish population usually did not speak the local language and was more urban, better educated, and wealthier than the local ethnic, and largely peasant, population. Thus the two groups historically had little occasion to come to understand and respect each other, and officially sanctioned pogroms against the Jews periodically legitimized and fueled anti-Semitism and its violent expression. During the first, brief Soviet occupation, many Lithuanians had witnessed Jews collaborating with the Soviet NKVD and purging their wealthy or educated neighbors. Evidence of some Jews as Communist leaders and sympathizers who thrived under the Soviet occupation and persecution of gentile Lithuanians then fueled a cycle of violence and revenge once the Soviets were driven out. Further, the Soviet deportation of national elites erased the upper level of educated ethnic Lithuanians, reducing its ability to contain the angry sentiments of the less educated social groups.

The first response to the German occupation by the ethnic Lithuanians was typical of that in many other Central European countries. The Lithuanians greeted the regime shift with immense relief, particularly since the chaos between the Russian retreat and the Nazi ascent gave Lithuanians an opportunity to reassert self-rule. German troops had just begun to enter Lithuania when on June 23 anti-Soviet resistance groups, led by the Front of Lithuanian Activists (Lietuvių Aktyvistų Frontas, LAF), openly revolted against the Soviets in order to meet the Germans as masters of their own country.[22] The city of Kaunas was taken two days before the arrival of General (later Field Marshal) Friedrich Wilhelm von Küchel's Wehrmacht divisions. Similarly, Vilnius was functioning under local administration by the time the German army arrived.

The Front of Lithuanian Activists had been organized in November 1940 by Lithuania's ambassador to Berlin, Colonel Kazys Škirpa. Its organizational and military strength lay in Lithuania's underground network of an estimated 36,000 members in 1941. The underground had ties to Germany, a natural ally because of its geographic proximity, its anti-Communist disposition, and its support for anti-Soviet forces. In December 1940, Berlin began preparing for Barbarossa, the plan to conquer Russia, and found it convenient to encourage Škirpa and the Lithuanian underground. The Germans expected to use the Lithuanian resistance movement as a fifth column when the attack on the Soviet Union began.

The Germans miscalculated. Most Lithuanians were not willing subjects of either Russia or Germany. Berlin was surprised, even shocked, when the Lithuanian insurrectionists captured the Kaunas radio station and proclaimed the restoration of Lithuania's independence governed by a Provisional Government. Berlin had simply hoped to use pent-up anti-Soviet emotions for military purposes without incurring any political obligations to the Lithuanians. Hitler's headquarters issued orders to disregard the insurrection and the Provisional Government. The Wehrmacht's daily reports on the Eastern front never once mentioned the rebellion or its success at restoring governmental services. However, the fact could not be totally suppressed. *Paris-soir,* on June 25, 1941, reported on its front page that a revolt had taken place in Lithuania, a new government had been installed, and independence declared. The newspaper, relying on information by the Italian state press agency, called the revolt "the first crack in the Russian bloc."

The Germans were not the only surprised party. The leader of the Lithuanian Activist Front, Kazys Škirpa, was also shocked by the turn of events. He had relied on German support ever since the summer of 1939, and in 1941, sensing Hitler's Barbarossa plan, had mistakenly persuaded himself that Berlin supported restoration of Lithuanian independence.[23] When the rebels of Kaunas announced Škirpa's appointment as prime minister of the Provisional Government, the Germans did not allow him to leave Berlin. Instead he was interned for the duration of the war. In Kaunas, his duties were assigned to Acting Prime Minister Juozas Ambrazevičius-Brazaitis, professor of literature and minister of education in the new government.

For six weeks the Provisional Government attempted to act as a governing institution, but for the most part the occupation authorities frustrated its work. Local control over the post office, telephone, press services, and transportation was taken over by the Germans, leaving the Provisional Government isolated and impotent. On August 5 Ambrazevičius-Brazaitis and his cabinet gave up. They announced the government was "suspending" activities. In a long memorandum announcing this decision they criticized German occupation policies, including the massacre of the Jews and Berlin's refusal to recognize Lithuanian sovereignty in exchange for Lithuania's readiness to help in the war effort against the Soviets.[24] In response, the newly installed Nazi Zivilverwaltung Adrian von Renteln insisted that the government was "dismissed."

Lithuania became a part of Heinrich Lohse's Ostland. On July 25, 1941, the Nazi Zivilverwaltung replaced its military administration. Von Renteln recruited former general Petras Kubiliūnas (1894–1946) as chief of the Vertrauensrat, a Council of Trustees. Kubiliūnas had been imprisoned by President Smetona for supporting a pro-German coup d'état in 1934. The Council of Trustees administered the infrastructure of local and regional government and in some respects even the central government, but its autonomy was very limited. Jews and Germans were exempt from Kubiliūnas's jurisdiction. The Lithuanian Activist Front was disbanded and its leader, Leonas Prapuolenis (1913–1972), was sent to the Dachau concentration camp.

The Nazi occupation did little to restore private property and the other institutions critical to a market economy. Industries nationalized by the Soviets were not restored to former owners but taken over and managed by specially established German companies. Titles to farmlands were not returned except on an extremely selective basis after 1943. The property of Lithuanian citizens who had been deported by the Soviets for the most part were administered by the Germans. In addition, farmers were required to meet high quotas of delivering agricultural products. Publications were very limited and the mass media heavily censored. Finally, in 1942, the Nazi regime began enacting its long-term strategy for the Baltic states by colonizing the countries with ethnic Germans and destroying the large and historically rooted Jewish population.

Persuaded that all hope of cooperation with the Germans was lost, the Lithuanians responded to the Nazi policies by organizing resistance against them. Three separate anti-Nazi movements, antagonistic to each other, existed on Lithuanian territory. A well-armed and disciplined Polish Home Army controlled segments of the Vilnius region and had infiltrated workplaces and German offices in the city of Vilnius. In the fall of 1941, the remaining Communist sympathizers gained a foothold after Moscow began using partisan groups of mostly refugee natives to sabotage German military activities.

The third and by far the largest resistance group, however, was the democratic-nationalist Lithuanian underground, which consisted of a coalition of a dozen political parties and other groups.[25] At first, Catholic-oriented groups organized their own coalition under central leadership while the left-oriented parties maintained a separate central organization. In late 1943 the Social Democrats united these resistance forces under the umbrella of the Supreme Committee for the Liberation of Lithuania. The committee elected Professor Steponas Kairys (1878–1964), a Social Democrat, as its first chairman. These groups published scores of underground periodicals, maintained military forces, and at one time managed clandestine radio broadcasts. They heavily infiltrated the local and regional, and even the central, administration of Kubiliūnas, including the state security office. To a large extent, this underground shaped Lithuania's public opinion through its publications and organizational network.

Although the goal of the Lithuanian resistance movement was similar to that of its anti-Nazi counterparts in Western countries, its tactics were rather different. Resistance leaders were convinced that the Western Allies would win against the Nazis and would help to restore Lithuanian statehood, as they had at the end of World War I. Thus, the Lithuanians opposed German economic, labor, and military recruitment policies deemed hostile to Lithuania's survival but supported German actions against the Soviets, who were perceived as an even bigger threat than the Germans.

From the end of 1941, Germany periodically requisitioned tens of thousands of workers for its factories. Recruitment of military manpower from prisoners captured and held in POW camps, many of whom mistakenly thought that they were joining units of a reborn Lithuanian army, had begun that summer. Altogether, during the occupation the Germans organized twenty such battalions of over 8,000 troops. In 1943, after the defeat at Stalingrad, Berlin decided to increase its use of Baltic manpower for military purposes.[26] As a result, occupation authorities attempted to organize Baltic Legions of Waffen SS in all three states. They were unsuccessful, however, in Lithuania. Lithuanian resistance to the enterprise humiliated the Nazis. On March 17, induction was stopped and the Lithuanians were declared unworthy of joining the SS. In retaliation, forty-six prominent intellectuals and public figures were sent to the concentration camp in Stutthof. In addition, the generalkommissar closed down the universities and some other schools in Vilnius and Kaunas.

Guerrilla attacks by Soviet partisans increased over the following year. In February 1944, the Germans tried again. They authorized Povilas Plechavičius, an immensely popular general, to recruit a Territorial Force of 10,000 men to be commanded by Lithuanian officers to fight Soviet partisans on Lithuanian territory.[27] The resistance saw in the project an opportunity to establish a nucleus national army and supported the general. Recruitment was a huge success, as volunteers exceeded the quota. In May, however, the Germans demanded the transfer of the newly recruited troops to the direct command of the SS. Plechavičius refused and his troops followed suit. On May 15 he was arrested and sent to the Salaspils concentration camp near Riga. After executing a number of the resisting troops, the SS disarmed and arrested about 3,500 men, who were sent to the Luftwaffe in Germany. The rest escaped seizure and fled to the forests. As a result of the German occupation, the Soviets estimated civilian population losses at a half a million people. Western scholars suggest a more realistic figure of 300,000–325,000.[28]

STALIN RETURNS TO LITHUANIA

Lithuania was retaken from the Germans by the armies of the Third Byelorussian Front. The front's commander, General Ivan Danilovich Tscherniakhovsky (1906–1945), killed in action in East Prussia, was buried in the center of Vilnius with a large monument to remind the Lithuanians that the Soviets were the new rulers of their country. At the end of 1991, with the consent of the general's daughter, his remains, along with the hated monument, were extracted and shipped for reburial in his native city, Uman', in the Ukraine. Kaunas fell on August 1, 1944, and the last of the German troops were driven out with the capture of Klaipėda on January 18, 1945. The Soviets advertised the participation of the 16th Lithuanian division in the taking of the port city. The division had been organized in early 1942 in Russia and from the spring of that year saw much action on its way to Lithuania. Over one-third of the division was composed of Jewish troops. Another third consisted of Russians, and the remaining third of Lithuanians.[29] After the victory on the Baltic, the 16th division was demobilized and sent home. It did not participate in the storming of Germany.

In a meeting with Baltic party and government leaders in July 1944, Stalin demanded assurances from Sniečkus, the Lithuanian leader, that the Lithuanian "national flag" would be flown over Vilnius as the Red Army took over.[30] The dictator wanted to emphasize the national, patriotic character of the war with the Germans. In the same vein, Lithuanian Communists boasted that only under their control did Lithuania rule all ancient lands since Vilnius was regained from the Poles in 1939 and the Klaipėda region from the Germans after the Allied victory. Until victory over Germany in May 1945, national traditions were tolerated—for example, candidates for the priesthood were exempted from military service.

With both Klaipėda and Vilnius regained, the republic's territory grew from 55,670 sq. km in 1938 to 65,200 sq. km in 1945. Its boundaries remained stable for half a century until Mikhail Gorbachev threatened, in 1990, to take away Klaipėda and some Vilnius territory in case Lithuania insisted on independence. At the Potsdam conference in 1945, Moscow was apparently prepared to claim a part of East Prussia on grounds that it was once inhabited by ethnic Lithuanians.[31] This demand proved to be unnecessary, however, since neither Truman nor Churchill asked for justification of this annexation to the Soviet Union, even when the province was incorporated not into Lithuania but into the distant Russian republic.

Though it grew in territory, Lithuania lost in population—and not only through deportations and arrests by Soviet rulers.[32] Lithuania's Germans (52,000) were repatriated to Germany in 1940–1941. Overall, the Nazi occupation resulted in the loss of one-third of a million people. Some 20,000 people, among them 6,000 Lithuanians, 8,500 Jews, and 3,600 Russians, retreated into the Soviet Union together with the fleeing Red Army in June 1941. Many perished. With the retreat of the Wehrmacht three years later, an estimated 70,000–80,000 Lithuanians escaped to the West from the returning Soviet forces. More than 60,000 of these reached Germany and other West European countries. From there, they were eventually able to emigrate to the United States, Canada, Australia, or Latin America. Another exodus was made possible by an agreement between the Lithuanian Communist government and the National Liberation Committee of Poland, signed September 22, 1944. Some 218,000 Poles—or Lithuanians feigning Polish heritage—including the strongly nationalistic and rather unwilling Polish Archbishop of Vilnius, Romuald Jalbrzykowski, left for Poland.

Casualties of the partisan war of 1944–1953 (at least 40,000), and the arrests and mass deportations between 1945 and 1951, added hundreds of thousands of victims. Estimates range from 200,000 to 300,000 or more. Neither natural population increases nor the mostly Russian immigration that followed the war could replace those losses. As a result, Lithuania's population in 1959 was smaller than it had been twenty years ago.

THE POLITICS OF COMMUNISM

Thus Lithuania was again incorporated into the Soviet empire. An occupation of half a century followed. This time the totalitarian system became fully entrenched and with it, a party-oriented social system. In the political sphere, Lithuania was forcibly socialized into Soviet norms and behavior. Culturally it had to accept Russian personnel as well as the widespread use of the Russian language. At the same time, Lithuanian Communists needed to legitimate their rule and tried to integrate these foreign institutions and norms as much as possible as elements of Lithuanian tradition. This endeavor required very complicated political maneuvers.

The returning Communist leaders, First Party Secretary Antanas Sniečkus, Chairman of the Council of Ministers Mečislovas Gedvilas, and Chairman of the Presidium of the Supreme Soviet Justas Paleckis, found their country devastated by the ravages of war, impoverished by the flight or deportation of its educated classes, and engulfed in a vast and strong anti-Communist insurgency.

The eradication of this insurgency and the economic reconstruction of the republic were the two most urgent tasks of the postwar rulers. To oversee the process, the Kremlin created a special Organization Bureau of the Central Committee for Lithuania on November 11, 1944 (1944–1947). It was chaired by Mikhail Suslov, first secretary of the Stavropol province, who could draw on his experience eradicating the anti-Soviet resistance in North Caucasus to destroy the Lithuanian rebels together with Sniečkus. Suslov served until he was promoted to Moscow in March 1946. There, he soon became a secretary of the Central Committee and eventually the editor of *Pravda*. Later, after he had reached the heights of influential Politburo membership, he acted on behalf of his old acquaintance as Sniečkus's sponsor and protector. Indeed, already in 1946, when still in Vilnius, Suslov reportedly saved Sniečkus's career after a Moscow commission compiled unlikely charges of favoritism and corruption against him.

The new regime had a host of administrative problems, but the most conspicuous was the shortage of trustworthy personnel. The local NKGB (Narodnyi Kommissariat Gosudarstvennoi Bezopasnosti, or People's

Commissariat of State Security) and NKVD (Narodnyi Kommissariat Vnu-trennykh Del, or People's Commissariat of Internal Affairs) and the state procuracy, as well as many other sensitive sectors of the economy, were staffed largely by Russians and operated directly under Moscow's bureaucracy. The deputy chief of the national secret police, A. Kobulov, defending Moscow against charges of russification, insisted that there were no Lithuanians available for needed positions. In 1948, of 299 district chiefs of secret police at the local level, only 18 were Lithuanians. The situation in the procuracy was better, but in 1948 only 46.5 percent of its employees were Lithuanians. Similar conditions existed in the Lithuanian Communist party. In 1947, only 18.4 percent of its membership was Lithuanian. Less than half of these members were entrusted with positions in the secret police, the internal ministry police, and other powerful agencies. The density of Russians in the higher administrative structure of the postwar period can be estimated from the fact that in accordance with Lavrenti Beria's policy of "korenization," or national strengthening, more than 3,000 leading Russian officials were later ordered to leave the republic.[33]

In time, the party as well as the administration would draw more personnel from the local population. By 1953, 38 percent of party members were Lithuanian; by 1965, this percentage had risen to 63.7 percent. In 1989, the year of peak party membership, the Lithuanian percentage was 70.5—an improvement, though still below the percentage of Lithuanians in the general population, which was 79.8. Meanwhile, Russians were overrepresented—in 1947, they constituted 59 percent of the party membership. This proportion gradually went down to 17.2 percent in 1989. The percentage of Poles rose to 4.4, while the share of the Jews declined from 7.9 percent in 1947 to 0.9 percent in 1989.[34]

Despite the fact that the party and the government were eventually dominated by ethnic Lithuanians, administrative practice was conducted in Russian, the lingua franca of the Soviet empire. Communications and accounting in virtually all economic institutions were also conducted in Russian. In education, from the early 1970s a doctoral thesis could no longer be written or defended in Lithuanian. Separate Russian language classes proliferated in higher education; the use of Lithuanian in radio and TV diminished.

The party, one of the tiniest in the Soviet Union, nevertheless grew in size, especially after 1965.[35] In part as a reaction to John F. Kennedy's compromise on Cuba in 1962, many Lithuanians saw the United States as unwilling to lift the Iron Curtain and came to accept Soviet rule as permanent and the Communist party as a legitimate institution for career and promotion purposes. Membership was no longer regarded as unpatriotic. One had to work within the system, it was said, to defend whatever national values were salvageable.

By the 1970s the party's membership had become more diverse and better educated. Underground loyalists, World War II veterans, and the local militia (*istrebiteli* in Russian; *stribai* in Lithuanian parlance) were gradually replaced by political idealists and intellectuals. From the early 1960s, the percentage of intelligentsia—professionals and employees with higher education—began visibly to grow, and by 1975 one-fifth of party membership had higher education. This increasing acceptance of the party by intellectuals signified a recognition that one could not advance professionally without it. Former prime minister of Lithuania Kazimiera Prunskienė has explained that she joined the party in 1980, at the age of thirty-seven, because her choice was "either to take the Communist party card, which was equivalent to permission for travel abroad on official business, or to stay professionally sterile."[36] Prunskienė classified party members of her generation in three groups: (1) active ideological thinkers and propagandists, (2) formal members who acquired membership for purposes of a career in the power structure, and (3) "superformal" members who compromised for purposes of professional growth and advancement not related to politics or power.

There were indeed very few pure Communists left since Marxism-Leninism as an ideology had died during the Khrushchev era. The rest made compromises with their conscience and their "consciousness was polluted," as Prunskienė put it, just as much as anyone else's in the Communist-dominated environment.[37] They learned to live with hypocrisy and adopted double lives: a public face for the regime and a small and circumscribed private sphere for themselves. Instances of party members allowing their babies to be secretly baptized were not unusual. Instead of "proletarian internationalism," this generation of intelligentsia promulgated "nationally" understood "socialism," even "national communism,"[38] and eventually supported the goal of independence. Overall, they acquired Soviet commitments without shedding the popularly held wish to preserve and advance Lithuania as a nation.

For almost half a century, from 1936 until his death in 1974, Antanas Sničkus held the reins of the Lithuanian Communist party.[39] He left an indelible, personal imprint on the apparatus of the Communist party and on the development of Soviet Lithuania. Sniečkus grew up the youngest of seven children in the family of a very prosperous farmer in southwestern Lithuania. His parents were kulaks, a class that Stalin destroyed. Young Sniečkus was infected by Communist ideas as a refugee from Lithuania in a Russian-supported high school for refugees in Voronezh during World War I. He started out as an intellectual Communist who betrayed his social class. He severed relations with his family, which, in turn, regarded him as an outcast. Sniečkus's mother fled to the West in the fall of 1944 and refused his request to return to Lithuania and rejoin him.

Becoming a party member at seventeen, he spent the 1920s training in Moscow and as an underground operative in Lithuania. He had started serving his second prison sentence in Kaunas when the Soviets occupied Lithuania in June 1940. Throughout his long career, he faced many potential pitfalls, purges, and dead ends. As the director of the State Security Department, for example, Sniečkus had the onerous task of arresting some 2,000 leading public figures before Lithuania's first Communist elections. But Sniečkus was lucky: He was a good inside manipulator capable of finding friends, a characteristic that helped to keep his position secure in future years. He overturned a Russian-directed Moscow conspiracy to replace him in 1946, escaped a purge by the unlucky Lavrenti Beria, and survived a confrontation with Nikita Khrushchev over Lithuania's agricultural and cultural policies. Khrushchev's commission was to recommend Sniečkus's dismissal on the very day Khrushchev himself fell from power.

Sniečkus also knew how to protect his own turf at home from ambitious local competition. His greatest rival was his old comrade Mečislovas Gedvilas, who complained to Moscow that Sniečkus was too timid. In response, Sniečkus had Gedvilas demoted from chairman of the Council of Ministers to the post of minister of education.

Ironically, like Sniečkus, Gedvilas would often circumvent Moscow for nationalist reasons. For example, he would authorize construction of only an "addition" to an existing school, which required no approval from Moscow. The old structure then would be torn down and the new "addition" completed as a separate building.[40] Gedvilas further gained respect by advocating an eleven-year secondary school system for the Baltic republics on grounds that the Lithuanians and other Balts needed an extra year to properly learn both their native language and Russian. An anecdote tells of an argument between Gedvilas and a Central Committee apparatchik. The latter insisted that Lenin's language, Russian, must take priority. Gedvilas is supposed to have retorted: "If so, Marx's native tongue should take absolute priority." Khrushchev's educational reform of 1958 confirmed the eleven-year secondary school system for the Baltics, though the rest of the Soviet Union stayed with its ten-year *desiatiletka* system.

First Secretary Sniečkus was brutal, close-mouthed, flexible, and ruthless, but after Stalin's death he no longer acted as the youthful Communist firebrand who almost casually signed orders of deportation for tens of thousands of families.[41] Instead, he became a political boss who played the Soviet system better than any of his local colleagues. He handled business politically through the party's Central Committee Secretariat, not directly through government ministries, and was mostly remembered for dissuading Moscow from pursuing economic expansion in Lithuania and so minimizing environmental devastation and the influx of a very large Russian immigration, as occurred in the other Baltic states. In the late 1950s through the 1970s he also gained a reputation and respect for quietly protecting intellectuals and national culture and for preserving the historical national castle of Trakai against the wishes of the Kremlin.

In the 1960s and 1970s, three political views could be distinguished among those in the politically articulate strata of the Lithuanian population.[42] The most widely accepted was the "autonomist" philosophy, which sought neither separation from Moscow nor elimination of socialism but seriously supported the ideals of Lenin's theory of nationality relations. The second was more daring. "National Communists" frequently thought that their present ties to Moscow hindered rather than helped Lithuania's progress and that Lithuanians themselves, not Moscow, should make decisions affecting national life. The third was a "traditional-liberal" view. Those with this outlook opposed Soviet rule, advocated a non-Communist society and statehood, and sought a genuinely democratic political order, however vague this concept was at the time. This view was heard only in the underground and only by dissidents. Sniečkus was no Lithuanian Kadar. He most likely agreed with the Ukraine's Vladimir Shcherbitsky that "national communism" was economically and politically unworkable.[43] His long reign thus represented the autonomist ambition of a politically savvy provincial boss.

POLITICS AND ECONOMY

In the postwar period, the economic reorganization of society was no less radical than the political restructuring. The regime tolerated small shops and private business for only two years. During this time the industrial sector was nationalized. The new land reform law, which imposed collectivization, began in early 1949 and was completed in 1952. Sniečkus is said to have argued in Moscow that collectivization should be delayed because the country was not yet ready for it, but Georgii Malenkov, Stalin's secretary, replied that the republic party secretary was to obey Politburo orders, not to question them. Threats and physical harassment were widely used to force the farmers to join the collectives. In a reference volume, *The Baltic States*, jointly issued by the publishers of Estonian, Latvian, and Lithuanian encyclopedias in 1991, Lithuanian authors estimated that 300,000 people were deported in the effort to crush the nationalist underground and ease collectivization.

A pre–Soviet era farmstead. (Photo by Rimantas Dichavičius. Used by permission.)

Although the number actually deported is probably smaller than this estimate, collectivization caused not only much suffering and demoralization among farmers but also an enormous drop in agricultural production. It took longer than a decade for Lithuanian output levels to recover. During this time, Stalin died and Khrushchev revised agricultural policies. The republic's leaders, however, helped the recovery. They reestablished Lithuania's specialty, meat and dairy products, and turned away from Khrushchev's love affair with corn. Eventually Lithuania became the most efficient meat and dairy producer in the empire, exporting 40 percent of the total to the Soviet Union, mostly to large cities such as Moscow and Leningrad.[44] Even in the best years, however, production by collective and state farms had to be supplemented by private plots of land. In 1989, for example, 21 percent of meat and 30 percent of eggs still came from these intensively farmed plots held by collective and state farm families.[45] Although the productivity of the Lithuanian farm worker was 47 percent higher in the republic than in the rest of the Soviet Union, it was much lower than in the United States, constituting only 16 percent of the U.S. figure.[46]

Lithuania's industrialization did not seriously begin until Stalin's death. Sniečkus is credited for convincing Stalin to overlook Lithuania while pushing for a quick industrial development in Estonia and Latvia. Lithuania's Baltic neighbors were also likely preferred by Stalin, however, because they already possessed an industrial infrastructure and some well-developed industries. Lithuania's partisan war, which created political instability and scared away Russian immigrants, also may have been a factor in Moscow's thinking.

Once industrialization began, it accelerated, grew in volume, and brought about dramatic economic and social changes. By 1990, industrial production accounted for 54 percent of the national product.[47] The share of agriculture was 25.3 percent. The rest fell to construction (10.1 percent), transportation (3.9 percent), and commerce (6.7 percent). Industries in the other two Baltic republics produced over 60 percent of their national product (Estonia 61.7 percent and Latvia 60.3 percent). In volume of output, according to the last chairman of Moscow's Gosplan, Yurii Maslyukov, Lithuanian industrial production was eighty-four times higher in 1989 than it had been fifty years ago, in 1940.[48] In some cases, the Soviets expanded what already existed, for example, food processing, furniture, textiles, construction materials, paper, and shipbuilding. The Soviets also developed the energy, machine building, metal working, chemical and wood products, and construction materials industries. In the 1980s, Lithuanians built large fishing vessels and made metal-cutting lathes and many consumer durables. The Lithuanians also refined gasoline.

Moscow's economic doctrine of central management was frequently articulated by economic and political writers. In 1972, Professor V. Kistanov reasserted in the authoritative *Voprosy ekonomiki* that, contrary to some proposals, economic rationality as perceived by Moscow, rather than national republic territory, should be the basis both for economic management and for state organization.[49] For years, territorial resource considerations were overlooked and the ethnic factor rejected in favor of a very centralized economy run from headquarters in Moscow. The only interlude in such policy implementation occurred during the Khrushchev era, 1957–1964, which had endeared this abstract art–bashing peasant leader to regional party bosses despite his many serious faults as party chief.

Yurii Andropov, who succeeded Brezhnev, had declared this centrally run, integrated Soviet economy to be the cornerstone of the Soviet state organization and the foundation on which Soviet nationality policy rested. Gorbachev, his heir in reform, also time and again warned that the loosening of economic integration (as distinguished from local management practices) would undermine the Soviet empire.

It was only in late 1980s when Gorbachev realized that he could not save the Communist empire without giving priority to strictly economic considerations. For Lithuania, this imperial economic policy produced not only high industrialization and voluminous production increases but also a decisive dependence on the Russian hinterland for resources as well as for markets. This dependency was conditioned in part by Lithuania's meager natural resources but institutionalized by highly centralized, specialized, and inflexible Soviet management practices that limited the republics to its captive market of barter (ruble) exchanges. Centrolit, for example, was the largest cast iron foundry in the Baltic region when in 1980 it was obliged to export 55 percent of its production to Russia. At the same time, metal-working enterprises in Šilutė, Lithuania,[50] 112 miles away from the foundry, had to import their cast iron from Armenia, Leningrad, and Kolomna in the Soviet Union, all more than 1,000 miles away.

The principle of specialization was key to the command economy. Following this economic doctrine, Moscow Gosplan built a single factory or two for supplying certain industrial parts for the entire country. Some of these factories were built in Lithuania. For example, a factory in Panevėžys was making virtually 100 percent of the compressors for pneumatic brakes for auto vehicles assembled anywhere in the Soviet Union. Another factory made 100 percent of all household electric meters.[51] A bathroom fixtures factory, Kaitra, molded 50 percent of the bathtubs and fixtures installed in new Soviet housing, and still another enterprise supplied 100 percent of Soviet TV channel changers. Through the extremely specialized and centralized structure of the economy, the disparate and distant elements of the vast Soviet empire were made interdependent.

Lithuania in the past has had to import 80 percent of its natural resources, including energy, from Russia and the other former Soviet republics.[52] The republic will be able to pump only 15.5 million tons of recently discovered oil in the next twenty years, but the country needs at least 7 million tons annually to serve its industrial and agricultural economy.[53] It will always be dependent on outside sources of energy and raw materials. Currently, Lithuania gets most of its oil from Bashkiria, most of its natural gas from Ukraine, and most of its coal from Russia, including nuclear fuel for the Ignalina power station. Cotton for textile mills comes exclusively from Central Asia, and much wood for furniture or paper from Russia's Far East. Various metals come from Ukraine. Among the unexploited resources there are large iron ore deposits in southern Lithuania, but the environmentalists will not easily agree to mining them. In 1982, Lithuania exported 80.5 percent of its industrial production to former Soviet republics, mostly to Russia (43.9 percent), and imported from them 89.1 percent of its goods and supplies, again mostly from Russia (47.3 percent).[54] Only 19.5 percent of production was exported abroad, primarily to the Third World and former Socialist countries. Imports amounted to a mere 11.9 percent.

According to the Soviets, the reward for such dependency has been a higher standard of living for the Lithuanian people. In 1989, Gosplan chairman Maslyukov indicated that Lithuanian enterprises paid wages 2 percent higher than the Soviet average, after Estonia, Latvia, and Russia. Lithuania's per capita income in the same year was 2,757.95 rubles—slightly higher than that of the Russian Federation and somewhat below Estonia and Latvia, but 9 percent above the Soviet average.[55] But this "prosperity" was purchased by making permanent an annual trade deficit of at least 1.5 million rubles.

Thus, Maslyukov articulated the standard Kremlin argument that Lithuania's relative prosperity was due primarily to budgetary and price support by the Moscow government, an argument that found some acceptance in Lithuania. According to Maslyukov, the Soviet Union had invested in Lithuania 50 billion rubles and covered its trade deficit.[56] Gorbachev would later insist that the amount of investment was 30 billion rubles.[57] The Lithuanian Bureau of Statistics, however, argues that a large part of the investment had been provided by the funds of Lithuanian collective farms and population savings. Second, industries had provided profits and foreign currency for Moscow's ministries, most of which were not passed on to Lithuanian factories.[58] Furthermore, Moscow did not include in its calculations budgetary expenditures by the Lithuanian government on housing, education, health, and pensions for workers imported from other parts of the Soviet Union to work in new factories or for military service. Economists further add that Moscow exploited Lithuanian slave labor in the gulag and deportation settlements, for which the Lithuanians were not paid or paid little. They argue that only when Moscow compensates for slave labor, imprisonment, deportations, and killings, the way West Germany did the victims of the Holocaust and the non-Jewish prisoners, will the accounts with Moscow be balanced.

The sociopolitical consequences of such radical industrial change have been commensurate with its scope. First, industrial development spurred the growth of the cities, the working class, and the professionals. The urban population grew from 28.3 percent in 1950 to 68.6 percent in 1989, a 40 percent increase.[59] The percentage of workers and professionals in industry increased to 30.2 percent, while the percentage of agricultural workers sank to 17.6 percent from 31 percent in the 1970s. Lithuania obviously is no longer a purely agricultural country and has developed many problems of social disorganization characteristic of urban modernization.

Another sociopolitical change produced by industrialization was demographic, namely, the immigration of Russians and other Slavs. The Russian percentage of the population has quadrupled, from 2.3 percent in

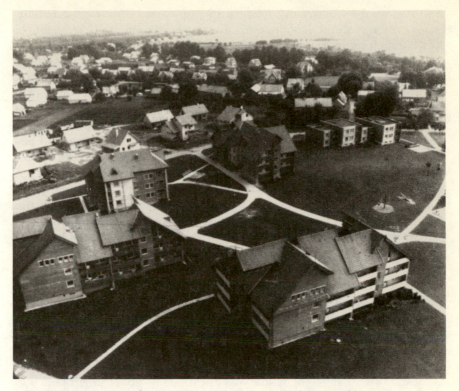

A Soviet-era suburban development. (Photo by A. Sutkus. Used by permission.)

1939 to 9.4 percent in 1989. The immigrants were not only managers and party or government officials but also included some factory workers, taxi drivers, store clerks, public transportation employees, and the like. Contrary to popular belief, the percentage of university graduates and professionals of Russian ethnic background was still higher than that of the Lithuanians in the late 1980s. Neither numerical nor percentage increases threatened the position of the autochthonous population as it did in Estonia and Latvia, but with the slight increase of the Byelorussians (1.7 percent, mostly in the city of Vilnius) and the Ukrainians (1.2 percent), the ethnic Lithuanian population declined to 79.6 percent in 1989.

The third major consequence of Soviet-style industrialization has been a staggering pollution of the environment. Industrial pollution, of course, is not unique to the Soviet Union, but it hit there much harder than in the industrialized Western countries. Low technological capabilities, the absence of much awareness of potential dangers, and the skewed priorities imposed by the Communist leadership aggravated ecological problems. Soviet rulers valued economic production goals and military achievements much more than health, social welfare, or the wholesomeness of the environment. Even such a relatively powerful regional leader as Antanas Sniečkus was for years afraid to show to his Moscow-appointed second party secretary, Valerii Kharazov, plans for the development of Lithuania's national parks—plans designed to constrain unreasonable industrial expansion. Moscow's recklessness has been unmistakably revealed in the horror stories on nuclear testing, the ruin of the Aral Sea, devastations of the Central Asian ecological environment, river pollution, and even pollution of some parts of Lake Baikal, the deepest body of fresh water on earth, not to speak of the nuclear accident in Chernobyl.

For Lithuania the cleanliness of the environment was not just a question of personal health but also of the national and ethnic survival of a community in the landscape it had occupied for centuries. By 1959, the Lithuanians had become sufficiently concerned to push for adoption of an environmental protection law, one of the first in the Soviet Union. Various regulations were added though not rigidly enforced. Environmentalists such as Professor Česlovas Kudaba, in carefully devised studies, warned of the potential dangers of the densely packed chemical plants, of heating plants releasing 74 tons of sulphur trioxide a day, of overdone drainage, and the like. In 1982–1984, scholars of the Academy of Sciences and other institutions prepared a plan for the "protection of nature in Lithuania until the year 2000" that on the whole was approved as government policy by the republic's authorities. The major problems, however, were not resolved. For example, water purification systems were installed here and there, but the country's second largest city, Kaunas, with a population of 430,000, still does not have a water purification plant.

The construction of huge chemical plants in the 1960s aggravated the situation. Major Lithuanian rivers–Nemunas, Nevėžis, Neris, and Mūša—became heavily polluted. Feeding their waters into the Baltic Sea, they contribute, together with the discharges from paper mills and from ships in Klaipėda harbor, to the environmental crisis of the Baltic Sea.

Pollution of the Baltic Sea, heavier on the more industrial Latvian coast than on the Lithuanian coast, frequently requires closure of otherwise brilliant white sand beaches at resort towns like Palanga in Lithuania. Special efforts were made by Lithuanian intellectuals to lobby for the protection of the Baltic shoreline in the late 1980s when Moscow decided to explore for offshore oil on the Lithuanian coast. With the help of Moscow's Russian environmentalists, this second Lithuanian victory against Moscow's planners was won. The first was the diversion of the construction of an oil refinery in the 1960s from the vicinity of the largest

Lithuanian river, Nemunas, to Mažeikiai, a border town between Lithuania and Latvia, so as not to turn the Nemunas into a national sewer line.

Another potential environmental disaster was found in the use of poisonous chemicals, mainly ammonia and chlorine, by some 150 industrial enterprises.[60] Inhabitants were exposed to as many as 33 grams of chlorine, more than ten times the potentially lethal amount.

The most environmentally dangerous legacy of the Soviet era, however, is the nuclear power plant at Ignalina. Built on the Chernobyl model and commissioned in 1983, it was to have five reactors and to become the largest nuclear power plant in the world. After the disaster in Chernobyl, Communist Lithuanian authorities unilaterally stopped funds for the construction of the third reactor. International and local authorities disagree on the potential danger of frequent accidents at the plant. The Swedes, interested in minimizing the danger for themselves, are willing to invest money to strengthen the plant's security system. Ignalina's danger to Lithuania became an ecological symbol of Moscow's suppressive and irresponsible rule over Lithuania. Moscow's insistence on further expanding Lithuania's chemical industries was a major factor in uniting the Communist intellectual elite in their support for the national reawakening movement of Sąjūdis in the summer of 1988.

POLITICS AND SOCIETY

Political and economic changes were accompanied by the reorganization of society and the reshaping of political culture. Lithuania became a part of the "new civilization" for which Sidney and Beatrice Webb had such high hopes in the 1930s.[61] The essence of this civilization, regarded by Soviet writers as a higher level of historical development, consisted of a party-oriented society that would forcibly replace the private system of social organization we usually refer to as civil society. Impressed by some material achievements and the semblance of stability and consent among the Soviet citizenry, Western observers have frequently failed to identify the essential role of suppression critical to this system. Although the identification of society with the state was its main characteristic, the system was organized around the ruling political party, which not only held a monopoly of power but dictated, enforced, and controlled the goals and norms of public and even private behavior. Although it was put in by force and by bloodshed, the system developed its own momentum that was dominated, as Alexander Solzhenitzyn showed, by an institutionally organized network of fear and lies.

Although the Communist regime enjoyed little real credibility, most citizens dutifully fulfilled their civic obligations and marched in state victory parades, laid wreaths at the tombs of Russian soldiers, and joined most of the myriad of social organizations designed to provide collective support and supervision for almost all aspects of social life. To do otherwise was to risk sanctions that ranged from job demotion or expulsion from school to incarceration in the local psychiatric hospital. Thus, after the Red Terror of Stalin's rule, when the specter of brute force, torture, and Siberian gulags terrorized the populace, the regime adopted a lighter touch.

Once the Soviet regime had destroyed Lithuania's initial resistance, it enlisted the population's compliance, largely on the basis of pragmatic and economic considerations. In an economy where money had little meaning, the primary access to housing and most goods and services was controlled by the Communist party through the individual workplace to ensure the desired behavior. To get into college, one needed to have been a Communist Youth member with a politically acceptable parentage. To get a good job afterward, the history of one's political and social activities was more important than grades. Once on the job, attendance at regular labor collective meetings and political study groups was mandatory. All along the process, any divergence from the dictated norms could be recorded by one of the many KGB informants among one's classmates, coworkers, neighbors, and telephone operators. On the surface, post-Stalinist society reflected stability and social participation. The free and willing expression of self-interest, however, which is the driving force of a true civil society, was anathema to the Soviet leaders, who simply relied on mechanisms of coercion more subtle than those employed by the original Bolsheviks.

The nature of the party-oriented society in Lithuania after World War II was evident in the treatment of its writers. In 1946, the newly formed Writers' Association was mobilized to enforce the official Soviet cultural policy in Lithuania.[62] At the October 1–2, 1946, meeting of Lithuanian writers, party secretary Kazys Preikšas (1903–1961) vigorously denounced writers of diverse ideological convictions simply to clarify the new prominence of political criteria.

Public condemnation of social leaders and opinionmakers was only the beginning. Writers, teachers, and especially leaders of the many social groups that existed under Smetona began to disappear in the gulags— people who earlier had generally supported liberal or Communist causes.

Religious institutions, especially the Catholic Church, were among those that suffered the most from the social controls.[63] Bishop Vincentas Borisevičius (1887–1947) was executed. Archbishop Mečislovas Reinys (1884–1953) of Vilnius was arrested and died in Vladimir prison. Bishop Pranas Ramanauskas (1893–1959), an auxiliary to Borisevičius, and Archbishop Teofilis Matulionis (1873–1962) of Kaišiadorys were deported and spent years in slave labor camps. Church organizations and their constituent units lost all legal rights. Like all property, church buildings were assigned to the state. Formal religious education was not allowed even in the church, while atheists had an exclusive constitutional right to conduct education and engage in communication. Church activities were put under the supervision of local government councils, law enforcement agencies, and the KGB. At the same time, russification, not only political but also cultural and linguistic, was accepted as something to which the Lithuanians needed to reconcile themselves. Speaking in 1958 at a time when discussion of "national communism" was in vogue, Sniečkus declared:

> It is very important that every working man realizes that the person who incites us against the Russian nation, who would like to tear the Lithuanian nation away from the Russian nation, is digging the grave for the Lithuanian nation. Either with the Russian nation, with all Soviet nations on the road to national progress—or imperialist slavery, the threat of destruction of the Lithuanian nation. There is no third road.[64]

Cultural policies reflected this view. Writings, art, traditions—anything related to keeping alive the collective national memory—was purged. History was rewritten and former leaders were branded as oppressors, guerrilla fighters as bandits. The Russian language was made the lingua franca not only in government but also in economic and cultural life. Books from Western languages could not be translated directly but only from their Russian translations. The regime sought to "de-nationalize" and assimilate the native population. In a fit of anger, Suslov is supposed to have said: *"Da, budet Litva, no bez litovtsev"* ("There will be Lithuania but without Lithuanians"). The goal was a Soviet man, a sovietized member of society without national loyalties though aware of his ethnic origins. The goal was never achieved, although it seemed to be for a time. Lithuanians ultimately had no choice but to accept Soviet rule if they wanted to survive.[65] This realism—acceptance with eyes open of a system based on fear and lies—never fully resolved the question of the legitimacy of Soviet power but nevertheless created a framework for the socialization and molding of new generations according to Moscow's needs. The regime made people preoccupied with a shortage of everyday goods so they would have no time for politics or public concerns. They learned how to handle the overlapping and overbearing bureaucracies, how to use illegal middlemen (*tolkachi*) and connections (*blat*), and how to turn to the second economy and the black market to meet centrally set economic goals. At the same time, personal and family perks took precedence over organizational or collective goals.

Thus, the schizophrenic Soviet reality demanded that official norms and rules be violated in order to achieve official goals. This left the people, especially the younger members of society who were disillusioned with communism and its promises and bereft of any belief or political ideology, alienated and cynical. Cynicism and the power of brute force became the philosophy of the ruling and managing elites. There also occurred a withdrawal into the privacy of friends and family and a search for purely private gratifications, pleasure, and forgetfulness. The prevailing attitudes did not foster the introduction of capitalism and democracy. The Soviet system furthered collectivism with the idea that the state, not the person, is responsible for people's welfare. The result, one philosopher has written, "was an infantilized man, a person who expected handouts from the state and society"[66] but who did not care to work hard or accept responsibility for himself. According to another philosopher, the Soviet experience left "an empty niche in political life in which a new layer of politicians will have to form itself."[67]

It was paradoxical that an ideology preaching selflessness and idealism should reap the opposite in reality. To escape the void, the people, especially the young, took to alcohol. Drinking became not just an occasion for weekend enjoyment but a way of life, a ritual, an everyday part of private and public transactions, even part of a job. Alcohol turned into a political tranquilizer that created and fueled apathy, low productivity, and irresponsibility. All Soviet reformers, including Gorbachev, tried unsuccessfully to stem this problem. The damaging influence of the sovietization of political culture can especially be appreciated in the 1990s, when Lithuania is struggling to structure a free market and forge democratic independence.

NOTES

1. Raymond J. Sonntag and James S. Beddie edited a collection of documents related to the pact in *Nazi-Soviet Relations, 1939–1941* (Washington, D.C.: Department of State, 1948). The best told story of the Nazi-Soviet pact is found in Anthony Read and David Fischer, *The Deadly Embrace* (New York and London: W. W. Norton, 1988). Very interesting and valuable documentary and journalistic information from the Soviet side has been compiled by Y. Felshtinsky, ed., *SSSR-Germaniya, 1939* (vol. 1) and *1939–1941* (vol. 2) (Vilnius: Mokslas, 1989).

2. Among various accounts by contemporaries, see Colonel Leon Mitkiewicz, former Polish military attaché in Lithuania, *Wspomnienia Kowienskie* (London: Veritas, n.d.).

3. For the story see Albert N. Tarulis, *Soviet Policy Toward the Baltic States* (Notre Dame, Ind.: Notre Dame University Press, 1959), pp. 128–138. Also see documents of Lithuanian ambassador Edvardas Turauskas, at the archives of the Hoover Institution on War, Revolution and Peace, Stanford University.

4. See Bronis J. Kaslas, "The Lithuanian Strip in Soviet-German Diplomacy, 1939–41," *Journal of Baltic Studies*, no. 3 (1973): 211–225.

5. For documents and witnesses' accounts see U.S. House of Representatives, Select Committee on Communist Aggression, *Third Interim Report*, 82d Cong., 2nd sess., 1954. Hereafter cited as *Third Interim Report*. Also see the valuable memoirs by Lithuania's last foreign minister who conducted negotiations with Stalin and Molotov. Juozas Urbšys, *Lietuva lemtingaisiais 1939–1940 metais* (Vilnius: Mintis, 1988).

6. See story, based on interviews with participants, in Mikolaj Iwanow, "The Byelorussians of Eastern Poland Under Soviet Occupation," in *The Soviet Takeover of the Polish Eastern Provinces, 1939–41*, ed. Keith Sword (London: Macmillan, 1991), pp. 262ff.; also Regina Žepkaitė, "Vilniaus atgavimo kaina," *Tiesa*, October 11, 1988.

7. See documents in *Third Interim Report*, esp. pp. 332–334.

8. In addition to the Soviets, one Western scholar, the Finnish historian Seppo Myllyniemi, lent credence to the story. In his *Die baltische Krise 1938–1941* (Stuttgart: Deutsche Verlags-Anstalt, 1979), pp. 105ff., Myllyniemi asserted that President Smetona sent Augustinas Povilaitis to Berlin in February 1940 to ask whether the Germans were ready to make Lithuania into a German protectorate and to offer help to achieve this objective. This assertion was based on the presumed record of a secret police interrogation of Povilaitis published several times in the Soviet Union. One version is "Kak burzhuaznye natsionalisty prodavali Litvu," in *Kommunist* (Vilnius) (1980): 36–37. The interrogation is also summarized in many works of Soviet Baltic historiography.

Myllyniemi considered this report corroborated by an entry in the diary of Werner Best, a high-ranking official in the Reichssicherheitshauptamt. The diary makes a note of Povilaitis's arrival. The Lithuanian presumably met with very high-ranking Gestapo leadership and received only vague answers. According to Best, Povilaitis expressed the desire for Lithuania to be under German influence. Myllyniemi inferred that Smetona agreed. In his June 1939 conversations with T. H. Preston, the British minister in Kaunas, Smetona had expressed the view that Lithuania would be occupied by either the Soviet Union or Germany, and that in the case of such calamity he preferred Germany because of its free-enterprise economic system. In various interviews with former Lithuanian officials, including enemies of Smetona's domestic and foreign policies, however, none of them have ever mentioned such a decision or manipulation by Smetona. The reason that Povilaitis visited—and not just once—with high-ranking German security officials was to discuss German and Lithuanian interests in the activities of the Polish underground in the newly acquired former Polish territories as well as their interests in the behavior of Soviet military garrisons in Lithuania. As earlier mentioned, from a fifty-year perspective, the nonogenerian foreign minister Urbšys flatly denied any real or contemplated pact with Germany by Smetona or any other Lithuanian leader on his behalf. See Urbšys, *Lietuva lemtingaisiais 1939–1940 metais*, p. 71.

The rumor reported in Lithuania by the *Bulletin of the Internal Security Department* stated, in February 1940, that shortly a delegation from Germany would come to Kaunas to offer a German protectorate to Lithuania. The Reich was concerned that Lithuania did not become a center of Polish resistance for the reconstruction of the Polish state. If Lithuania accepted this offer, Soviet garrisons would withdraw and be taken over by German military contingents. This change was rumored to enjoy Soviet support. After the switch, the Soviets persumably would return the entire Vilnius territory and the Germans the Suwalki triangle. See Turauskas archives, Hoover Institution, Stanford University.

9. See Kazys Musteikis, *Prisiminimų fragmentai* (London: Nida, 1970); also Juozas Audėnas, *Paskutinis posėdis* (New York: Romuva, 1966).

10. Interview in *LeFigaro* (Paris), reprinted in *The Observer* (Chicago) (November/December 1991): 5.

11. *Gimtasis kraštas,* November 22–28, 1990, pp. 1–2.

12. Petras Griškevičius, *Lenino keliu didžiuoju* (Vilnius: Mintis, 1975), p. 14.

13. The most interesting information and insights into the work of Dekanozov are found in Juozas Vaišnoras, "Istorijos kryžkelėje: Iš atsiminimų apie 1940–uosius," *Pergalė,* no. 10 (1988): 126–145. An analysis of the "synthetic" revolution of 1940 can be found in a number of sources. One of the earliest is Tarulis, *Soviet Policy Toward the Baltic States;* see also my brief chapter in V. Stanley Vardys, ed., *Lithuania Under the Soviets* (New York: F. A. Praeger, 1965), pp. 47–61. A strictly comparative short analysis of the Baltic transformation in the summer of 1940 is also found in my "The Baltic States Under Stalin: The First Experiences," in Keith Sword, ed., *The Soviet Takeover of the Polish Eastern Provinces 1939–41* (London: Macmillan, 1991), pp. 269–291. See also Romuald J. Misiunas and Rein Taagepera, *The Baltic States: Years of Dependence, 1940–1980* (Berkeley: University of California Press, 1983), pp. 15–47.

14. Transcript in *Third Interim Report,* pp. 341–344; also Tarulis, *Soviet Policy Toward the Baltic States,* pp. 211–215.

15. B. Vaitkevičius, ed., *Lietuvos TSR istorija,* vol. 4 (Vilnius: Mokslas, 1975), p. 15.

16. Bernard Newman, *The New Europe* (New York: Macmillan, 1943), p. 207.

17. See, for example, *Literatūra ir menas,* February 25, 1989, p. 13.

18. U.S. Department of State, *Bulletin* 3, no. 57 (1940): 48.

19. See Mečislovas Gedvilas, *Lemiamas posūkis* (Vilnius: Vaga, 1975), p. 99; also Juozas Vaišnoras, minister of finance of the "people's" government, "Istorijos kryžkelėje," *Pergalė,* no. 10 (1988): 126–145.

20. *Tarybų Lietuva,* November 12, 1940, p. 1.; ibid., November 26, 1940, p. 1.

21. Texts of documents in *Third Interim Report,* pp. 523–528.

22. Story of the insurrection by Zenonas Ivinskis, "Lithuania During the War: Resistance Against the Soviet and Nazi Occupants," in V. Stanley Vardys, ed., *Lithuania Under the Soviets* (New York: F. A. Praeger, 1965), pp. 61–84; Seppo Myllyniemi, *Die Neuordnung der baltischen Länder, 1941–1944* (Helsinki: 1973), pp. 72ff.; Kazys Škirpa, *Sukilimas* (Washington, D.C.: 1973); Dr. N. E. Suduvis, *Allein, ganz allein* (New Rochelle: Freunde der litauischen Front in Europa, 1964). Also Algirdas M. Budreckis, *The Lithuanian National Revolt of 1941* (Boston: Lithuanian Encyclopedia Press, 1968); Misiunas and Taagepera, *The Baltic States: Years of Dependence, 1940–1980,* pp. 44–67.

23. Cf. memoir by Bronius Aušrotas, in *Draugas* (Chicago), March 21, 1992, p. 3; see Edvardas Turauskas, *Lietuvos nepriklausomybės netenkant* (Chicago: Lietuviskos knygas klubas, n.d.), p. 277. Turauskas was the second in the hierarchy of the

Foreign Ministry of Lithuania in 1939–1940. He and Lithuanian diplomats in Western countries were rather critical of Škirpa's pro-German politics.

24. Text in E. Rozauskas, ed., *Nacionalistų talka hitlerininkams* (Vilnius: Lietuvos TSR Mokslų Akademija, 1970), pp. 35–41.

25. In addition to the works listed in footnote 22, for studies of the German occupation and resistance activities of 1941–1944 see Povilas Zičkus, Algirdas Vokietaitis, and Vladas Zilinskas, *Laisves beieskant* (Chicago: LLKS, 1983); also K. Pelėkis, *Genocide: Lithuania's Threeford Tragedy* (Germany: Venta, 1949).

26. *Lietuviškoji tarybinė enciklopedija*, vol. 6 (Vilnius: Mokslas, 1980), p. 611.

27. The general's biography was written by Petras Jurgėla and Paulius Jurkus, *Gen. Povilas Plechavičius* (Brooklyn: Karys, 1978).

28. For the Soviets, see *Hitlerinė okupacija Lietuvoje* (Vilnius: VPMLL, 1961), pp. 431ff. For Western sources, check Misiunas and Taagepera, *The Baltic States: Years of Dependence, 1940–1980*, pp. 275-226, and Adolfas Damušis, *Lietuvos gyventojų aukos ir nuostoliai antrojo pasaulinio karo ir pokario 1940–1959 metais* (Chicago: Laisvę Fondas, 1988), pp. 13ff. These sources include estimates for all population losses. For information specifically on the Holocaust in Lithuania, including statistics, see Dov Levin, "Lithuania," *Encyclopedia of the Holocaust*, vol. 3, ed. Israel Gutman (New York and London: MacMillan, 1990), pp. 895–899.

Pogroms against the Jews in June 1941 were initiated by Einsatzgruppe A under Brigadefuhrer Franz Stahlecker. In a number of localities, some Lithuanians collaborated in the executions. Some other Lithuanians, among them the family of future president Vytautas Landsbergis, hid and saved their Jewish neighbors. For an archival documentation see Helmut Krausnick and Hans-Heinrich Wilhelm, *Die Truppe des Weltanschauungkrieges* (Stuttgart: Deutsche Verlags-Anstalt, 1981). Recent (1989–1992) Lithuanian periodicals address various aspects of the tragedy. The weekly *Atgimimas* (through 1991) has periodically published lists of people who helped persecuted Jews.

29. Cf. Vaitkevičius, *Lietuvos TSR istorija*, p. 128.

30. See Gedvilas, *Lemiamas posūkis*, p. 239.

31. P. I. Kushner, *Etnicheskie territoriii i etnicheskie granitsy* (Moscow: Academy of Sciences, 1951). This book is an extremely well-documented demographic and historical study.

32. For figures in this section see Lithuanian Information Institute, *Lithuania: Survey*, 3rd ed. (Vilnius: Republic of Lithuania, 1992), pp. 6–8; *The Baltic States: A Reference Book* (Tallinn-Riga-Vilnius: Estonian, Latvian, Lithuanian Encyclopedia Publishers, 1991), pp. 176–177; also Vaitkevičius, *Lietuvos TSR istorija*, p. 112; *Lietuvių enciklopedija*, vol. 5 (Boston, 1955), p. 148. Data given by these sources must be considered as approximate, not necessarily definitive. They sometimes differ: For example, estimates of the numbers of Jews able to flee before the German advance vary. Cf. Levin, "Lithuania."

33. See Vytautas Tininis, *Gimtasis kraštas*, December 19, 1991–January 2, 1992, p. 12; see also an article by Eugenijus Grunskis, *Gimtasis kraštas*, October 31–November 6, 1991, p. 7.

34. Partijos Istorijos Institutas, *Lietuvos komunistų partija skaičiais, 1912–1975* (Vilnius: Mintis, 1976), pp. 120–123; *Express informacija*, published for the 20th

Conference of the Lithuanian Communist Party, December 1989. See *Tiesa*, December 20, 1989, p. 1.

35. *Tiesa*, December 20, 1989, p. 1.

36. See Kazimiera Prunskienė, *Gintarinės ledy išpažintis* (Vilnius: Politika, 1991), pp. 9–10.

37. Ibid.

38. Vytautas Radaitis, *Komunistas* (Vilnius), no. 9 (September 1966): 15–19.

39. The leadership of Sniečkus is analyzed with the help of official sources, private interview material, and studies by Vytautas Tininis in *Politika* (Vilnius), no. 13 (1991): 20–25; ibid., no. 14 (1991): 23–28; *Lietuvos rytas*, March 17, 1992, p. 7; ibid., March 18, 1992, p. 7; *Gimtasis kraštas*, December 19, 1991–January 2, 1992, p. 12; document texts published in *Gimtasis kraštas*, August 1–7, 1991, p. 7; and current periodicals. These studies are based on newly accessible archival documents.

40. Gedvilas, *Lemiamas posūkis*, p. 85.

41. See text of the order he signed on September 28, 1951, decreeing "the resettlement beyond the bounds of Lithuania *up to* 40,000 kulaks with families who are sabotaging the activities of collective farms" (my italics), *Gimtasis kraštas*, August 1–7, 1991, p. 7.

42. For purges and political attitudes see V. Stanley Vardys, "Modernization and Baltic Nationalism," *Problems of Communism* (September–October 1975): 44ff.

43. Vladimir V. Shcherbitsky, "The International Significance of the Experience of National Relations in the USSR," *Kommunist* (Moscow), no. 17 (1974): 22.

44. Report by the Commission to Draft a Plan for the Restoration of Lithuania's Independence, Supreme Soviet of the Lithuanian SSR, *Lietuvos rytas*, March 6, 1990, p. 3.

45. Statistics in *Atgimimas*, no. 7, February 16, 1992, p. 7.

46. *Tiesa*, April 14, 1990, p. 2.

47. Lithuanian Information Institute, *Lithuania Survey*, 3rd ed. (Vilnius: Republic of Lithuania, 1992), p. 35; also *The Baltic States in Figures* (Helsinki: Statistics Finland, n.d.), p. 9.

48. *Izvestiia*, March 10, 1990, p. 1.

49. V. Kistanov's article is entitled "Leninist National Policy and the Division of the USSR into Economic Regions," *Voprosy ekonomiki* (Moscow) (December 1972): 56–65.

50. Strumskis, *Lietuvos ryšiai su Rusijos Federacija*, p. 29.

51. "Running Out of Gas?" *Time*, April 30, 1990, pp. 44–45. Also my interview, summer 1991.

52. *Tiesa*, March 7, 1992, p. 1.

53. *Tiesa*, November 9, 1991, p. 1.

54. Strumskis, *Lietuvos ryšiai su Rusijos Federacija*, pp. 20–21.

55. See Yurii Maslyukov in *Izvestiia*, March 10, 1990, p. 1; Western calculations by U.S. Census Bureau, *Statesman's Year Book; Wall Street Journal*, September 12, 1991, p. 20; and AP research, chart in *Norman Transcript*, September 9, 1991, p. 20. The question of economic advantages versus political sovereignty for Lithuania is cogently argued by Alastair McAuley, ed., in "Economic Constraints on Devolution: The Lithuanian Case," *Soviet Federalism, Nationalism and Economic Decentralization* (New York: St. Martin's Press), pp. 178–195.

56. Maslyukov, in ibid.

57. See *Tiesa,* April 14, 1990, p. 2.

58. See answer by the chief of the Lithuanian Statistics Bureau, in ibid.

59. Lietuvos Statistikos Departamentas, *Lietuvos statistikos metraštis 1989 metai* (Vilnius: Informacinis-Leidybinis Centras, 1990), p. 32.

60. See *Lietuvos aidas,* March 5, 1992, p. 8.

61. Sidney and Beatrice Webb, *Soviet Communism: A New Civilization?* (New York: Charles Scribner's Sons, 1936), pp. 1119ff.

62. See Lietuvos Mokslų Akademija, Lietuvių Literatūros ir Tautosakos Institutas, *Rašytojas pokario metais* (Vilnius: Vaga, 1991), esp. pp. 43–120.

63. See V. Stanley Vardys, *The Catholic Church: Dissent and Nationality in Soviet Lithuania* (Boulder and New York: East European Quarterly, Columbia University Press, 1978).

64. *Tiesa,* February 13, 1958, p. 4.

65. Cf. V. Stanley Vardys, "The Baltic States in the Soviet Union," in *The Soviet Union and the Challenge of the Future,* vol. 3, ed. Alexander Shtromas and Morton A. Kaplan (New York: Paragon House, 1989), pp. 455–460; V. Stanley Vardys, "Recent Soviet Policy Toward Lithuanian Nationalism," *Journal of Central European Affairs* 23 (October 1963): 313–332; also my article in *Ateitis,* no. 11 (1976): 19ff.

66. Bronius Kuzmickas, article on characteristics of today's Lithuanian, *Atgimimas,* no. 45, November 16, 1992, p. 14.

67. Aleksandras Dobryninas, *Literatūra ir menas,* February 1, 1992, p. 2.

▪ FOUR ▪

Resistance, Survival, and Reform

The bloodless takeover in the summer of 1940 let the Soviet propaganda machine claim that the Lithuanians willingly, even eagerly, accepted Soviet rule and incorporation. Soon, however, opponents of the new regime organized themselves into an armed underground that belied the legitimacy of the Soviet regime. Their first major show of force was the insurrection against the Soviets on June 23, 1941. This event cost the Lithuanian rebels some 4,000 casualties but hastened the Red Army's withdrawal and gave the Lithuanians a basis of power in the face of encroaching German divisions.

During the following half century the Lithuanian resistance to the Soviet occupation changed forms and turned into a struggle for national survival. In 1944–1952, Lithuanians fought the reestablishment of Soviet rule and sought the restoration of Lithuanian sovereignty. The partisans totally rejected Soviet power as illegitimate and fought it by the force of arms. After the destruction of partisan insurgency, peaceful groups of dissidents challenged individual Soviet policies by offering alternative social proposals and ideological perspectives. Many dissidents continued the struggle to restore Lithuanian sovereignty but did so by peaceful means of organization and communication.

Both types of challenges were considered crimes punishable by severe sentences of incarceration and exile. After Stalin's death, there arose a third type of resistance to the Soviet system. This resistance did not aim at abolishing Soviet rule or legal structures but at preserving and defending national culture, traditions, and values within the Soviet system. It even used Communist institutions and other legal means available in the Soviet system to pursue its own objectives. Thus, the initial form of Lithuanian resistance to Soviet rule, armed struggle, evolved into political and then cultural resistance. All three forms of resistance deeply influenced the evolution of Lithuanian political culture and kept alive the spirit of national survival.

THE PARTISAN WAR

The insurgency against the Soviets began spontaneously in different parts of the country during the summer and fall of 1944.[1] The Soviets blamed the Germans and later charged Western intelligence agencies with supporting it. Neither the Germans, the Americans, nor the Western Europeans initiated or fueled the partisan war, however. In 1944 the insurgents inherited leftover German armaments and communications equipment. Some of them underwent training in German insurgency schools and were parachuted into Lithuania, but they followed their own political agenda.

The partisan movement spread quickly. During its years of highest strength (1944–1947), its ranks included at least 30,000 armed men who lived clandestinely in the forests. The Soviets claimed that the main formations of the partisans were defeated in 1948. Nevertheless, the partisans were still active in 1952 and fully ended their campaign only in 1956 when the last commander of partisan forces, Adolfas Ramanauskas-Vanagas, was captured.

Tens of thousands of young men and women took on this seemingly hopeless challenge against the Soviet Goliath. Life in the forests was dangerous—most perished after an average of only two years. There are several explanations for their decision to confront the Soviets by the force of arms. First, the regime did little to allay Lithuanian fears that the ruthless and terroristic Soviet rule of 1940–1941 would not be repeated. Instead, mass deportations, begun in 1945, forcible collectivization, and individual arrests seemed to demonstrate the regime's unwillingness to make peace with the population. Later, after Stalin's death, even Lithuanian Communist party leaders acknowledged that their own deviations from "Socialist legality" "misled" many "innocent" people into armed resistance to Soviet rule.[2]

Second, the militarily successful insurrection of 1941 showed that, under the right circumstances, the Red Army and its Communist leaders were not invincible. Thus, there was hope of victory. This expectation was reinforced, indeed inspired, by the international image of the anti-Nazi resistance. According to this perception, the Soviet Union and the Western nations were not allies but cobelligerents who cooperated only to fight the common Nazi enemy. Once Hitler was defeated, differences between the United States and the Soviet Union would lead to a war. This rift would ostensibly let Lithuania and other nations occupied by the Soviets shake off Soviet rule to rejoin the international community of nations. It was only a matter of time before this would happen. Soviet rule, in other words, was considered to be temporary, and national victory was possible. In the meantime, joining the guerrilla forces seemed to offer people a chance to win time for the nation and to provide for their own personal security in light of oppressive Soviet demands and threats.

Finally, the richness of community life during the years of independence had created social structures of support that helped to sustain risky activity. Crosscutting membership in numerous social and political groups provided social cohesion to help sustain the momentum developed by the nationalist underground in 1940–1941 and during the Nazi occupation of 1941–1944.[3] Although many of the nationalists had been arrested by the Nazis in 1944 or had joined the refugees, leaving the underground in disarray, the military arms of these organizations had survived. The remaining nationalist forces were thus able to engage in organized military action. This support helped mobilize the patriotic idealism that inspired many, especially the young. High school seniors commonly left school to join their "forest brothers" as a group, sometimes with their favorite teacher.

The Soviets did their best to picture the insurgency as a "war between classes"; however, the ranks of partisans included people from all walks of life. The poorer strata of rural population were not worse but probably even better represented among the guerrillas than within the Communist party.

In 1945–1947, the entire fighting force of more than 30,000 was organized into nine regions. Only two of these succeeded in integrating themselves under a single command. In January 1946, the partisans united into the United Movement for Democratic Resistance. The military arm of the movement was separate and subject to a new political organization, the Supreme Committee for the Reconstruction of Lithuania. The movement's tactics changed from military to political. In August, however, the plan fell into the trap of Soviet state security. The Soviets encouraged centralization with infiltrated agents. They planned to control partisan communications with the West and then to destroy the movement itself by arresting its leadership. They almost succeeded. Centralization was stalled, however, until 1949, when the partisans reorganized into Lithuania's Movement of Freedom Fighters (Lietuvos Laisvės Kovotojų Sąjūdis).

Internally, the organization consisted of three layers: active partisans in their bunkers hidden on farms or in the forests; "passive" fighters who continued in civilian life but were infrequently called upon to perform special tasks; and "supporters" who helped with intelligence, supplies, and shelter. The political goal of the partisan movement was to remove the Soviet government and establish an independent democratic republic founded on the tradition of Christian ethics and the principles of Western liberal democracy. The partisans considered themselves legitimate successors to the authority of the free Lithuanian state. They not only refused to recognize the legitimacy of Soviet rule but also maintained their own institutional infrastructure, including the courts, and expected the population to obey their decrees. The guerrillas pursued an obstructionist strategy against the dominant Soviet regime. They would threaten potential new recruits to positions of local authority and other local enforcers of Soviet policies. Officials who cooperated with the Communists too eagerly were either warned, punished, or simply liquidated. The partisans further obstructed the collectivization of farms and the general stability of government by cutting the lines of communication, confiscating needed agricultural products, and destroying the units of militia and special (NKVD) forces that the Soviets had mobilized against them. In the political process, their target was elections. The partisans promulgated the boycott of local elections and penalized those who participated.

Obstruction of the Soviet government represented only one side of partisan activities. The movement also published underground newspapers, documented Soviet crimes, and protected the lives and property of the civilian population against marauding gangs and military units.

Since armed insurgency was very widespread, it seriously impaired Soviet rule. Victory over the guerrilla forces became the first priority of the reestablished Soviet government. The task of destroying the partisans fell on SMERSH (the military counterintelligence organization), the Ministry of Internal Affairs, and the Ministry of State Security (at that time called the NKVD). In the summer of 1944 Moscow moved troops into Lithuania. However, these trained soldiers, who had just completed the deportations of the Chechen-Ingush, the Kalmyks, and the Crimean Tatars, did not have much initial success. In September, General Sergei N. Kruglov, Beria's deputy in the Commissariat of Internal Affairs and former deputy chief of SMERSH, came to Lithuania demanding sterner measures against the partisans. A cruel and brilliant strategist, Kruglov moved beyond a strictly military approach to organize the local population against the partisans, by armed provocation if necessary, to create the semblance of a civil war.[4] The forests were periodically combed and intelligence services were called into action. Beria's future successor declared an open season on the partisans, encouraging the use of any means, including torture and punishment of any kind, to destroy them.

Accordingly, a number of measures were taken. The NKVD organized a network of local militia called *istrebiteli* (Russian for "destroyers"), who later were given the name of "people's defenders." These were men of military age given military privileges and exempted from service in the war still being fought in Germany. The NKVD's department, or *spetsotdel*, on "bandits" intensified efforts at infiltrating the insurgency movement—a plan that yielded good results. Extreme measures were used against partisans caught in the field of battle and against their supporters. Torture was so common that the partisan leadership usually assumed that secrets would be divulged. Those captured received long sentences in the gulag. Their families were persecuted, and their homes were burned down. Bodies of dead partisans were exposed in the marketplaces of provincial towns, as police watched to see whether civilians—frequently taken there by force—would identify the dead. Thus, for security reasons and to protect their families, the partisans frequently committed suicide, usually in a way that made recognition more difficult. Partisan leader Juozas Lukša-Daumantas, who returned to Lithuania from the West in 1951, and the journalist Julius Butėnas ended their lives in this manner rather than surrendering to the Soviets. At other times, the Kremlin lured the partisans out of the forests with the carrot of amnesty. Thousands used the opportunity to return to legal life but usually ended up either as NKVD infiltrators, informers, or prisoners in the Vorkuta coal mines or Far Eastern lumber camps.

The partisans retaliated against the Soviet strategy of total war. The result was a national bloodbath. According to Soviet sources, there were 40,000 casualties of the partisan war—20,000 on each side. Non-Soviet Lithuanian sources place the numbers at 30,000 each. Exact figures will probably never be known. It is reasonably safe to say, however, that in proportion to the total population, casualties in the Lithuanian guerrilla war were not less than those in Algeria against the French. The outcome was different in the two countries largely because of the behavior of the occupying power.

Although the partisans did not achieve their ultimate goal of Lithuanian independence, the historical legacy of their struggle belied the legitimacy of the official regime. The spirit of patriotic commitment of the generation of the 1940s was passed on to the new generation educated under the Soviets, thus making their socialization into the "Soviet man" more difficult. Furthermore, the Soviet handling of the insurgency created a very large group of permanently disaffected population who were denied normal participation in society and whose children were barred from higher education and better jobs. They never forgot the suffering inflicted on them and remained a social force that would support continued resistance to the regime. Thus, resistance in Lithuania would never be violent again, but it would continue.

THE DISSIDENT MOVEMENT

After the partisan movement was destroyed, continued opposition to Communist rule found expression in the peaceful defense of national, religious, and human rights.[5] In the late 1960s and the 1970s, three separate but overlapping directions crystallized in the dissident movement: defense of the rights of the Catholic Church and of believers of any denomination; advocacy of national rights and self-determination; and advancement of human rights, which included the monitoring of their violation by the regime. According to data compiled by a Western scholar, in 1970–1977 two-thirds of all dissident demonstrations in Lithuania were of a religious nature and one-third dealt with the topic of national rights.[6]

In comparison to activities in other Soviet republics, dissident activities in Lithuania were very widespread. In 1965–1978, 10.3 percent of all demonstrations and protest events in the Soviet Union—not counting the publications of the underground press—occurred in Lithuania, which had only 1.3 percent of the total Soviet population.[7] Similarly, Lithuania had the greatest per capita number of underground periodicals.[8] All of these statistical figures are imprecise, but they give an impression of the role, scope, and character of dissent in Lithuania until 1987. In particular, the Prague Spring of 1968 excited many in the Baltic republics. During this time, the incidence of individual acts of defiance, such as raising the national flag, increased. In 1968–1970, the courts sentenced 103 persons for anti-Soviet activities while the KGB "preventively" handled another 375.[9]

In comparison to the Russian dissident movement of intellectuals, scientists, and writers, the Lithuanian movement extended beyond the upper social echelons to include rural and urban workers. Lithuanian dissidents did not have prominent scholars or professionals, such as Andrei Sakharov or even Sergei Kovalev, in their ranks, and the numbers of university faculty were few; however, the Lithuanian underground included and kept close ties with the underprivileged strata of the population, the workers and collective farm peasants. This connection helped to make the Lithuanian dissident underground into a more widespread social mass movement. Religious dissent activities, in particular, broadened the popular support of the opposition and constituted the loudest and earliest voices of political grievance.

By the middle of the 1960s, the church had been debilitated. In 1961, as a part of Khrushchev's attack on religion, Moscow had tightened up its already restrictive antireligious legislation, which was later implemented in Lithuania's criminal code of 1966. The authorities pressed for a more strict enforcement of this code by local government agencies and for prosecution of those who violated it, especially those engaged in teaching religion to children. In 1970–1972, three priests and an elderly woman were sentenced to prison terms for this "crime." This was a warning to clergymen as well as laymen. A new drive of atheist indoctrination was begun in 1963. At that time, the regime sought to choke off preparation of new priests. This was done by limiting enrollment at the only licensed theological seminary to twenty-four students in the 1965–1966 school year and then to thirty in subsequent years. Annually, more priests died than were ordained. Finally, the country had only one reigning bishop left in six dioceses. Two bishops were in internal exile. Church administrators were severely constrained by the commissioner for religious affairs and had to obtain his approval to conduct ordinations, make appointments, or transfer clergymen. Communist leaders privately boasted that the church would be dead within two decades.

The clerical church administration at that time was weak, scared, and compliant. In 1968, several parish pastors seized the initiative to demand the opening of doors to the theological seminary. The tactic of direct petition, supported by many figures, had been employed by Bishop Valančius in the nineteenth century to get what he wanted from the Tsarist government, but it was new in the 1960s. A new Soviet law passed in 1968 allowed petitioning of government. Petitioners thus could not be arrested. Of course, they could be silenced. The Soviet administrators attempted to do just that with the first Catholic petitioners, but the petitioning activity spread like wildfire. It embraced many topics and was endorsed by thousands of people, all of whom could not be imprisoned. The petitioners demanded the return of exiled bishops, the publication of prayerbooks, the lifting of diverse rules that impeded the practicing of the sacraments, and the abolition of discrimination in utility rates to churches. The best known of these petitions was a letter to Secretary General Leonid Brezhnev. It was sent to him in December 1971 through the Secretary General of the United Nations, Kurt Waldheim. This petition, asking not only for a theoretical but also a practical guarantee of freedom of conscience, was signed by 17,054 people and became an international event.

The routing of this petition indicated that the new generation of dissidents well understood not only the value of using Soviet laws for promoting their objectives but also the importance of public opinion for getting satisfaction of their grievances. The view that international opinion would create pressures on the Soviets to satisfy the dissident demands of religious or human rights was shared with the Moscow dissidents, who in 1968 started publishing the *Chronicle of Current Events.* Lithuanian dissidents as well as those of other republics were supported in this endeavor by Western radio broadcasts, which disseminated news about dissident activities.

Numerous petitions were signed by thousands despite KGB harassment. The largest number of signatures collected on one petition was 148,149. This petition, presented in 1979, requested the return for religious use of a newly built church in the port city of Klaipėda. The church had been seized by the government as soon as its construction was completed in 1961.

The authorities, however, disregarded virtually all the petitions and the Catholic dissidents switched tactics. On March 19, 1972, they began the publication of the *Chronicle of the Catholic Church of Lithuania.*[10] The

Scene on the unique "hill of crosses," near the medieval city of Siauliai, which became an important symbol of Lithuanian national and religious resistance to sovietization. (Photo by A. Sutkus. Used by permission.)

clandestine publication shared the philosophy of Moscow's *Chronicle*. Its publishers kept in close contact with liberal Russian dissidents such as academician Andrei Sakharov. In seventeen years, from 1972 to 1989, the Lithuanian *Chronicle* published eighty-one voluminous issues to become the "uncensored voice of Lithuania."[11] At first, it covered national issues as well, but later it focused exclusively on the suppression of religious freedom while other dissident publications, such as the journal *Aušra*, raised the nationalist agenda. In 1991, it was revealed that the *Chronicle* was edited until 1983 by Rev. Sigitas Tamkevičius, S.J., appointed bishop in 1990. After Tamkevičius's arrest and sentence in 1983 on unrelated charges—the KGB never found out who the editors were—the editor was Jonas Boruta, S.J., a young scientist who had become a priest after graduating from an underground theological seminary.

The periodical attempted to redress the Vatican's uninformed or even misinformed view of the condition of the church in Lithuania, believing that the West would exercise important pressures on Soviet policy if the truth were known. It also opposed compliance with Soviet prohibitions, especially those against religious education and ordination, because compliance legitimized popular fears that top church administrators and clerics were in the employ of the KGB. More than a dozen people were arrested and imprisoned for helping with the production of the *Chronicle*. One of them, secret nun Nijolė Sadūnaitė, sentenced to a long term of labor camp and exile, gained international recognition for her courageous and articulate struggle in the religious underground.

In 1978, after the election of Pope John Paul II, five Catholic clergymen established a Catholic Committee for the Defense of the Rights of Believers. The purpose of this group was to achieve for believers equal rights with the atheists, constitutionally as well as practically. The committee collected and publicized voluminous case materials on religious discrimination of individual Catholics and non-Catholics and organized many petitions and protest demonstrations. One of its leaders, Rev. Alfonsas Svarinskas, was arrested and sentenced in the spring of 1983. His colleague Rev. Sigitas Tamkevičius, was sentenced late in the same year. Another member, Rev. Juozas Zdebskis, earlier sentenced for teaching religion to children, was mysteriously killed in an auto accident.

Strong religious protest and dissidence overlapped and mutually nourished the patriotic sentiment that resurfaced after Stalin's death. In 1956, students in Kaunas and Vilnius shocked the authorities by holding massive demonstrations of solidarity with the Hungarian revolution. The demonstrations occurred on November 2, 1956, All Souls' Day, which traditionally attracts hundreds and thousands of people to commemorate the dead.[12] The religious occasion turned into a patriotic demonstration. Demonstrators sang the national anthem, produced a Lithuanian tricolor, and marched down the main thoroughfare of the city before being dispersed by the police. Similar demonstrations were held in the famous Rasos cemetery of Vilnius. Hundreds of young people were arrested immediately or tracked down years later.

In the 1970s nationalist protest again became a public issue. On November 23, 1970, Simas Kudirka, a forty-year-old radio operator on the Soviet fishing vessel *Sovetskaia Litva*, jumped aboard the U.S. Coast Guard cutter *Vigilant*, which was moored alongside the Soviet ship at Martha's Vineyard, Massachusetts.[13] His defection did not succeed because the Coast Guard admiral allowed the Soviets to board the *Vigilant* and seize Kudirka. Back in Lithuania, Kudirka received a ten-year prison sentence, but not before declaring the dedication of his generation to Lithuania's independence and to democracy. The case received international attention and also stirred up people in Lithuania.

A roadside shrine in the Lithuanian countryside, 1970s. (Photo by Rimantas Dichavičius. Used by permission.)

Two years later, on March 14, 1972, the largest nationalist upheaval of the postpartisan era began in Kaunas, a city then of 300,000 population known for its critical disposition toward the Soviets. Romas Kalanta, a nineteen-year-old high school senior, immolated himself in protest against the Soviet occupation of Lithuania and to attract the world's attention to Lithuania's oppression. Formally a member of the Komsomol, but actually a nonconformist long-haired youth, he lit a match and burned himself to death at the centrally located theater park.. The act was premeditated, organized in advance by a rebelling Lithuanian hippie group to which Kalanta belonged.[14] The police insisted on a private funeral but thousands of students and workers, upon learning that the scheduled funeral would not take place, spilled into the streets. They locked arms and marched down the main street overturning police cars, waving the Lithuanian flag, smashing the windows of Communist party quarters, and singing the national anthem. Special troops were called in because the police could not subdue the crowds. Some 500 people were arrested, but ultimately only eight were held for trial. The rebellion, as the residents of the city referred to it, continued on May 19. The flames of Kalanta's self-immolation spread. Several other people in provincial towns were reported to have repeated Kalanta's deed. Shortly afterward the youth of Vilnius rioted at an international sports competition. They refused to stand up for the Soviet anthem and tried to march into the center of the city.

Moscow became alarmed. Representatives of the Central Committee of the Communist party were sent to investigate. On the surface, the response of party secretary Sniečkus was moderate, mostly verbal. Soon afterward, however, a number of officials and journal editors lost their positions—or were transferred to other, less responsible duties. In October the trials of the eight alleged leaders of the demonstrations were held. The KGB then moved in to liquidate ethnographic study groups that, according to the party secretary for ideological affairs, masked nationalist activities. A number of group members were arrested and received prison sentences. Still others lost their positions or were dismissed from schools.

In addition to engaging in religious and nationalist dissent, the Lithuanians initiated a very active group of human rights monitors. Established on December 1, 1976—a year after President Ford, Brezhnev, and other leaders had signed the Helsinki agreement, which was to guarantee human rights in the Communist countries of Europe—this "Helsinki" group became the main exponent of human rights in Lithuania until 1978, when all its leaders were dispersed. The purpose of the Helsinki group was to monitor Moscow's compliance with the Helsinki agreement in human rights and to register violations of the agreement. The Lithuanian group was one of the three active in the Soviet Union and, after Yurii Orlov's committee in Moscow, the most energetic as a monitor. The organizer of the Lithuanian group was Viktoras Petkus, a twice imprisoned activist of the Catholic movement. Its membership included Rev. Karolis Garuckas, S.J., the poet Ona Lukauskaitė-Poškienė, the activist of the Jewish emigration movement Eithan Finkelstein, and another poet, Tomas Venclova. The group published a long list of documents on individual cases beginning with a thorough documentation of the discrimination and oppression of the Catholic Church. After the arrest of Petkus, the silencing of Finkelstein, the deaths of Garuckas and Poškienė, and the departure of Venclova, dissident activity again became less prominent.

The 1970s also witnessed an expanding cooperation between Baltic dissidents. In 1979, they published a statement articulating the legal and philosophical rationale for the restoration of statehood to Lithuania, Latvia, and Estonia. The statement was drafted in commemoration of the fortieth anniversary of the Molotov-Ribbentrop pact of August 23, 1939, and was addressed to several parties: the Soviet government, the West and East German governments, the signatories of the Atlantic Charter, and the Secretary General of the United Nations, Kurt Waldheim. In their letter,[15] the Balts rejected Soviet rule as imposed by force and demanded the reversal of the consequences of the 1939 pact. After reviewing the sequence of events, the signers declared that "the Molotov-Ribbentrop pact was a conspiracy between the two greatest tyrants in history—Stalin and Hitler—against peace and humanity; it also inaugurated World War II. We consider the date of August 23rd the day of shame." Well argued, this appeal showed familiarity with the secret documents of the 1939 pact, which the Soviets denied even existed, and with more recent international law documents that included self-determination as a right. Curiously, however, the 1975 Helsinki provision on self-determination was included only as an afterthought. The Baltic signers requested a fourfold action from the world community of nations: (1) that the Soviet Union publish the "full contents" of the Molotov-Ribbentrop pact together with all the supplementary secret documents; (2) that the governments of East and West Germany "publicly pronounce the Molotov-Ribbentrop pact to be void from the moment of its signing" and help the USSR to "liquidate" the consequences of the pact; (3) that the signatories of the Atlantic Charter condemn the pact and its consequences "from the position of their moral responsibility"; and finally (4) that Kurt Waldheim raise the question of Baltic freedom in the United Nations.

The declaration was signed by forty-five Balts, including thirty-seven Lithuanians, four Latvians, and four Estonians. The Lithuanian signers included four priests; the future leader of the Lithuanian Freedom League, Antanas Terleckas; and some members of the Lithuanian Helsinki group. Among the Estonians were university professor Juri Kukk and ornithologist Mart Niklus. The Baltic declaration was endorsed by academician Andrei Sakharov and four other prominent dissidents in Moscow. It was especially galling to the Soviets because of its mention of Hitler and the internationally reverberating reminder of how the Baltic states became Soviet property. The KGB had no mercy for the signers, who disturbed Soviet complacency and challenged their historical lies.

An important aspect of dissident activities was the publication of underground periodicals. As earlier noted, Lithuania had a reputation for having proportionally the largest number of dissident publications in the Soviet Union. In addition to the *Chronicle of the Catholic Church of Lithuania*, there periodically appeared more than a dozen journals. The list included *Aušra* (The Dawn), *Rūpintojėlis* (The Caring, Sorrowful Christ), *Lietuvos ateitis* (Lithuania's Future), *Dievas ir tėvynė* (God and Country), *Tiesos kelias* (Way of Truth), *Vytis* (The Knight), *Laisvės šauklys* (Herald of Freedom), *Pastogė* (Shelter), *Lietuvos archyvas* (Lithuanian Archive), *Varpas*

(The Bell), *Alma mater, Perspektyvos* (Perspectives), and others. Most were of a symbiotic patriotic-Catholic orientation, although *Laisvės šauklys* and *Vytis* placed greater emphasis on nationalist issues. A thoroughly academic *Perspektyvos*, edited by Vilnius university teacher Vytautas Skuodis and two friends, one of them secondary school teacher Povilas Pečeliūnas and the other journalist and poet Gintautas Iešmantas, published articles of diverse ideological content, including a paper by the Lithuanian Communist Association, a dissident Communist group that advocated Lithuania's secession from the Soviet Union. Articles discussing Eurocommunism and secession were provided by editor Iešmantas, a former Communist who had lost his job because he had rebelled against the system by remaining, at least for a time, a committed Marxist. His was the most prominent attempt to create a Lithuanian national-Communist opposition until the Gorbachev reforms ten years later. In this sense, the amalgam of nationalism and communism had much less ideological currency in Lithuania than it did in the two other Baltic countries.

The dissidents paid a price for their exercise of free speech. At least fourteen collaborators—typists and distributors—of the *Chronicle of the Catholic Church of Lithuania* were sentenced to long prison terms or exile. The editors of *Perspektyvos* met with the same fate. Several members of the Catholic Committee for the Defense of the Rights of Believers and the Helsinki monitoring committee were either killed, imprisoned, or confined to psychiatric hospitals. Altogether, in the 1970s and early 1980s Communist authorities incarcerated more than 150 prisoners of conscience.

THE STRUGGLE FOR CULTURAL SURVIVAL

Although cultural sovietization and linguistic russification continued in Lithuania after Stalin's death, the "thaw" of the early Khrushchev years and the politically more relaxed atmosphere eased personal fears and encouraged many writers, artists, filmmakers, scholars, and even government bureaucrats to test the limits of the Communist party's tolerance. When the party attempted to reimpose formulas of Socialist realism as guiding principles for literature and the arts, an ongoing jousting match began between the censors and the creative intelligentsia. Whereas the latter saw in political changes some openings for the reassertion of national cultural values, the former imposed limitations set at the outer limits by Soviet nationality theory.[16]

According to Bolshevik doctrine, nationality development had to be guided by three principles.[17] The first was Lenin's idea of two nations in each nation, the "bourgeois" and the "proletariat," and consequently, "two different cultures in each national culture."[18] The bourgeois culture had to be destroyed. Thus, the national heritage of every culture the

Soviet state absorbed had to be reexamined and purged of "nonproletarian" elements. This task was left to local bureaucrats and Moscow officials.

The second principle was Stalin's idea that Socialist culture was the same for all nationalities. It differed only in its linguistic and strictly ethnic mode of expression. Thus, culture was national in form but uniformly Socialist in content. By the 1950s, "Socialist content" was interpreted through the perspective of Russian culture and "national in form" was limited in reality to figurative realism, regardless of nationality.

Finally, the third principle of nationalism made clear the limited potential for the expression and development of cultural differences. According to the Soviets, nationalities developed and progressed through a dialectical process of two tendencies, "flourishing" (*rastsvet*), on the one hand, and "rapprochement" (*sblizhenye*), on the other. The synthesis of the dialectical process was the replacement of national cultures by a merger (*sliyanye*), or assimilation, of nationalities into the Russian medium, a goal sought by all Soviet leaders since Stalin. At the 22nd Party Congress in 1961, Khrushchev reiterated this position by announcing that the Communists did not intend to conserve national differences forever.[19] Across the many nations of the Soviet Union, therefore, cultural expression was largely dominated by slight variations on proletarian themes, such as boy-meets-girl-meets-tractor.

The surviving Lithuanian intelligentsia understood the Communist threat to national identity but also saw opportunities for resisting its implementation. The force of official policy depended much on bureaucratic politicians and on the participating intelligentsia itself, many of whom began to push for a more liberal, traditional interpretation of national culture, testing the limits of Communist orthodoxy.

The first major literary figure to test the cold waters of Socialist orthodoxy was Vincas Mykolaitis-Putinas with the novel *The Rebels* (1957), which was used for an opera libretto of the same title. The book dealt with the insurrection against the Russian empire in 1863. It passed the book censors in 1957, but the staging of the opera, composed by Julius Juzeliūnas, was not permitted until twenty years later, in 1977. Also during the "thaw" period, a young writer named Vytautas Rimkevičius published a novel called *The Students* (1957) that pictured—against the background of philosophical discussion—nationalist demonstrations in Kaunas on All Souls' Day in 1956, the time of the Hungarian revolution.

A decade later, Justinas Marcinkevičius, a well-known poet and an early supporter of the Communist regime as well as party member, came out with *Mindaugas* (1968) and other plays on topics of Lithuanian national history. His sensitive lyrics about Lithuania's anguished fate made him one of the most popular and respected poets in the land. Authors Juozas Glinskis and Romualdas Lankauskas, poet Sigitas Geda, and critic

Vytautas Kubilius defied the canons of Socialist realism forbidding discussion of the ills of society and especially the flaws of its rulers. In his play, *The House of Courage*, Juozas Glinskis depicted the reflections of imprisoned priests in a thinly veiled critique of the duplicity and absurdity of Soviet life.

Most literary deviation dealt with national and broadly human issues of existence and freedom. The list of authors writing in such a fashion was impressive. But the censorship and closed atmosphere under the Communist party's secretary for ideological affairs, Lionginas Šepetys, forced many authors and intellectuals to leave the system in the 1970s since most had gotten too famous to simply be repressed. Tomas Venclova, the poet and human rights activist, had many privileges as the only son of a prominent Communist writer and government official, but not enough to freely publish. Despite state interference, his famous writings helped introduce Lithuanians to modern Western poetry and ideas, but ultimately he sought emigration to the West. Similarly, Jonas Jurašas, the famous artistic director of the Kaunas theater, fled the constant interference in his theater productions to work in the United States; the young novelist Saulius Kondrotas defected; and the well-established novelist Icchokas Meras emigrated to Israel.

The Lithuanian Artists Association was quite subversive. Although in the immediate postwar period its Stalinist administrators had thrown out or silenced some distinguished members of the group, the association eventually became a hotbed not only of artistic but also of political heresy. Its younger members fought the conservatives in the Vilnius Art Institute and elsewhere. Baltic triannual exhibits, alternately held in Vilnius, Riga, and Tallinn, provided a means whereby artists could struggle for greater freedom of artistic expression. In 1972 and 1975 Moscow forbade these exhibits, but they were continued later. The typical attitude of many artists was depicted, tongue in cheek, by a distinguished Lithuanian painter, Antanas Gudaitis, who in 1972 wanted to exhibit a painting entitled "The Prodigal Son." In this self-portrait, Gudaitis pictured himself among pigs.[20] The authorities understood the message and removed the artist from the Exhibitions Committee membership. His friends, however, were not afraid to write a letter to Secretary Sniečkus defending their colleague and demanding his reinstatement.

A number of other activities contributed to the Lithuanian cultural resistance, such as official designation of many churches as architectural monuments protected by the state. This practice saved a number of church buildings from desecration and devastation. By using such tactics the Lithuanians were also able to restore national monuments such as castles or palaces deemed to belong to the national treasure of architectural culture. Sniečkus had to endure Khrushchev's wrath over the restoration of the fourteenth-century castle of Trakai. The shrewd university rector Jonas Kubilius worked to preserve the Lithuanian character and traditions of Vilnius University while staying politically viable. In the end, he, like First Secretary Sniečkus, survived his Communist counterparts in Moscow.

The cultural establishment in Lithuania also included apolitical intellectuals such as the metaphysical, even religious, poet Jonas Juškaitis and musicology professor Vytautas Landsbergis, the future leader of Sąjūdis and president of the republic. The latter wrote almost exclusively on Mykalojus Čiurlionis, a composer and painter of national tradition whom the elder Venclova, along with his colleagues, had been able to rescue from the purge of unorthodox artists during the Stalin era.

As in other Soviet republics, the creative intelligentsia led the development of national traditions within the Communist regime. The group was too large to be ideologically or attitudinally monolithic. Many of them had been influenced by the blandishments and power of the Soviet empire or

The fourteenth-century castle of Trakai near Vilnius, from which medieval western Lithuania was controlled. (Photo by A. Sutkus. Used by permission.)

believed in Marxist ideals, especially during their school years. Many were Communist party members seeking opportunistic career guarantees. A small minority pushed hard at the limits of sanctioned behavior with little compromise of their work or beliefs. The sculptor and poet Vytautas Mačiuika, for example, had been arrested for his association with the partisans as a teenager. Three times he escaped from the Gulag and was saved for productive life by people considered totally faithful to the regime. Mačiuika has considered himself "Lithuania's partisan whose resistance is continued by his sculpture and his writings."[21]

Generally, however, the attitudes of generations changed over time. The nationally conscious and active intellectuals of the 1970s differed from their partisan forebears and from dissidents in their public acceptance of Soviet rule. They paid the Communist party at least an occasional tribute and were willing from time to time to be used for tasks that strengthened the empire. The philosophy that conditioned their behavior has been well articulated by the nonagenarian Lithuanian scholar Juozas Matulis, who for at least two decades presided over the Lithuanian Academy of Sciences: "If a person will not adapt himself to the environment, he will simply perish."[22] He tells a story of how he saved eighty-three graduate students from dismissal from the Academy of Sciences. Sniečkus and two other party secretaries, Kazys Preikšas and Vladas Niunka, demanded in a specially called meeting that he dismiss the group. When Matulis inquired as to why he should do so, the secretaries answered that "one crosses himself, the other goes to church, etc.," Matulis said.[23] Matulis countered the accusations by asserting that the students were "good workers" and that therefore he would not issue an order of termination. He suggested to Sniečkus and his colleagues that if they wanted them thrown out, they should write the decree themselves. They did not, and the students stayed on eventually to become useful scientists. The demand to compromise and survive, however, fostered hypocrisy.

The rampant hypocrisy among Lithuanian intellectuals forced a sort of schizophrenic behavior upon them that took a heavy toll on their psyches. An example was the suicide death in 1980 of the young novelist Bronius Radzevičius, who hid his best work and could only postmortem be celebrated as a talented author. Recent investigations of Lithuanian KGB archives suggest that some former pillars of national culture had bought their freedom of expression by agreeing to become KGB informers. For the price of collaboration and compromise, therefore, the public protection of national traditions and resources was made possible.

Although developments in the 1970s and early 1980s show that Lithuania's religious dissidents helped to improve the position of the Catholic Church and kept alive the spirit of resistance, the influence of writers, artists, and scholars legally struggling to preserve the national memory was ostensibly more visible. The creative intelligentsia represented the intellectual elite to which Communist rulers needed to pay careful attention, which they did. Without a single comprehensive philosophy to provide the underpinnings or structure for mass opposition, it was the personalities of this segment of society, not the dissidents of the 1960s through the 1980s, who organized the reform movement Sąjūdis, successfully exploiting the Gorbachev reforms to eventually unseat the Communist regime and declare Lithuania a free and sovereign state.

GLASNOST' COMES TO LITHUANIA

Soon after Mikhail Gorbachev, an apparatchik of the younger generation, was elected to the position of CPSU general secretary in March 1985, he set out to restructure and energize the economic sector of the country and turn around its drastically declining productivity. Persuaded that the obstacle to restructuring was rooted in the inefficient and dogmatic party and government bureaucracy, the new leader chose new tools for their rejuvenation, namely, democratization and openness (*demokratizatsiia i glasnost'*).

Democratization would open up the ossified ranks of the bureaucracy and draw into public life and the economy people from outside the party ranks currently alienated from the political process. Openness, though at first not understood as complete freedom of expression, would allow criticism of the system and bring about a resurgence of intellectual creativity. The population would be newly motivated to work harder for the goals of the Socialist system. To light a fire under recalcitrant bureaucrats uninspired by the restructuring, or *perestroika*, Gorbachev encouraged establishment of "informal" groups to spur the Communist party and other bureaucracies to action.

Glasnost' arrived in Lithuania later than in Moscow or Estonia or even much more strictly regimented Latvia. When Vitalii Korotich of Moscow began his no-holds-barred reporting in his refurbished magazine *Ogonëk*, Lithuania's press was still very tame. Several reasons explain Lithuania's reticence. First, doubts about the permanence of Gorbachev's rule and ubiquitous cynicism about Moscow's neverending series of reforms restrained the acceptance of glasnost'. Like most Soviet citizens everywhere outside of Russia, Lithuanians greeted official proclamations with fear, apathy, and alienation. Second, Lithuania's national survival was less threatened by Soviet rule than Estonia's and Latvia's. The Lithuanian percentage of the population was a stable 80 percent, whereas the Estonian and Latvian populations in those two Baltic nations hovered close to 50 percent, prompting a greater urgency for change. Finally, Lithuania's Communist regime was led by particularly mediocre and conservative apparatchiks. In February 1987, Petras Griškevičius, who took over as first secretary after the death of Antanas Sniečkus in 1974, conceded that perestroika was a "revolutionary process" but spoke about glasnost' more like the conservative Politburo member Yegor Ligachev than like the reformer Gorbachev and frowned upon the demand to fill in historical "white spots," or sensitive, censored topics.[24] Thus, the beginning of the end of the Soviet era was punctuated by the fits and starts of a cautious society.

Predictably, the traditional dissidents were the first to seize upon the more relaxed political atmosphere in Moscow. They organized a demonstration on August 23, 1987, to commemorate the anniversary of the signing of the Molotov-Ribbentrop pact. Similar demonstrations were held in Riga and Tallinn at the same time, but the Vilnius meeting was the smallest. Because the dissident movement had been more widespread in Lithuania, the Lithuanian regime held staunchly to a conservative attitude and severely denounced the demonstrators' intentions. The demonstration of August 23, however, was only the modest first trickle of the groundswell of future opposition.

In November 1987, there occurred a revolt among the creative intelligentsia. The Artists Union published a scathing letter critiquing the lack of real reform in Lithuania and demanded promises of political change.[25] Shortly thereafter, Griškevičius died of a heart attack.[26] He was succeeded by Ringaudas Bronislovas Songaila, the chairman of the Presidium of the Lithuanian Supreme Soviet, a lifetime nomenklatura apparatchik who followed in his predecessor's footsteps and kept the brakes on political reform. In response to the possibility of a public observation of Lithuania's Independence Day in February 1988, Songaila brought in a concentration of military personnel carriers and allowed various police measures, some of them violent, to prevent the Lithuanians from gathering.[27] Instead, the authorities organized their own "celebration meetings" in which they did not commemorate the anniversary but vilified the U.S. president and Congress. President Reagan had issued a proclamation supporting the objective of Lithuanian independence and inviting a commemoration of the anniversary.[28] A large group of U.S. senators also had written to Mikhail Gorbachev asking that Soviet authorities not interfere with the festivities.[29] Soviet president Andrei Gromyko came to Vilnius ten days before February 16 to denounce "the lunatics abroad" who did not understand how "mighty" was the Soviet power in Lithuania.[30] None of this stopped the commemoration of independence, however. Banished from streets and meeting halls, the celebrating crowds flooded the churches where special masses were said and sermons preached. The authorities then harassed the pastors who had allowed such "anti-Soviet" acts to take place.

Although traditional dissidents were ready to try the limits of reform with action, intellectuals moved more slowly to increase their latitude and avail themselves of glasnost'. On December 1, 1987, at a meeting of the Writers Union, a group of leading critics and poets took to task the editor of their professional weekly, *Literatūra ir menas* (Literature and the Arts). One writer protested the editor's fear of publishing a collectively signed letter that took issue with one of the republic's leaders. A poet, Sigitas Geda, complained about censorship and demands to make changes in his poetry before publication, and Vytautas Kubilius, a highly respected literary critic known for his lack of ideological orthodoxy, derided the editor's "good relations" with the leadership of the Writers Union, suggesting that this did not help perestroika. Then he bluntly told the gathering:

> Society is indignant about the weekly's facelessness, writers are ashamed to contribute. . . . This decaying newspaper can be revived only by contributors who think originally and courageously. Are the reserves of Lithuanian intellectual talent so poor that we cannot find our own V. Korotich [editor of *Ogonëk*]?[31]

Another writer, the ambitious and aggressive Communist Vytautas Petkevičius, loudly insisted that the atmosphere for creative activity in the republic was still oppressive and bluntly faulted Communist party activists as "men of little talent and ability" who should be "put in their place" and never again allowed "to drown out the creative and sane mind of our nation." Antanas Drilinga, the editor of the weekly, survived for another year, but the newspaper started becoming "original and courageous" and inspired others to follow suit.

Soon the Lithuanian "Korotiches" and "Chaklays" began to make their appearance in the weekly *Gimtasis kraštas* (Native Country) and the daily *Komjaunimo tiesa* (Komsomol Truth). A member of the new party leadership in the Writers Union, Algimantas Čekuolis, returned from his diplomatic post in Spain to spearhead the further development of glasnost' in Lithuania. He took over the editorship of *Gimtasis kraštas*, a weekly aimed at Lithaunians abroad but read locally as well, and turned the ridiculed propaganda rag into a forum for increasingly vocal reformers who consistently shocked their readership with unflinching exposures of the system's sins and bold political demands. In the spring of 1988, for example, Čekuolis published the text of the banned national anthem of the Lithuanian republic and argued for its reinstatement. Although he was a party member, like many of his colleagues Čekuolis carved out a niche of political legitimacy by distancing his approach from that of the traditional dissidents. His weekly, for instance, suggested that the *Chronicle of the Catholic Church of Lithuania* was edited and printed in New York and

Chicago, that dissidents were "extremists," and that virtually no one wanted to celebrate Lithuania's independence.[32] Even as intellectuals pushed at the limits of political reform, therefore, they tried to stay within the line of official legitimacy that traditional dissidents had crossed long ago. Although the two groups shared fundamental nationalist commitments, differences in their strategies were bound to come to a head.

At the April meeting of the Artists Union, a forum for lectures and adult education, Arvydas Juozaitis, a philosopher at Vilnius University and an Olympic medalist, introduced historical evidence for the illegality of the Soviet regime in Lithuania in an unprecedented lecture on "Political Culture and Lithuania." As a result, questions were raised publicly for the first time about sensitive historical issues, such as the guerrilla war against the Soviets. That war was subsequently exonerated from the charge of "banditism" and publicly acknowledged as a legitimate act of national self-defense against marauding occupiers.[33] Simultaneously, intellectuals from various quarters began raising other political demands in controversial media coverage. In its plenary meeting of April 4, the Writers Union proposed that the Lithuanian language be declared the official language of the Lithuanian SSR and that June 14 become an official day of mourning for Stalin's victims.

The dissidents planned to commemorate the anniversary of Stalin's deportations with a meeting on May 22. The authorities this time did not respond with police measures and harassment but organized a competing meeting instead, to be held on May 21. The meeting of May 21 was sponsored by the official organizations of the republic's writers, artists, composers, and architects as well as the government of the city of Vilnius. In anticipation of the denunciation of Stalin's deportations of non-Communist Lithuanians, the gathering stressed the suffering of Lithuanian Communist leaders under Stalin and the help extended to the deportees of 1941 by Lithuanian Communist leaders in Russia. Since attendance at this demonstration was virtually risk-free, it took some wind out of the sails of the dissidents' meeting the next day. Their demonstration was sabotaged further when officials brought in powerful loudspeakers to drown out the voices of dissident speakers with loud, happy music. *Gimtasis kraštas* denounced those speakers as "extremists" who gave the new political climate an "anti-Soviet," "demagogical" color. Among the transgressions of the organizers was the display of the flag of "bourgeois" Lithuania—the same one that was reinstated as the official state flag one short year later.[34] The police eventually dispersed some demonstrators. Although official estimates reported that these numbered only around 500, some estimates went as high as 3,000.[35]

The Lithuanian press had discarded most taboos of the past by 1989 and felt free to raise the most sacrosanct issues. Stalinist crimes were disclosed in brutal detail, the suffering inflicted on deportees was described in memoirs, and Katyn-type massacres, such as the mass executions of prisoners in Pravieniškės or the bestial killings by torture in the forest of Rainiai in 1941, were brought into the daylight. Crime and accident reports were published with regularity and theoretical discussions of the ills of the single-party system became commonplace. Interviews with Catholic Church representatives, news about the new bishops appointed in spring 1989, and items about the Pope became a part of journalistic reporting. Nearly every new social or political group printed its own publication: Some were only 4–6 pages long, but each was produced with the relish of people long suppressed from expressing themselves freely. Soon hundreds of new bulletins and gazettes flooded the newsstands. No theme or image was exempted, including pornography, and no public institution, except, at first, the KGB, escaped the critical attention of both old and new periodicals. The Moscow program of glasnost' had unleashed numerous voices in Lithuania that would soon come together in action.

THE EMERGENCE OF CIVIL SOCIETY AND SĄJŪDIS

The proliferation of new associations added to the emerging happy cacophony of an increasingly diverse press as new groups formed and old ones severed their ties with Moscow. The diversity of actors outside of the traditional Communist party power structure bore witness to the sudden emergence of a civil society formerly hidden under the superficial monolith of Soviet political culture. What started as support for Gorbachev's intended "pluralistic socialism" in Lithuania turned into a struggle for democratic pluralism as well as national liberation. The Lithuanian Movement for Restructuring (Lietuvos Persitvarkymo Sąjūdis), or simply Sąjūdis (Movement), quickly became the main focal point of the emerging groups and was the engine that drove social and political change in the republic.[36]

Sąjūdis was born in the Lithuanian Academy of Sciences after Lithuanian intellectuals enviously observed the establishment of the People's Front by Estonian intellectuals. On May 23, 1988, the academy established a commission to propose changes in the Lithuanian SSR constitution needed to accommodate Gorbachev's reforms.[37] Three days later, the academy hosted two distinguished Estonian economists from the Estonian Academy of Sciences to discuss their unprecedented model for economic sovereignty. The determination to establish a similar Lithuanian group quickly was solidified by two current events, namely, the election of Lithuanian Communist party delegates to Gorbachev's 19th Communist Party Conference and the decision by Moscow to expand the Lithuanian chemical industry.[38]

The first mass meeting of Sąjūdis, June 1988. (Photo by R. Urbakavičius. Used by permission.)

Although the 19th Party Conference was heralded in Moscow as an expression of a new political era, in Lithuania the regime picked delegates "the old way," that is, they were in effect appointed by the party leadership, contrary to the instructions of the Central Committee in Moscow. Industrial ministers in Moscow betrayed the same mistrust of democracy and reform. They decided unilaterally to expand the chemical giants in Jonava, Kėdainiai, and Mažeikiai—cities already choking from air and water pollution. Riding roughshod over Lithuanian authorities, Moscow's ministries angered most of those outside the Lithuanian power structure and many within it. A meeting held on the same day in the hall of science at the palace of Verkiai discussed the question, "Can we overcome bureaucracy?"[39] The participants were persuaded that they might if they were united, which they were. It was there that the idea of creating a core group of movement leaders was first expressed.

On June 3, a public meeting was held ostensibly to discuss upcoming amendments to the Soviet constitution proposed by Gorbachev. Instead, an "initiative group," consisting of thirty-six prominent scholars and intellectuals, was elected on the spot in a large room packed to overflowing capacity.[40] Thus was born the Lithuanian Movement for Restructuring (Sąjūdis). The event had been secretly orchestrated earlier and a list of about ten members chosen beforehand. However, activists insist that over two-thirds of the membership of the "initiative group" were spontaneously suggested in an act of popular will by the audience. Although formally established to push the party along officially approved political goals, the Lithuanian Sąjūdis would inevitably differ from the Estonian Front to become a parallel and eventually victorious center of political power in Soviet Lithuania.

Initially, Sąjūdis sought to walk a fine political line between the Communist party, on the one hand, and the dissidents, on the other. After kicking out Stasys Imbrasas, a section chief of the Central Committee, from a meeting, Sąjūdis was declared hostile to the powers that be.[41] At the same time, dissidents considered Sąjūdis a tool of the Soviet oppressors because it was allowed to operate legitimately. At first, Sąjūdis wanted to ensure its ability to operate and decided that the new movement would not accept into its midst "people who have attempted to propagate extremist ideas."[42] These "extremists," of course, were dissidents, many of whom had spent years in prisons or concentration camps. Kazys Saja, a distinguished Lithuanian playwright, found such an attitude "strange" and "immoral." Former political prisoners were to be excluded "so their 'soiled' names would not offend high functionaries." "What irony!," Saja said. "It was these people who first had the courage to say that the king is naked. Stalinists loaded them to camps, psychiatric hospitals; they were forced to emigrate, and we, additionally, beat them over the head—their emotions, you see, their maximalist philosophy considerably differs from ours."[43] Eventually, Sąjūdis became a mass organization; participation became open to all, including dissidents and political prisoners.

The new organization held its formal Founding Congress in Vilnius on October 22–23. It was attended by 1,021 delegates chosen by professional organizations of Vilnius and Kaunas and elected from territorial areas of the republic as well as from political, cultural, and social groups.[44] Sąjūdis used the Great Diet of 1905 as a model for its congress. It also met in Vilnius and demanded autonomy for Lithuania in Tsarist Russia—becoming the first empire nationality to raise such a demand. The rulers of the republic did not participate as delegates. By social background, 299 delegates were born in peasant or collective farm families, 202 came from working families, and 459 had grown up in white-collar families. Occupationally, the largest group consisted of scientists and artists, writers, and other professionals. Educationally, 177 had advanced academic degrees, 693 were university graduates, 4 had only a primary education, 11 had an incomplete secondary education, 41 had completed their secondary education, and some others had special technical education.

A large majority of the delegates—980 (96 percent)—were Lithuanian; in addition, 8 (0.8 percent) were Russian, 6 (0.6 percent) were Jewish, 9 (0.9 percent) were Polish, and 13 represented other ethnic minorities. If compared to minority percentages in the population, the Russians and Poles were much underrepresented. This happened because delegates were elected from groups supporting Sąjūdis but there virtually were no such groups in Russian and Polish diasporas. To their later regret, in their patriotic enthusiasm and preoccupation with the restoration of Lithuanian history and language in society, Sąjūdis organizers had neglected to make a purposeful effort to recruit among these two minorities. A great majority of the Russians and the Poles stayed aloof despite declarations in the Sąjūdis program demanding recognition of "equal social, economic and cultural rights and freedoms for all citizens of the Lithuanian SSR, irrespective of race, nationality, religion and customs" and the right to develop their own languages, cultures, and state-supported native language schools.[45]

Obviously, this was a Lithuanian middle-class gathering, dominated—characteristically for Eastern Europe—by intellectuals. True to Lithuanian tradition, most of these intellectuals were of an overwhelmingly humanistic or social sciences background. The congress elected the movement's assembly (seimas) of 220 members, which in turn chose the 35-member governing council. Locally, Sąjūdis had territorial, workplace, professional association, and operational committees. Initially, the participants refused to choose a chief executive officer; however, political developments soon made it necessary.

As its formal program, Sąjūdis claimed its overall goals were to "support and deepen" the perestroika process started by the all-union Communist party;[46] achieve "sovereignty" in all areas of life within a "Leninist" Soviet federation; and pursue a "pluralist society" with no one "usurping" political power. Among the programmatic goals were a Western-style guarantee of civil rights, elimination of Stalinism and "stagnation," exposure of Stalin's crimes, and punishment of the epoch's criminals.

The movement went on record as a group that considered "national consciousness and expression as important factors of social renewal." Although it fell short of claims to independent statehood, in concrete policy terms Sąjūdis supported separate Lithuanian citizenship, control of immigration, and Lithuanian as the official language of the republic, coupled with a guarantee of the rights of minorities. The program further opposed a "state monopoly" over culture and demanded the establishment of a "national" school system and broad cultural contacts with foreign countries. It especially emphasized the need to restore the teaching of Lithuanian history at schools, asserting that "knowledge of history is an integral part of any nation's consciousness" and that the "Lithuanian nation has a dramatic history and traditionally draws its vitality from the past."

The congress decided against a formal organization of the movement since this would involve not only formal membership but also the creation of a much detested "bureaucracy." Thus, in contrast to the Latvian Popular Front, the Lithuanian Movement for Restructuring did not have dues-paying members but only participants and activists, the latter moving the wheels of local organizations. Lists of just the activists were kept. As a result, the movement's leadership could only estimate the group's size. In the winter of 1989, Sajūdis's president, Professor Vytautas Landsbergis, placed membership between 100,000 and 500,000.[47]

The leadership of Sajūdis represented a coalition between Communists and non-Communists, the latter playing a relatively more prominent role since December 1988. A survey of political attitudes among members of the movement's Diet was conducted by the Executive Council's sociological research center to gather data about the leadership's affiliations and views. The questionnaire was answered by 186 out of 220 members of the Diet.[48] According to this survey, 32 percent were members of the Communist party and 3 percent were members of the Komsomol. Sixty-one percent did not belong to any party, and 4 percent were affiliated with the newly established Democratic party and "other" parties. Only one of the reporting 186 members "sympathized" with the Communist party, however; 37 had sympathies for the Democratic party; 34 for the Christian Democrats; and 14 for Social Democrats. Three members felt an affinity to the Nationalist party (the old Tautininkai party of President Smetona), 5 to the environmentalist "Greens," and 1 to the Lithuanian Freedom League. An absolute majority (95 percent) said they supported a multiparty system in Lithuania; not a single one favored one-party rule. However, only 18 percent wanted Sajūdis to become a political party, whereas 47 percent were against such formalization.

Programmatically, Sajūdis underwent changes after its inception on June 3, 1988. Its initial direction was expressed in the slogan "Openness, democracy, and sovereignty." Its national program, however, was radicalized by the political process of the summer of 1988 through the winter of 1989. In October 1988 Sajūdis sought "sovereignty" in the Soviet federation, but by the end of November it already advocated "moral independence," and by February 1989 it wanted "spiritual" independence. In April the Sajūdis assembly publicly declared that "partial sovereignty is impossible," that "sovereignty [means] the independence of the state," and finally that "a sovereign country cannot be part of another country." Thus, in less than a year Sajūdis had begun to advocate political independence and secession from the Soviet Union.[49] During that time, it helped to spawn a number of smaller support groups representing regions, professional groups, and countless social and political interests and provided momentum for other organizations severing ties with their Moscow superiors.

The Lithuanian Artists Union, true to its tradition of independence, was the first to break with the central organs, doing so even before the formal declaration of the republic's sovereignty in May 1989. Following the declaration, the Writers Union and other professional groups began to end their subordination to central headquarters and registered themselves as independent Lithuanian organizations. Similarly, environmental groups such as Zhemyna became more vocal and adamant in their demands for "greener" policies.

In June 1989, the Lithuanian Komsomol formally broke with Moscow to become "Lithuania's Communist Youth Association" instead of a branch of the "All-Union Leninist Communist Youth Association," its status for over forty years. A survey of Komsomol members conducted in May 1989 revealed that 49 percent of the respondents wanted the organization to be transformed into other youth organizations, whereas 26 percent thought it should be liquidated altogether.[50] Soon a variety of groups for young people became popular, including Boy Scouts and Girl Scouts, Young Lithuania (a nationalist young people's organization), the Heirs of Gediminas (named after the Lithuanian Grand Duke of the fourteenth century), the Followers of Kudirka (named after the leader of national awakening at the end of the nineteenth century), and the Catholic youth group Ateitis. Meanwhile, the Komsomol kept losing membership. Youth associations were joined by dozens of others, including environmental groups, temperance unions, deportee associations, associations for the protection of political prisoners, associations fostering Baltic friendship, women's groups, and even the Catholic Caritas, which planned the establishment of orphanages, nursing homes, and private schools.

In addition to political demonstrations, Sąjūdis organized other events or profited from rallies sponsored by kindred groups. One of those was the tour of rock music festivals in July 1988 led by architect and musician Algirdas Kaušpėdas, a member of the National Council of Sąjūdis and a leader of one of the best-known rock groups. Another was the huge rally for the environment held in Kaunas. The August 2, 1988, rally, sponsored by the environmental group Atgaja, like U.S. protest rallies, combined political speeches with a rock music concert, again directed by Algirdas Kaušpėdas. The event represented the culmination of a week-long tour of the country by the sponsors, who preached about the governmental neglect of the environment in Lithuania. The rally was attended by 500,000 people. It was a critical week that brought news of the movement outside urban areas to Lithuania's heartland.[51]

Algirdas Kaušpėdas, leader of the rock group "Antis," uses political theater to spread popular support for change. (Photo by R. Urbakavičius. Used by permission.)

Twenty demands directed to the authorities were adopted at the rally. Among them were requests to stop the installation of the third Chernobyl-type reactor in the Ignalina nuclear power plant and to discontinue the construction of a special HES power plant at Kaišiadorys and instead to spend 100 million rubles to build a water purification plant for the city of Kaunas, which so far had no such facility and was spewing raw sewage. Expansion of the giant cement works at Naujoji Akmenė was also opposed—it worked solely for Moscow's benefit and profit—and substitution of natural gas for the use of highly polluting mazoot was demanded to run the existing power plants.

A new ecological group, Zalieji (the Greens), spawned by Sąjūdis, organized an event to "join hands" around the Baltic Sea on September 3 with activists of all the border nations. On September 16–17, Sąjūdis gathered 10,000 activists to form a human ring around the Ignalina nuclear power station and focus on the dangers it represented. Since local authorities refused permission for holding a demonstration, the crowds entertained themselves by planting trees, watching plays, and listening to songs about Chernobyl.[52] The Movement for Restructuring gathered 287,000 signatures for a petition asking the United Nations and the director of the International Atomic Energy Agency to establish an international commission for the examination of the plant's safety. "Green" events also included a boycott of dairy products to demand state-sponsored quality control over milk production so it would not be contaminated either by cattle sickness or chemicals, as apparently was the case in large parts of the country in 1988.

Non-Communist political parties, too, soon emerged. The first was the Lithuanian Democratic party, initially very popular among members of Sąjūdis's Diet. It advocated left of center social and nationalist policies. This group was joined by the Christian Democratic party, the Social Democratic party, the Greens, and even the Nationalist party, presumably the successor to the ruling party of independent Lithuania's last president, Antanas Smetona. Dissidents found it difficult to define their role in such radically different circumstances. They dispersed their efforts: Some effectively organized hunger strikes to help the release of all prisoners of conscience; others chose strictly political activity; and still others revived the Helsinki Watch Committee or joined groups supporting prisoners and deportees or honoring the memory of postwar anti-Soviet partisans. Most of the new parties were small and politically amorphous but gave Lithuanian intellectuals their first chance to develop endogenous political skills and ideologies.

The unleashed energies and sentiments of society also turned to public names and symbols. Generally, periodicals abandoned their Communist symbols and dropped the label "Soviet" or "Communist." The reformist daily *Komjaunimo tiesa* (Komsomolskaya pravda), for example, was renamed *Lietuvos rytas* (The Morning of Lithuania) by its far-sighted editor, Gedvydas Vainauskas. Monuments and street names were reclaimed. Thus, the city of Kapsukas, named after the founder of the Lithuanian Communist party, was again called Marijampole (The City of Mary), the name it bore until 1955. Historical and national monuments removed or destroyed by the Soviets reappeared almost overnight.

Lithuanian minorities, too, organized themselves to assert their national identity and make their voices heard in politics. In addition to the Russians and the Poles, the Germans, the ancient Karaims, and the Byelorussians formed cultural societies. Lithuanian Jews, a small remnant of once the largest minority group in the country, also founded their associations. Jewish leaders closely cooperated with Sąjūdis. The president of the Association of Lithuanian Jews served as a member of Sąjūdis's ruling council. The republic's Communist authorities, encouraged by Sąjūdis, began to address Jewish sensitivities and needs. A monument by Arbit

Dissidents hold a hunger strike for the release of Lithuanian political prisoners, August 1988. (Photo by R. Urbakavičius. Used by permission.)

Blatas, a New York artist of Lithuanian roots, was to mark the location of a Vilnius ghetto during the World War II Nazi occupation. Other monuments to honor the Holocaust victims were planned and eventually built. Restoration of Jewish cemeteries destroyed by the Nazis and abandoned to the elements by the Soviets were begun by groups of volunteers. A museum of Jewish culture was authorized. Even a "Maccabee" sports club was established and accepted into the world federation of such clubs. Lithuanian Jews resumed direct relations with world Jewish organizations.

Finally, with international borders opened more generously by Gorbachev's liberal policies, the Lithuanians passionately plunged into a search for international contacts. By the summer of 1988, anticipating the introduction of economic autonomy for the republic by Gorbachev, the Lithuanian government sent dozens of managers and economists to Western Europe, the United States, and Canada to seek economic investment. In turn, delegations from abroad, including those of the European parliament, visited the republic. Most of all, for economic and cultural reasons the Lithuanians sought to restore their ties to Lithuanian emigration in the West, and in turn, a number of Americans and Canadians have moved to Lithuania in order to work and consult.

The best example of the input received through such exchanges, at least in the realm of academics, was the participation of Western scholars in the reestablishment and work of the University of Vytautas Magnus in Kaunas.[53] Originally founded in 1922, it was closed down by the Soviets in 1950. After it was reestablished in 1989, Western scholars were invited to reorganize its academic structure following the U.S. model. One-half of its faculty senate consists of Western academics who teach in U.S., Canadian, Australian, and European universities. Its top administrators are U.S. professors of Lithuanian origin, but scholars from everywhere in the Western world are invited to teach and help a new generation reclaim its lost heritage of Western intellectual thought.

The Western diaspora since has financed the numerous visits of activists and scholars to the West, provided funds for the hiring of consultants, supplied computers or communications technology, and acted as a conduit of information and resources to help the newly emerging Lithuanian activists and groups find broader access to international organizations such as the Peace Corps and various UN-sponsored entities.

THE LITHUANIAN FREEDOM LEAGUE

The Lithuanian Freedom League was born in the underground. First mentioned in 1978, for a decade nothing was heard about the league, very likely because its moving spirit, the dissident historian Antanas Terleckas, was arrested and spent long years in a labor camp. It apparently was established "as a counterbalance to the primarily religious focus"[54] of the Catholic-dominated dissident movement, but it was virtually unknown until its members reemerged in 1987, the first among civic groups to test the credibility of glasnost'. It was a small group. In late September 1988, it claimed only 803 registered members.[55] As a public organization, it included both Catholic dissidents and those, like Terleckas, who maintained that the Catholics did not sufficiently focus on nationalist issues. Some Catholic clergymen were active in its leadership, however. Its core support came from former dissidents, political prisoners, anti-Soviet partisans, and deportees. As an opinion poll of May 1989 indicated, its popularity rating was much higher than that of the Communist party but much lower than that of Sąjūdis. Some leaders of the Movement for Restructuring were happy to see the league confronting the Communist regime because it saved Sąjūdis from being labeled "extremist."[56] That adjective belonged to the league. However, others of Sąjūdis's leading circle reportedly considered the league a competitor. Generally, Sąjūdis intellectuals looked at the league with "disdain"[57] because the league's leadership was less educated and sophisticated. The league, in turn, considered Sąjūdis leaders too moderate because they had shown a willingness to compromise with the Communists.

The league, indeed, has been not only much less compromising than Sąjūdis but also much more willing to confront the Communist authorities. It pushed Lithuanian society to use Gorbachev's glasnost' for the republic's national renewal. On August 23, 1987, the league commemorated the anniversary of the signing of the Molotov-Ribbentrop pact. This was the first public demonstration in decades to pierce the national conscience of the intellectuals and it shocked Griškevičius's conservative leadership. In 1988, the league provoked Songaila's regime into an officially approved remembrance of Stalin's purges, deportations, and crimes by staging—without the required permit—a demonstration to commemorate the deportations of 1948 from Lithuania. A group of "doers" instead of "talkers," in 1987–1989 the league was quick to call people into the streets. The demonstrations attracted from 3,000 to 50,000 participants. The largest ones were held on September 28, 1988, November 26, 1988, and January 10, 1989. The first was in remembrance of the transfer of Lithuania to the Soviet sphere of influence by the Nazi-Soviet agreement of 1939. The second demonstration—held without any participation by Sąjūdis because Brazauskas's government pressured the movement not to cooperate with the league—demanded the resignation of the officials who had frustrated the adoption of the sovereignty declaration by the Supreme Soviet. The third, cosponsored by the Lithuanian Democratic party, the National Youth Association, and the Helsinki group, but not Sąjūdis, demanded outright independence and the airing by the United Nations of the "colonial" status of the Baltic states.

These demonstrations were organized to serve the two main purposes of the league, namely, to awaken the Lithuanian national consciousness and, second, uncompromisingly to promote the idea of Lithuanian independence.[58] The league's "ultimate ideal," as stated in its manifesto, was "a free Lithuania in a confederation of European nations."[59] Programmatically, the league supported most of Sąjūdis's program but disagreed with its early interpretation of the concept of sovereignty. The league, as already stated, consistently advocated full independence, which meant Lithuanian control not only of domestic but also of foreign and defense policies. The group therefore from the very outset demanded annulment of the Stalin-Hitler nonaggression pact of 1939 as well as the withdrawal of the Red Army from Lithuania at a precisely agreed time. All of this meant secession from the Soviet Union, a point that Sąjūdis had withdrawn from the resolutions of its founding congress at the insistence of Algirdas Brazauskas, the new first secretary of the Communist party.[60]

The league's main achievement was the radicalization of the Lithuanian Movement for Restructuring and even of the Lithuanian Communist party. The group also helped to bring about a faster pace of emancipation than had been expected by the main players of the drama. The Communist party resented the league. The leadership of Sąjūdis was divided. Thirty-eight percent of the movement's legislative assembly favored close cooperation with the league, but 49 percent supported collaboration only if the league would change its confrontational tactics.[61]

Disagreement on tactics really indicated differences of policy. For example, the league publicly called for a boycott of the elections to Gorbachev's newly reorganized Supreme Soviet on grounds that, as an occupied country, Lithuania should not participate in the occupier's political process. This view was rejected not only by Sąjūdis but also by an overwhelming majority of the population. After 1987–1989, the voice of the league became shrill, the issues it chose to argue inconsequential. After the declaration of independence in 1990, it began to fight the now free government with almost the same intensity it had fought the Communists in the past. The group's popularity in the country sank to near zero. Effective as a voice of dissent in the years of total Communist domination, the league's leadership failed to adjust to the requirements and responsibilities of free public life. It continued to resist the system, but did not manage to become a positive decision maker and political actor.

YEDINSTVO:
THE RUSSIAN AND POLISH MINORITIES

If Sąjūdis succeeded in uniting or establishing a modus vivendi with all "informal" Lithuanian groups that, like Mao's hundred flowers, now bloomed on the political field, it had less luck with Lithuania's largest minorities, namely, the Russians and the Poles. Smaller minorities—the Jews, Byelorussians, Tatars, Karaims, and others—generally supported reforms as advocated by Sąjūdis and institutionalized by the republic's government. In contrast, the Russians and Poles—with sizable exceptions—opposed these reforms and made alternative policy proposals on some burning issues. For example, they opposed the choice of Lithuanian as the official language and made counterproposals. The Russian and Polish minorities in 1989 constituted 9.4 percent and 7 percent of Lithuania's population, respectively, compared to 79.6 percent for the Lithuanians.[62] The Russians had a majority in the city of Snieūkus (now renamed

Visaginas), where the main industry is the Ignalina atomic power station. The Poles possessed majorities in two *rayons* (counties), the rural Vilnius and Šalčininkai counties of eastern Lithuania.

The massive scope and emotional currents of national rebirth intimidated these minorities. Sąjūdis, in particular, was seen as encroaching upon Russian and Polish interests. After Sąjūdis's founding congress on October 22–23, 1988, a new "informal" organization, Vienybė-Yedinstvo-Jednosc (Unity), was established to articulate and defend the perceived interests of the Russian and Polish minorities. It was composed, presumably, of all nationalities, but in reality most of its members were Russians and Poles. At first, *Sovetskaia litva* and *Czerwony sztandar,* Russian and Polish dailies published in Vilnius, served as forums for this rather odd Russian-Polish coalition. On November 11, the republic's press published a declaration adopted at the new group's founding meeting that explained its objectives.[63] As far as Gorbachev's reforms were concerned, its program was much more orthodox than that advocated by Sąjūdis. Yedinstvo clearly declared the primacy of the Communist party, professed loyalty to the perestroika process as formulated in Moscow, and favored the traditional Communist "mutual enrichment" of national cultures; it also stated opposition to discrimination based on nationality. The group strongly objected to the adoption of Lithuanian as the only official language of the republic. That opposition brought together many Russians and Poles to unite in this organization. Its coordinating national headquarters were apparently under the leadership of Nina Andreeva of Leningrad, the reactionary opponent of Gorbachev's perestroika.

Yedinstvo demanded that the question of official language be decided by legislation under a restructured republic government. It suggested that the unicameral legislature be replaced by a bicameral structure in which one house would represent the population at large while the other represented equally all nationalities, large and small, living in Lithuania. This house, "the council of nationalities," would have the "functions of the highest institution in deciding questions involving national processes and intranational relations."[64] Until such a legislature was established, the question of official language should not be discussed, the organization's leaders said. Valerii Ivanov, representing Yedinstvo at a meeting of Communist party activists, formally demanded reorganization of the legislature as well as the removal of the Lithuanian flag from the Lithuanian Communist party offices.[65] In a public demonstration in Vilnius on February 12, 1989, that attracted a crowd estimated at 80,000, Yedinstvo threatened workers' strikes and refusal to pay Communist party membership dues if the decree on Lithuanian as the official language was not squashed in two weeks.[66] Yedinstvo members denounced Sąjūdis supporters as "separatists," "extremists," "nationalists," and "Nazis,"[67] all very bad words in the Soviet Union. Sąjūdis activities, it was suggested, should be limited to economic and social issues. At various demonstrations attracting thousands, Yedinstvo leaders said that people of all nationalities should have a right to use their native languages in all state, economic, social, and political affairs, that students in special schools and institutions of higher education should be taught in their native languages, and that autonomous territories should be established for each nationality group. At the February 12 demonstration, unsigned leaflets were distributed declaring that "the only good Lithuanian was a dead Lithuanian" and inciting the people to action: "Russians and Slavs! Under the flag of great Russia we will take Lithuania!"[68]

Associations of smaller nationalities, namely, the Jewish associations, the Byelorussian group Syabryna, the Tatar, Latvian, Estonian, Mordovinian, Karaim, and German societies, and the Ukrainian Community of Lithuania, denounced the February meeting as an activity of "great Russian chauvinism" and Yedinstvo as a very negative organization because it opposed efforts by all of Lithuania's nationalities to restrain "the pretentious monopolistic claims" of the center (Moscow). These nationalities, their statement said, supported the implementation of the decree making Lithuanian the official language.[69]

The Poles had some specific demands. Polish spokesmen asked for the retranslation of Poland's first TV program on the Lithuanian network, for an increase in the number of Polish kindergartens and secondary schools, for Polish as a language of instruction in universities, for more positions for Polish academics, and for the establishment of a Polish consulate in Vilnius.[70] The matter of the consulate had apparently already been agreed upon between Moscow and Jaruzelski. An interview with Jan Sinkiewicz, an editorial board member of *Czerwony sztandar* and the president of the newly formed Association of Lithuania's Poles, revealed that the Poles wanted to transform Vilnius into a cultural-political Polish center for the entire Soviet Union, working in close cooperation with the Warsaw government.[71] Organized Poles have dissociated themselves from the Lithuanian-run Cultural Foundation, which supported Polish activities. On May 12–13, Poles in the Vilnius area demanded the establishment of territorial Polish autonomy in Lithuania. The rayon of Šalūininkai actually declared such autonomy.

In its founding conference of May 13–14, 1989, Yedinstvo was captured by extremists of the city of Vilnius led by Valerii Ivanov. As a result, the organization split. Many delegates walked out. Two dozen leading figures, including some founding members, withdrew from the organization altogether, denouncing the conference as an "example of how extremism endangers democracy."[72] In the view of the protesters, the organization had been "discredited" and "did not become an integral part of Soviet Lithuania's political system" as apparently was expected. Ivanov's group, they said, was playing a dangerous game with unknown consequences. Lithuania did not need Karabakh or tanks on its streets. The fledgling Center for Russian Culture also denounced and dissociated itself from Yedinstvo, suggesting that the way to deal with the Lithuanians was to pursue a "dialogue of mutual respect" so that "the equality of Lithuania's citizens" was "achieved by common efforts."[73] In February, impressed by Yedinstvo's ability to stage a demonstration with 80,000 participants, Lithuanian authorities promised that Yedinstvo would be consulted and given an opportunity to influence the drafting of legislation implementing the language law.[74] The group's disastrous performance, and its split in May, however, considerably if not fatally reduced its political importance and ability to influence political change.

Minority representatives attributed the rise of their opposition to Sąjūdis's insensitivity to Russian and Polish needs. The Kremlin's representatives said the same. The Lithuanian Movement for Restructuring may have made political mistakes but its declarations have been liberal to minorities, except that it did not support the idea of territorial autonomy. The background of Russian and Polish attitudes was complex. Most of Lithuania's Russians and Poles were working-class people who felt threatened by the sea of national flags and other symbols of national awakening. The Polish intellectual elite was very small. Most of it had left for Poland at the time of repatriation in the late 1940s. The Russian elite was the most populous among the non-Lithuanian ethnic groups. The Russians, in addition, were mostly immigrants—and felt insecure. All must have felt endangered by the language decree, which required all state employees to learn Lithuanian in two years. Most of them had never learned Lithuanian and had not intended to learn it, even though they permanently lived in the republic. Neither group wanted to accept minority status despite the fact they were minorities in Lithuania, a feeling probably similar to that of the poor white minority in many counties of the U.S. South that originally refused to accept the civil rights revolution.

The establishment of a separate association of Lithuania's Poles in May 1989 led to a lively dialogue between the Polish representatives, on the one hand, and republic authorities and Sąjūdis leaders, on the other. In Warsaw, on June 26, 1989, Brazauskas and Jaruzelski signed an agreement obliging the Lithuanian and Polish Communist parties to extensive cooperation, including numerous exchanges to profit Lithuania's Polish minority.[75] On July 10, Lithuania's Supreme Soviet appealed to the Poles, asking them to withdraw legislation passed in the Šalčininkai district of

Brazauskas (right), Šepetys (left), and others in torch-light procession to Vilnius Cathedral after the opening day of Sąjūdis's founding congress, October 22, 1988. (Photo by R. Urbakavičius. Used by permission.)

private schools and suggested that the principle of separation of church from school embedded in constitutional law should not apply to private educational institutions.

Reformers both outside and inside the Communist party have received the church's support. However, the church did not directly participate in political competition. The leadership of Sąjūdis generally supported the rights of the church and its appropriate place in society, but its president, Landsbergis, was at pains to stress that, unlike the Polish reform movement, the Lithuanian movement did not develop around the church; instead, according to him, the church came to the movement.[81]

In reality, the church at first was cautious. It wanted to be sure of the directions and goals of Sąjūdis. An absolute majority of clergymen did not want to participate in politics directly, and the church no longer had large numbers of intellectuals on its side. This was a change from the days before Soviet annexation, when, for many intellectuals, religion was not confined to church attendance but provided the underpinnings of a philosophy of culture and politics that inspired active lay participation in these crucial fields of Lithuanian life. Sąjūdis nevertheless was sympathetic to religion and friendly to the restoration of the status of the

Catholic Church. Most Sąjūdis reformers as well as Lithuanian Freedom League supporters, if they were not believers, at least considered the Catholic tradition as part of their national heritage.

The Catholic Church began to face the issue of direct political participation in the 1990s, when four clergymen were nominated by Sąjūdis and elected to parliament. One of those was Msgr. Alfonsas Svarinskas, an energetic and aggressive former political prisoner and a leading dissident in the Lithuanian underground movement for human rights. He was chosen by Sąjūdis to fill a vacancy that had occurred in the fall of 1991. Svarinskas, it may be added, confronted a candidate of the formerly Communist Lithuanian Democratic Workers Union and won by an overwhelming majority. In his view, Catholic priests have "played a special role in the fight against the Communists. They follow no private interests." He believes that "priests should take part in politics" because the parliament does not sufficiently devote itself to religious questions.[82] As is well known, however, the Vatican forbids clergy from running for government positions. Svarinskas nevertheless received permission to become a candidate from Cardinal Vincentas Sladkevičius. Svarinskas would relinquish his seat, he said, if the Vatican so commanded. Svarinskas's view on the clergy's participation in politics was not shared by other clergymen and became a divisive issue. In 1992, the bishops forbade clergymen to run as candidates for parliament and asked them to refrain from partisan campaigning. A Christian Democratic party was founded on February 16, 1989, but it is small and does not seek to speak for the church. It also may be added that in 1990 Pope John Paul II reestablished a Lithuanian church province within current Lithuanian boundaries, including Vilnius and Klaipėda, and divided it into two archdioceses. The Kaunas archdiocese is currently ruled by Cardinal Vincentas Sladkevičius, who spent thirty years in internal exile under the Soviets. The archdiocese of Vilnius is governed by Archbishop Audrys Bačkis, former Papal Nunzio in the Netherlands and an official in the Vatican curia who grew up in the West.

Thus, in June 1988 the Lithuanians began the march to autonomy that culminated in a declaration of independence on March 11, 1990, and was crowned by international recognition in August–September 1991. The drama, as it unfolded, played in four acts: (1) the rise of grassroots groups promoted by Gorbachev to help with perestroika, the process that led to the formal establishment of the Lithuanian Movement for Restructuring (Sąjūdis) on October 20–23, 1988; (2) the struggle of wits and ballots between Sąjūdis and the Lithuanian Communist party, which resulted in a formal declaration of the republic's sovereignty on May 18, 1989; (3) the demise of the Communist party's ruling monopoly and the severance of its alliance with Moscow by March 1990; and finally, (4) the total Communist loss of power, the declaration of independence, and the battle with

Gorbachev and the Kremlin for the recognition of independent statehood from March 11, 1990, through September 1991.

NOTES

1. For this discussion of the partisan war, information was drawn from the following Western and Soviet sources: V. Stanley Vardys, "The Partisan Movement in Postwar Lithuania," *Slavic Review* 22 (September 1963): 499–522; Kestutis K. Girnius, *Partizanų kovos Lietuvoje* (Chicago: Į Laisvę Fondas, 1987); Thomas Remeikis, *Opposition to Soviet Rule in Lithuania* (Chicago: Institute of Lithuanian Studies Press, 1980); V. K. Tauras, *Guerrilla Warfare on the Amber Coast* (New York: n.p., 1962); Arvydas Anusauskas and Vytautas Kucinskas, *Lietuvos laisvės kovos* (Vilnius: Žaltvykslė, 1991); Juozas Daumantas, *Fighters for Freedom* (New York: Maryland Books, 1975). This last monograph is a memoir of life as a partisan by partisan leader Juozas Lukša.

Of interest to students of partisan relations with Western intelligence agencies is Tom Bower's *Red Web: M16 and the KGB Master Coup* (London: Aurum, 1989). Unfortunately, the book is useful only for interviews the author conducted with KGB officers or agents who had infiltrated British intelligence and thus were able to destroy the liaison some Western agencies attempted to establish with the partisans. Otherwise it gives a very unbalanced treatment of the partisan problem in the three Baltic republics. Soviet sources include a series of books and pamphlets published in 1960–1968 that discuss various aspects of partisan activities. They are based, on the whole, on KGB records and interrogations of captured partisans. One of the first books was M. Chienas, K. Smigelskis, and E. Uldukis, *Vanagai iš anapus* (Vilnius: VGLL, 1960). A second edition was published a year later.

2. *Tiesa*, February 8, 1962, p. 3; *Pravda*, October 24, 1961, p. 4.

3. See Roger Peterson, "A Community-Based Theory of Rebellion," *European Sociology* 34 (1993): 47–78.

4. Testimony by Colonel Burlitsky, a former NKVD officer, to the Committee on Communist Aggression, U.S. House of Representatives, *Fourth Interim Report of the Select Committee on Communist Aggression*, 83rd Cong., 2nd sess. (Washington, D.C.: U.S. Government Printing Office, 1954), pp. 1372ff.

5. For further information on the Lithuanian dissident movement see V. Stanley Vardys, *The Catholic Church: Dissent and Nationality in Soviet Lithuania* (Boulder and New York: East European Quarterly, Columbia University Press, 1978); also his "Lithuania's Catholic Movement Reappraised," *Survey* 25 (Summer 1980): 49–73; "Human Rights Issues in Estonia, Latvia, and Lithuania," *Journal of Baltic Studies* 12 (Fall 1981): 275–298; and "Pogrindžio rezistencija Lietuvoje," *Ateitis*, no. 4 (1982): 102–110. See also Thomas A. Oleszczuk, *Political Justice in the USSR: Dissent and Repression in Lithuania, 1969–1978* (Boulder and New York: East European Monographs, Columbia University Press, 1988); Thomas Remeikis, *Opposition to Soviet Rule in Lithuania*; and Alexander R. Alexiev, *Dissent and Nationalism in the Soviet Baltic* (Santa Monica: Rand, 1983). The only memoirs by a prominent dissident translated into English are by Nijolė Sadūnaitė, *A Radiance in the Gulag* (Manassas: Trinity Communications, 1987).

6. See David Kowalewski, "Dissent in the Baltic Republics: Characteristics and Consequences," *Journal of Baltic Studies* 10 (1979): 310ff.

7. See David Kowalewski, "Lithuanian Protest for Human Rights in the 1970s: Characteristics and Consequences," *Lituanus* 25 (1979): 45.

8. *Soviet Analyst* 11, no. 16 (August 16, 1982), p. 5; Joshua Rubenstein, *Soviet Dissidents: Their Struggle for Human Rights* (Boston: Beacon Press, 1980), p. 258.

9. See Vytautas Tininis, "1972 metai: Gegužė, sudrebinusi Lietuvą," *Lietuvos rytas*, May 13, 1992, p. 3.

10. English translations of individual issues of the *Chronicle of the Catholic Church of Lithuania* were published by Lithuanian Catholic Religious Aid, Brooklyn, New York. A Lithuanian text, published in ten volumes, is *LKB Kronika* (Chicago: Lietuvos Kronikos Sajunga, 1974–1992). An article entitled "LKB Kronika" by the editor of this work, Bishop Sigitas Tamkevičius, S. J., explaining how *Kronika* originated and how it was edited, was published in a Chicago monthly, *Laiškai lietuviams* 18 (May 1992): 154–164. For a succinct, well-written history of Lithuania's Catholic Church, including the Soviet repression period, see Saulius Sužiedelis, *The Sword and the Cross* (Huntington: Our Sunday Visitor Publication Department, 1988).

11. *Soviet Analyst* 4, no. 4 (July 3, 1975): 6.

12. Texts of eyewitness accounts of the Vilnius and Kaunas demonstrations appear in Remeikis, *Opposition to Soviet Rule in Lithuania*, pp. 274–278. They are taken, respectively, from *Lituanus*, nos. 1–2 (1962): 64, and Elena Juciute, *Pėdos mirties zonoje* (New York: 1974), pp. 393–395.

13. Kudirka's story is more fully presented in Algis Rukšėnas, *Day of Shame* (New York: David McKay, 1973); also U.S. Congress, House of Representatives, *Attempted Defection by Lithuanian Seaman Simas Kudirka: Hearings Before the Subcommittee on State Department Organization and Foreign Operations of the Committee on Foreign Affairs*, 91st Cong., 1st sess.

14. See, for example, Barbara Jancar, "Religious Dissent in the Soviet Union," in *Dissent in the USSR*, ed. Rudolf Tökes (Baltimore: Johns Hopkins University Press, 1975), p. 226; also André Martin and Peter Falke, *Christus stirbt in Litauen* (Aschaffenburg: Paul Pattlach Verlag, 1977), pp. 19ff.

15. Text in V. Stanley Vardys, "Human Rights Issues in Estonia, Latvia, and Lithuania," pp. 289–292.

16. On the intricacies of censorship in Lithuania see Tomas Venclova, "Translation of World Literature and Political Censorship in Contemporary Lithuania," *Lituanus* 25 (Summer 1979): 5–26. For more details on the struggle for national culture after Stalin, see Romuald J. Misiunas and Rein Taagepera, *The Baltic States: Years of Dependence, 1940–1980* (Berkeley: University of California Press, 1983), pp. 159ff.

17. See V. Stanley Vardys, "Reflections on the Theory of Soviet Nationality Policy," in *Sowjetsystem und Ostrecht*, ed. Georg Brunner et al. (Berlin: Duncker and Humblot, 1985), pp. 263–277.

18. V. I. Lenin, *Polnoe sobranye sochinenii*, 5th ed., vol. 24, p. 129.

19. *XXII S'ezd Kommunisticheskoi Partii Sovetskogo Soyuza* (Moscow: Gosudarstvennoe Izdatel'stvo Politicheskoi Literatury, 1962), p. 217.

20. See Irena Kostkevičiūtė, "Dailė tarp prievartos ir pasipriešinimo," *Literatūra ir menas*, May 16, 1992, p. 10.

21. Interview with Vytautas Maūiuika, *Literatūra ir menas,* May 9, 1992, p. 4.

22. Interview with Juozas Matulis, *Tiesa,* April 2, 1992, p. 5.

23. Ibid.

24. See Petras Griškevičius's article, "Persitvarkymo centre žmogus" (The focus of perestroika is man), *Pergalė* (Vilnius), no. 2 (February 1987): 3–11 passim.

25. *Literatūra ir menas,* November 14, 1987, p. 5.

26. Cf. Alfred Erich Senn, *Awakening Lithuania* (Berkeley: University of California Press, 1990), p. 24.

27. See interview with militia general Stasys Lisauskas, the minister of the interior, in *Gimtasis kraštas,* April 7–13, 1988, pp. 1–2.

28. See *Radio Free Europe Research Situation Report, Baltic Area,* March 24, 1988, pp. 31ff.

29. Ibid.

30. See *Tiesa,* issues of February 3–6, 1988.

31. *Literatūra ir menas,* December 1, 1987, pp. 2, 5.

32. *Gimtasis kraštas,* no. 26, June 23–29, 1988, p. 3; no. 18, May 4–10, 1988, p. 2; no. 22, May 26–June 1, 1988, p. 3.

33. See reports by Saulius Girnius, *RFE/FL Research, Baltic Area 12,* February 16, 1988, pp. 37ff.; *Baltic Area 15,* May 20, 1988, pp. 29ff.

34. *Gimtasis kraštas,* June 23–29, 1988, p. 3.

35. Ibid.

36. *Sąjūdžio žinios,* no. 2 (1988): 1.

37. Ibid., p. 2.

38. Ibid.

39. Ibid.

40. Ibid.

41. *Sąjūdžio žinios,* no. 2 (1988): 4.

42. *Gimtasis kraštas,* no. 24, June 9–15, 1988, p. 3.

43. *Atgimimas,* no. 3, October 15, 1988, p. 8.

44. *Atgimimas,* no. 7, November 15, 1988, p. 7.

45. *The Lithuanian Reform Movement: Sąjūdis* (Vilnius: Sąjūdis, 1989), p. 38. Unless otherwise indicated, all quotes from the Sąjūdis program come from this source.

46. See "Lietuvos Persitarkymo Sąjūdžio bendroji programa," *Atgimimas,* no. 3, October 15, 1988, pp. 6–7 passim.

47. Interview in *Tygodnik powszechny* (Cracow), February 5, 1989, p. 5.

48. Data secured by Lithuanian Information Center, Brooklyn, New York, press release, April 7, 1989.

49. Statement by Sąjūdis Assembly, April 1, 1989. See *Lithuanian Reform Movement: Sąjūdis, Lithuanian Way,* vol. 1 (Vilnius, 1990), p. 54.

50. *Komjaunimo tiesa,* June 16, 1989, p. 4.

51. *Radio Free Europe Research, Baltic Area 10,* September 9, 1988, pp. 21–22.

52. Press release of the Lithuanian Information Center, Brooklyn, New York, September 19, 1988. Some experts, however, considered the Greens' campaign to block construction of the third nuclear reactor misdirected. Instead, this unit should have been installed so that the first reactor, which was old, technologically inferior, and more dangerous, could be dismantled. See interview with Lithuanian nuclear expert Rimvydas Jasiulionis in *Der Spiegel,* no. 46 (1992): 195–196.

53. See Barton Bollag, "U.S.-Style Campus in Lithuania Is Seen as a Model in the Region," *Chronicle of Higher Education*, November 13, 1991, pp. A43ff.

54. *The Lithuanian Reform Movement: Sąjūdis*, p. 45.

55. Ibid.

56. Ibid.

57. Ibid.

58. *Lietuvos Laisvės Lyga*, no. 1, November 10, 1988, pp. 1ff.

59. *The Lithuanian Reform Movement: Sąjūdis*, p. 46.

60. Ibid., p. 34.

61. Poll of members of the assembly, press release of April 7, 1989, by the Lithuanian Information Center, Brooklyn, New York.

62. *Tiesa*, May 26, 1989, p. 2.

63. *Tiesa*, November 11, 1988, p. 3.

64. Ibid.

65. *Tiesa*, November 17, 1988, p. 3.

66. *Atgimimas*, no. 7 (20), February 7, 1989, p. 4; *Tiesa*, February 14, 1988, p. 3.

67. *Komjaunimo tiesa*, February 15, 1989, p. 1.

68. See *Gimtasis kraštas*, March 30–April 5, 1989, p. 7.

69. See text in *Atgimimas*, no. 7 (20), February 7, 1989, p. 4.

70. *Czerwony sztandar*, September 4, 1988, summarized in *Atgimimas*, no. 4, October 21, 1988, pp. 6–7. A lengthy agreement on cultural and economic exchanges between the Polish and Lithuanian CPs was signed in Warsaw by Wojcek Jaruzelski and Algirdas Brazauskas. See *Tiesa*, July 2, 1989, p. 4.

71. See *Komjaunimo tiesa*, May 6, 1989, pp. 1–2.

72. *Tiesa*, May 18, 1989, p. 4; see also *Sovetskaia Litva*, May 16, 1989, p. 3.

73. *Komjaunimo tiesa*, May 20, 1989, p. 4.

74. *Tiesa*, February 14, 1989, p. 4.

75. *Tiesa*, July 2, 1989.

76. *Tiesa*, July 11, 1989.

77. *Gimtasis kraštas*, July 28–August 3, 1988, pp. 1, 4–5.

78. Arvydas Matulionis, *Lietuva ir Sąjūdis*, p. 103.

79. *Gimtasis kraštas*, May 11–17, 1989, p. 4.

80. *Atgimimas*, no. 8, November 22, 1988, p. 8; no. 9, November 29, 1989, p. 4.

81. Quoted in *Our Sunday Visitor*, November 17, 1991, p. 21.

82. *Tygodnik powszechny* (Cracow), February 5, 1989, p. 5.

· FIVE ·

Sąjūdis and the Party: The March Toward Independence

Following the establishment of the initiative group of Sąjūdis on June 3, 1988, Lithuania's social and political life became charged with intense and diverse activity. The country's political stage became dominated by the struggle for influence between the Movement for Restructuring and the Communist party. Sąjūdis did not have a formal part in the system. It functioned as merely an "informal" organization. The mobilized masses quickly conferred upon it factual legitimacy and political power, however, which the ruling party could not afford to disregard.

This struggle for influence differed from normal democratic competition for two reasons. First, while Sąjūdis gave voice to public opinion and relied on private donations for support, the Communist party controlled the media, law enforcement, and financial resources. Second, both groups, but especially the Communist party, had to consider the political demands of an outside force, namely, Moscow. In other words, the contest was trilateral, between Sąjūdis, the Lithuanian Communist party, and the Kremlin.[1] Sąjūdis was the outside challenger to power. The party's position was complicated and weakened by the fact that many of its own most distinguished intellectuals, artists, writers, and professionals actively joined the "other" side. This indicated a factional party split and threatened party unity. Paradoxically, the apparent betrayal also held a promise of allowing the party to control or influence Sąjūdis or ultimately come to a consensus with that organization without loss of face. Indeed, relations between Sąjūdis and the Communist party proved to be both a struggle for influence and a process of consensus building.

One can distinguish four phases in the relationship between the party and Sąjūdis: (1) from June 3, 1988, the establishment of the Sąjūdis initiative group, to October 22–23, the founding congress of the new organization; (2)

from October 22–23 to November 18, the fateful meeting of the Supreme Soviet of the Lithuanian SSR; (3) from November 18 through the elections for Moscow's new parliament in March 1989 and the vote on Lithuania's sovereignty on May 18, 1989; and finally, (4) the nine months from May 18 to the party's loss of power beginning in March 1990. The first period can be characterized as a time when Sąjūdis was gathering strength and the Communist party was attempting to influence or to contain it. The second period saw growing political consensus and the acceptance of the Estonian federalist model for Lithuania. The third began with bitterness, disappointment, and conflict, which radicalized Sąjūdis and spelled defeat for the party but opened avenues for cooperation and consensus in the post-election period. Finally, the nine months between May 1989 and March 1990 witnessed the erosion of the organizational strength of the party, its desperate effort to save itself by cutting ties to Moscow, and ultimately the demise of Soviet rule in Lithuania.

THE REFORMERS RALLY THE MASSES

The Movement for Restructuring used the summer of 1988 to gain wide and popular support. It reached out to the masses and provided a forum for diverse and festering points of view. As a Lithuanian sociologist put it, Sąjūdis gained prestige and respect by "serving as soil for growing diverse plants." Since the movement initially had no access to the media, it relied on mass meetings, demonstrations, and public events, announced by word of mouth, to spread the message. Meetings were held to discuss burning issues of the day. These included justice for exiles deported in 1941–1952 and the release of current political prisoners; environmental pollution and health hazards; "sovereignty" and the true history of Lithuania's incorporation into the Soviet Union; the status of the Lithuanian language; economic independence; mistreatment of recruits by the Red Army; and many other long repressed and controversial topics. Thus, these public meetings quickly became occasions for venting anger, for giving expression to pent-up emotions accumulated through five decades of hypocritical and oppressive Soviet rule, and for articulating demands for reform.

At first, Sąjūdis had to compete with the Lithuanian Freedom League. The dissidents were the first to call a commemoration of the Soviet mass deportations and attracted 6,000 participants. A Lithuanian tricolor was flown for the first time on this occasion. Ten days later, Sąjūdis called for an open "farewell" meeting. This event, which issued directives for the Lithuanian party delegates elected to the 19th Party Conference in Moscow, drew 50,000 people.

At the demonstration, Sąjūdis speakers voiced dissatisfaction with the secret elections of the conference delegates but stayed well within the official limits by couching their language in the rhetoric of perestroika. The group endorsed the ideas of the 27th All-Union Communist Party Congress and insisted that the 19th Party Conference shift government to the executive offices, or soviets, as distinguished from the party. It also advocated restoration of the republic's sovereignty in accordance with original Leninist principles. Sąjūdis wanted delegates to "secure guarantees" for the democratization of party and government activity; secure protection of the environment; grant various rights to republican rule; declare Lithuanian the official language of the republic; establish constitutional courts at all-union and republic levels; and ensure "possibilities" for "direct" republic relations with foreign countries.[2]

Encouraged by the success of the bon voyage meeting, Sąjūdis organized the welcome of delegates returning from the party conference on July 9. Some 100,000 people attended. More flags were flown and more patriotic speeches were made.

The mass demonstrations reached an apex on August 23 at the Vingis Park in Vilnius with a meeting attended by an estimated 250,000 people.

Communist and non-Communist leaders demonstrate in solidarity against Moscow (left to right: A. Brazauskas, academician J. Požėla, K. Prunskienė, V. Landsbergis), July 9, 1988, in Vingis Park, Vilnius. (Photo by R. Urbakavičius. Used by permission.)

The event commemorated the anniversary of the signing of the Stalin-Hitler nonaggression pact that had signaled the impending loss of independence for Lithuania. Mass participation exceeded all expectations.

The meeting featured a taped speech by independent Lithuania's last foreign minister, Juozas Urbšys, who was too frail to attend. He had personally negotiated with Stalin and Molotov in 1939 and told the story of the imposition of Soviet will on Lithuania. Stalinism was soundly denounced. One speaker said, "A religion has not yet been invented which could forgive all the crimes of Stalinism."[3] Another suggested, "If Tsarism created a prison of nations, Stalinism established a 'slaughterhouse of nations.'"[4] National flags and emblems now abounded, and the crowd was invited to sing the previously banned anthem of independent Lithuania. Sąjūdis announced its demands for publication of the text of the Nazi-Soviet pact with its secret protocols, for the opening of archives, for the rewriting of history texts for schools, and for the restoration of Lithuanian

Lithuanians protest the Molotov-Ribbentrop pact at Vilnius's Vingis Park, August 23, 1988. (Photo by R. Urbakavičius. Used by permission.)

sovereignty. It was an emotional occasion that was significant in still another way. By organizing it and making the demands that it did, Sąjūdis squarely put itself in the tradition of dissidents, who as early as 1979 had demanded both Soviet and German denunciation of this pact. In less than three months, priorities had shifted from the needs of perestroika as defined by Moscow to the requirements of political reform as perceived by the Lithuanians.

THE PARTY FIGHTS BACK

The Lithuanian Communist party leadership, leery of the Restructuring Movement from its inception, watched its spreading influence with great apprehension. The party, it must be conceded, had reluctantly begun to listen to Gorbachev's drums: A study of the republic's future economic self-management model was begun, and a strengthening of the republic's constitution was initiated in May. Glasnost' was extended to allow discussion of forbidden topics such as deportations or the partisan war. At the 19th Party Conference in Moscow, First Secretary Songaila dared to repeat the popular demand that Lithuanian be made the official language of the republic and supported many of the postulates raised by Sąjūdis. The party leadership supported efforts for more self-government and autonomy.

At the same time, Songaila condemned informal groups that wanted to move "outside of [the] political system" or to "dictate their will to party organizations." He also anxiously urged greater party influence over their activities.[5] There was too much glasnost', he said, in some segments of the periodical press that were publishing "unfounded assertions of doubtful ideological value."[6] Not used to public pressures, the party did not know how to react to Sąjūdis's political initiatives or to public discussion of truths long distorted by the Communist regime. Glasnost' revelations had cost it credibility, prestige, and deference. Fear was disappearing as people could no longer simply be told what to do; they needed to be persuaded. Only occasional voices came forward, such as that of Party Secretary Brazauskas, favoring concessions to the symbols and sentiments of outpouring patriotism. But even Brazauskas confessed to confusion when he first saw the national flag flying: Should he speak or should he quit? The party simply did not know how to respond.[7] In contrast to Brazauskas, Ringaudas Songaila, the Lithuanian first secretary, decided to contain and slow down the initiatives of the Movement for Restructuring, which smelled to him of "nationalism." The movement was denied access to all state media, and its activities did not receive fair and unbiased coverage. Party and government authorities in Vilnius, Kaunas, and many provincial localities discouraged the movement. Local party officials frequently demanded that Communists who joined the movement resign from the party. Of the thirty-two delegates chosen to the 19th Party Conference in Moscow, only five attended the bon voyage meeting organized by Sąjūdis.

The escalating conflict became of concern to Moscow. On August 11–13, 1988, Alexander Yakovlev, Gorbachev's reputed right-hand man in the Politburo, came to Vilnius to sort out the situation after doing the same in Riga. He did not give comfort to the Lithuanian party leadership. Instead, Yakovlev strongly supported glasnost', insisting that eventually everything would have to be revealed one way or another. He also prodded the party leadership to become more active in directing change. The Lithuanian Politburo was advised to avoid confrontation and to harness the "national factor" as a force for reform.[8] If this required co-option of national traditions and concerns, so be it. In an interview with the *New York Times* two months later, Yakovlev ridiculed the qualifications of Baltic popular front leaders ("composers" know nothing about economics) and derided Baltic demands for independence (Baltic republics are not self-supporting and cannot become viable units).[9] He shared the Kremlin's view that was again articulated by Moscow's visiting Politburo member Nikolai Slyunkov in November: The economy of the Soviet Union was a single system not to be taken apart. Thus, the Kremlin believed that, unlike economic issues, democratic and ethnic development would not destabilize Soviet rule and therefore was not dangerous. It might even be helpful to perestroika. Taking this view was the most serious mistake Gorbachev made.

Yakovlev's visit resolved the Lithuanian party leaders' doubts about satisfying nationalist demands. On August 18, 1988, the national flag and anthem of independent Lithuania were granted coexistence alongside "state" (Communist) symbols.[10] On August 20, a decree established Lithuanian geography and history as separate instructional subjects in schools, and assurances were given that preschool children would be taught in the native language. The teaching of Russian was not to begin until the third grade; teachers of Lithuanian in Russian schools were to receive the same 15 percent salary bonus that teachers of Russian in Lithuanian schools had been receiving for years.[11]

The chairman of the Council of Ministers, Vytautas Sakalauskas, also announced that the Lithuanian government had ended its financial support for the installation of the third nuclear reactor at the Ignalina nuclear plant. Construction would be stopped until questions of safety could be satisfactorily answered. This was an unprecedented act of defiance of central ministries.

Furthermore, Second Secretary Nikolai Mitkin publicly declared that Communist membership in Sąjūdis was legal since this movement was not an opposition party. Local apparatchiks were told not to oppose the election of Communists participating in Sąjūdis activities to party leadership positions. He also permitted non–party members to participate in party meetings. Nevertheless, Mitkin stressed that there is "a historically developed one-party system that has proven its value and nobody has the right to revise this."[12]

After Yakovlev's visit the party also allowed television coverage of some of Sąjūdis's activities. Thus, Lithuanian television ran a program over an hour long summarizing the demonstration of August 23, 1988, commemorating the signing of the Stalin-Hitler pact of 1939. Although the program was considered biased and distorted by many, the silence was nonetheless broken.

To clear the air and discuss some issues, such as those surrounding political prisoners, glasnost', and the KGB, on August 30 the movement's leaders met with the chairman of the Lithuanian KGB, Eduardas Eismuntas. According to Eismuntas, the three-hour meeting helped to produce "more mutual confidence" but, he said, "In many circles the movement is [still] viewed with suspicion." He expected Sąjūdis to "mature" and advised it to publicly acknowledge the party's primacy and to demonstrate it by using not only "national" (Lithuanian) but also "state" (Communist) flags and symbols. He could not understand what sort of relations members of the movement could have with the Voice of America or why Sąjūdis "closely collaborated" with the Lithuanian Freedom League and other organizations of "anti-Soviet disposition." Finally, he advised the movement to have more non-Lithuanians in its ranks and leadership.[13]

The meeting with the chief of the KGB indicated that the Lithuanian Communist leadership had not withdrawn its objections to the "national" aspects of the movement's activity. Indeed, the armistice between Sąjūdis and the party leadership did not continue for long. On September 14, the Lithuanian Politburo regurgitated the KGB's attack, saying Sąjūdis did not represent the entire population of Lithuania; it was "mononational." It cooperated with "extremists who openly propagate separatist sentiments." Some of the movement's leaders kept communications with "Western radio 'voices' and with the reactionary part of Lithuanian emigration."[14]

The Politburo further criticized the movement's press:

In its pages the editorial board of *Sąjūdžio zinios* [Sąjūdis News] allows vulgar, insulting attacks on some party and government functionaries; it frequently distorts the real situation in the republic, demeans victories of socialism achieved by the people, incites passions, and propagates historical conceptions of doubtful value. In its pages, it [the bulletin] has published without commentary a letter by American senators and much other material of an inciting, provocative nature.

As if regretting permission for press, radio, and television coverage of Sąjūdis activities, the Politburo urged the media not just to report mass meetings as positive events, but "at the same time to criticize the movement's erroneous positions."[15]

The movement had no equivalent forum for response, but in its bulletin a prominent lawyer and elected deputy to Gorbachev's All-Union Congress, Kazimieras Motieka, dryly noted: "The republic party leadership is upset that the movement fights for perestroika much more actively and decently [than they do]."[16]

In the end, First Secretary Songaila's preoccupation with the defense of apparatchik prerogatives and with the hunt for "nationalists" in Sąjūdis backfired on the party and even ended the personal careers of party leaders.

THE CONFRONTATION
AND THE FALL OF PARTY LEADERS

On September 28, 1988, the Lithuanian Freedom League (LFL) organized a demonstration in Vilnius to mark the anniversary of the Molotov-Ribbentrop pact. Although the LFL was refused a permit, thousands gathered in Gediminas Square. As soon as Antanas Terleckas, one of the leaders of the LFL, began speaking, about 500 riot police and Internal Ministry troops arrived. Wearing helmets and plexiglass shields, the police charged the crowd four times in twenty minutes. They struck with rubber truncheons, and the demonstrators responded by throwing stones and bricks. A number of people were beaten up, including a member of the Lithuanian television crew. Ten demonstrators were injured and twenty-five arrested. Some policemen also were hurt.[17]

The use of police against the demonstrators and the beatings they administered greatly angered the public. The incident, after a summer of very peaceful gatherings, became a scandal. It was blamed on Songaila, without whose approval the police could not have been used. Public indignation swelled. The Movement for Restructuring demanded an investigation, and on September 29 a demonstration was held in front of the Central Committee building. It was the first time that Sąjūdis had actively supported the LFL, its radical competitor.

The matter of police violence was raised again within days at the 13th Plenum of the Central Committee. Thousands of Sąjūdis and LFL picketers

Soviet Lithuanian police break up a protest by the Lithuanian League, September 28, 1988. (Photo by M. Baranauskas. Used by permission.)

demonstrated outside the Central Committee building. Inside, Professor Bronius Genzelis, secretary of the Vilnius University party organization, declared that responsibility for the incident lay not only with LFL leader Antanas Terleckas, who allegedly had provoked it by his confrontational tactics, but most of all with "our Central Committee." He said, "It is slowly losing people's confidence; it is responsible because it does not attempt to understand the process of development in our country." He ended the "lecture" by proposing that First Secretary Songaila "think over whether he is capable of leading the republic's party organization."[18]

The top two party secretaries, Songaila and Mitkin, rallied their forces for defense. Songaila appealed to Gorbachev and Central Committee apparatchiks in Moscow. Gorbachev is said to have supported Songaila, but representatives of Moscow's leadership visiting Vilnius were more inclined to sacrifice Songaila and Mitkin in the unrealistic expectation that their removal would help the Lithuanian Communist party co-opt Sąjūdis and regain the upper hand.

The party daily, *Tiesa*, did not report Genzelis's suggestion that Songaila resign, but by October 20, Lithuania had a new first secretary.

Songaila was pensioned off after only ten months in office. Algirdas Brazauskas, longtime secretary for industrial affairs and a Communist leader who attended meetings of Sąjūdis, was chosen to lead the party. Substantive changes followed quickly. The Presidium of the Supreme Soviet passed an unprecedented decree just before the movement's inaugural congress rehabilitating all the deportees of 1941–1952. It ordered compensation for "economic damages" inflicted upon them at the time.[19] In a press conference with foreign and Soviet journalists held on the eve of the congress, Brazauskas praised the church's contribution to perestroika and announced that the church of St. Casimir in Vilnius, which had been converted into a museum of atheism, was to be returned to religious use.[20] In his speech to the congress, Brazauskas further promised reconstruction of the monument of three crosses, which towered over the city until 1951, when it was dynamited. The crosses were erected in 1916 to commemorate the early Christian martyrs in Lithuania, and the promise to rebuild them pleased the Lithuanian as well as the Polish population.

THE HONEYMOON AND THE BREAK

The founding congress of the Restructuring Movement on October 22–23, 1988, was held peacefully and with the permission of the Communist party. Roughly 1,000 registered voting delegates representing 1,000 supporter groups met surrounded by scores of press representatives, TV crews, dignitaries, and guests. The gathering was a massive, festive telecast, as promised by the party, live on the Lithuanian TV network. Radio provided simultaneous translation for the non-Lithuanian-speaking population.[21] As an Estonian journalist observed in the congress hall,[22] emotionalism was heightened by a night torch parade and a Catholic mass said in open air in front of the illuminated white cathedral at Gediminas Square. Never before under Soviet rule had such a religious event been allowed in public, not to mention being nationally televised. Excitement and euphoria pervaded the ranks of delegates, who were made conscious of the historic importance of their work.

The congress adopted over two dozen resolutions addressing a wide range of issues, from sovereignty to the mistreatment of a Lithuanian soldier by the Red Army. The case of Arturas Sakalauskas, who had shot his torturers after being gang raped and for weeks physically abused by his fellow soldiers, had become a national cause célèbre and a subject of a documentary produced by a Leningrad film studio. Brazauskas was received with enthusiasm by the congress. A respected politician, he became Gorbachev's man in Lithuania, where he enjoyed a reputation for being a political moderate and a defender of the republic's interests. In his speech, Brazauskas revealed that three days previously, before his appointment to the first secretary's position, he had seen Gorbachev. The general secretary, relayed Brazauskas, sent greetings to the Lithuanian "people" and to Sąjūdis itself, which Brazauskas called a "positive" force for perestroika. Brazauskas, too, opined that a single-party system left room for societal associations. The Lithuanian Communist party, he said, had made mistakes concerning the Movement for Restructuring, but a "more objective" evaluation had emerged in the past two Central Committee plenums. Referring to the perceived declining ability of the party to deal with the new political developments, the first secretary said, "One should not jump to the far-fetched conclusion that the party is incapable of evaluating the situation in a timely and appropriate manner."[23] Appealing to the congress, he asserted, "On matters of principle we think alike."[24] The movement and the party did seem to share political views concerning a number of important issues, namely, economic autonomy, revision of the republic's constitution, and some aspects of the new all-union electoral law.

As a savvy man of politics, Brazauskas reminded his audience how far the party had already had gone to meet the public's and Sąjūdis 's demands. Indeed, the party, especially after the violent debacle on September 28, tried to ingratiate itself to Lithuanian society and sentiment. The use of traditional national symbols increased, and on October 7, in an

Outside parliament before the vote on declaring sovereignty, November 1988. (Photo by R. Kuginys. Used by permission.)

emotional ceremony that brought the crowd of tens of thousands to tears and dancing, the national tricolor of independent Lithuania was raised on the tower of the historical castle of Gediminas in the heart of the capital city.

Despite the convergence of some common goals, however, the sense of collaboration between the movement and the party generated by the congress did not last longer than six weeks. It broke over a disagreement on the concept of sovereignty as Lithuanians proceeded to discuss the proposed economic autonomy and other constitutional issues raised by Gorbachev.

On October 5, *Tiesa* published the "principles" for the republic's economic self-government. These principles were agreed upon on September 21–23 at a Riga meeting of state planners, economists, and mass movement leaders from all three Baltic republics.[25] They addressed the issues of sovereignty and federalism more strongly than the newly revised Lithuanian constitution had. The Baltic model also radically differed from Moscow's vision of a revised economic management of republics and territories.

The Balts proposed that title to all land, mineral resources, outer shelf areas, forests, and space of their territories belong to the republics. They wanted the management and use of these resources to be decided by republic supreme soviets, not by Moscow.[26] In addition, they felt that banks, enterprises, transportation, energy, and communications networks should be free of central management.

Thus, republic jurisdiction would extend to all local government and management questions. It would cover economic policies; republic and local budgeting; social, economic, and demographic development; taxation; prices; wages; and economic incentives. The republics further would have the power to control banks and the circulation of money, to establish currency, and to set rates of exchange, even as the ruble would still be accepted as common currency in the Soviet market. Finally, the Balts wanted the right to independently decide all matters involving their international economic activities.

According to this model, the government in Moscow would only manage defense enterprises, foreign relations, and other programs common to the entire country or to several republics. Certain deductions would be made from republic budgets to finance these expenses. These radical "principles" obviously garnered the party's support, since the chairman of the state planning committee could not sign without official sanction.

In addition to the document outlining the principles of the desired economic organization, Sąjūdis and the party also had to consider a draft of a new Lithuanian constitution. This draft was prepared by a group of scholars sponsored by the Lithuanian Academy of Sciences to establish a legal framework for the new economic model and to reflect changes initiated by perestroika in the political, social, and cultural sectors of society. The first draft was completed on September 21; the second, somewhat amended draft was approved by the Diet of Sąjūdis on November 13.[27]

On the question of sovereignty, the second draft was more bold and precise than the first. It proposed that the legal basis of relations between Moscow's central government and the republics would be contractual. Defense, foreign affairs, and all-union budgets would belong to a "mixed" jurisdiction; a delegation of these functions could be withdrawn from the center "if the activities of the USSR organs contradicted the interests of the Lithuanian SSR." Lithuania would have the right to secede. Article 70 provided that Soviet laws would be valid only if they did not "contradict the constitution of the Lithuanian SSR." This draft was submitted to the Supreme Soviet of the republic with the expectation that it would be considered at its November 17 meeting.

Gorbachev's proposed amendments to the Soviet constitution and the draft of the new electoral law were other problems of immediate importance. The movement's Diet resolved, on November 13, that the proposed amendments were "undemocratic and contrary to the spirit" of the 19th Party Conference and therefore should be rejected. Similarly, Sąjūdis found the electoral law to be "undemocratic" because it did not guarantee equal voting rights to people or equal representation to republics but instead strengthened the bureaucratic system of governance.[28] The movement made furious efforts to persuade Gorbachev that it was imperative to postpone the consideration of his proposals, sending him a telegram on November 2. On November 8 representatives of all three Baltic popular fronts met in Riga where they articulated their position that the constitutional amendments should provide legal guarantees for economic and institutional autonomy. They decided to appeal to the people for support and called for a massive petition to the Kremlin.[29]

On November 9 the council of the Lithuanian Movement for Restructuring met with First Secretary Brazauskas and other top officials of the republic, who supported their tactics. That evening, Sąjūdis speakers made an appeal on the movement's regular TV program asking for signatures to a petition demanding postponement of a decision. Within a week, 1.8 million signatures were collected in Lithuania. The petition papers filled thirty-one sacks and had to be transported by truck; Lithuanian authorities refused government transportation. As Jonas Mikelinskas, a distinguished writer, later said, this was really a popular referendum on independence from Moscow.[30] An absolute majority—some 75 percent—of the republic's adult population supported it.

There was little doubt that party leader Brazauskas and most of his colleagues supported economic autonomy and shared many of the criticisms Sąjūdis had of Moscow's constitutional amendments and the proposed electoral law. In the presence of Politburo member Nikolai Slyunkov, Brazauskas blamed the increasing economic difficulties of the republic on Moscow's continued practice of centralized management and insisted that only economic independence could facilitate economic upswing and recovery.[31] He agreed with Sąjūdis that Gorbachev's proposed amendments betrayed "a tendency to seek further centralization of government and management," suggesting that their adoption would create additional difficulties for the promised expansion of union republic rights. He called the new centralism "impermissible." Brazauskas also criticized the electoral system.[32] Like Sąjūdis leaders, he suggested that the announced procedures and rules would "practically" eliminate direct and secret elections. He thought it regrettable and unfair that republic representation in the House of Nationalities would be reduced to seven all-union organizations. Why is it, he asked, that only central organizations would be able to elect representatives to the Conference of Deputies?

It seemed that Sąjūdis and the party held enough in common to decide these matters, especially under the pressure of public opinion. The party's support crumbled very quickly, however, under Moscow's pressure.

The Kremlin became concerned with Baltic developments in the summer of 1988. Politburo member Alexander Yakovlev visited Lithuania and Latvia in August. Members of Soviet press organizations and TV reporters avoided informing the rest of the USSR about the political changes in Lithuania. *Pravda, Krasnaia zvezda,* and *Izvestia* frequently chose to report only slanted impressions, sometimes outright falsehoods. Moscow's anxieties increased after the Riga agreement of September 21–22 on the principles of Baltic economic autonomy. Although publicly Gorbachev considered the Lithuanian developments a "normal" part of the perestroika process,[33] the height of organized opposition to Gorbachev's constitutional amendments alarmed leaders in the Kremlin.

Two days after the beginning of the campaign for signatures to postpone consideration of Moscow's constitutional changes, Politburo members arrived in Tallinn, Riga, and Vilnius to restrain Baltic opposition. Victor Chebrikov visited Estonia; Vladimir Medvedev, Latvia; and Nikolai Slyunkov, Lithuania. Slyunkov was not as direct in Lithuania as Chebrikov was in Estonia because he found more cautious attitudes among Lithuanian party leaders. Nevertheless, he publicly warned that renewal was possible only if reform "strengthen[ed] the unity of republics" instead of loosening it.[34] Chebrikov failed to intimidate the Estonians. On November 17 they declared the supremacy of the republic's legislature over Moscow's. The Kremlin reacted with dispatch: Brazauskas was immediately called to Moscow to be warned against following the Estonian example. The Lithuanian Supreme Soviet was to consider this same matter on November 18. Gorbachev at that time was in India. Brazauskas very likely met with Politburo "experts" on the Baltics, namely Slyunkov, Medvedev, Chebrikov, and their aides.

The Lithuanian party caved in. On November 18, Lithuania's Supreme Soviet changed Articles 77, 168, and 169 of the constitution to make Lithuanian the official language and to legalize the old flag and anthem. The legislature also asked that Moscow's Supreme Soviet postpone consideration of amendments to the national constitution until the republics had a chance to rewrite their own constitutions and criticized Gorbachev's electoral law. They refused, however, to declare Lithuanian law supreme.[35] This was done diplomatically in hopes of not antagonizing Sąjūdis. The revision of the Lithuanian constitution was not rejected; the issue was simply skirted. Chairman of the Supreme Soviet Lionginas Šepetys, party secretary for ideology and propaganda, stymied discussion by simply refusing to accept motions to revise the relevant articles— 11, 31, 37, and 70.[36]

Representatives of Sąjūdis who attended the session were incensed. The crowd outside the Supreme Soviet building, in a festive mood waiting for the anticipated declaration of supremacy over Moscow, became furious. Deputies emerging from the building were treated with visible hostility. TASS poured salt into the Lithuanian wound by reporting that the Lithuanians "rejected" the Estonian proposal. Denials by Sąjūdis and by the republic's leaders, including Brazauskas, could not correct the distortion spread by all-union TV and press reports. For the supporters of Lithuanian reform, the Supreme Soviet's decision meant "betrayal of Estonia," a "stab in the back to Estonia," and "treason." The Lithuanian deputies were called "bootlickers." Even the decision on the Lithuanian language, flag, and anthem, to which party leaders pointed as a great achievement, did not console the masses, who largely saw this decision as the opportunistic, Communist manipulation of national symbols. What the crowds of supporters remembered and felt were the jilted expectations.

DAMAGE CONTROL BY BRAZAUSKAS
AND THE RISE OF LANDSBERGIS

Brazauskas tried to repair the damage. On November 19, in a dramatic TV speech that he reportedly prepared with great difficulty, the first secretary tried to explain the decision. Adoption of provisions related to legal sovereignty over Moscow's laws, he said, would have been "confrontational" and would "legalize secession" and the "refusal to obey USSR laws." "The road to sovereignty," he went on, "is extremely complicated, enormously long, and all of our actions must come from a deeply felt sense of responsibility. Quick, thoughtless decisions would only hurt us in pursuing the main goal."[37] He appealed for a slower pace of action and called not only on Soviet World War II "veterans" but also on the Catholic clergy "correctly to understand decisions that we made." Cardinal Vincentas Sladkevičius obliged by stressing that on the road to change, "of great importance will be our own determination, resolution, tenacity, and unhurried, wise steps toward always new achievements."[38] His statement seemed to endorse Brazauskas's plea for patience.

The Supreme Soviet decision shattered, at least for the time being, the newly established cooperation between the Communist party and Sąjūdis. It also caused internal problems for the movement's leadership. It was finally acknowledged that the Movement for Restructuring was not merely an auxiliary helper to the party or just a lobbyist but a political competitor. "There is a contest going on," confirmed Brazauskas. "Sometimes [Sąjūdis] must learn to lose. We [the party], too, sometimes lose."[39]

But the Movement for Restructuring did not want to lose. It reacted swiftly, loudly, and decisively. Sąjūdis leaders quickly lobbied among Supreme Soviet deputies for a special session of the legislature on November 25, that is, before the key meeting of Moscow's Supreme Soviet. Fifty-seven deputies agreed, but 117 were needed, and ultimately the party's opposition to legal sovereignty prevailed. In the view of Brazauskas, such a session would have produced nothing but "deeper confrontation, which nobody in Lithuania needs."[40] The council of the Restructuring Movement then blasted the leadership of the legislature for "procedural violations" that manipulated the outcome of the vote and admonished the three leaders of the Supreme Soviet responsible: Chairman of the Presidium Vytautas Astrauskas, Secretary Jonas Gureckas, and Chairman of the Supreme Soviet Lionginas Šepetys. They were voted "no confidence" and ways were investigated to have them recalled. Eventually, all three paid the price for their pro-Moscow disposition and timidity. In the meantime, the movement's leadership acknowledged its political power and vowed to use it in various forms of "moral" protest. Spiteful of the current defeat, the council declared "moral independence" and on November 20 stated,

No political requirements of the situation can restrain the free will of Lithuania. Its will is its highest law. Only Lithuania can decide and execute its laws. Until this principle becomes legal norm, only those laws will be respected in

Lithuania which do not restrain Lithuanian independence. Disobedience to laws which violate our independence may incur juridical responsibility but they do not transgress against morality.[41]

The strong reaction caused dissension among the supporters and the leadership of the Restructuring Movement itself. Long discussions showed unanimity on the goal of sovereignty for Lithuania but also revealed disagreements on what sovereignty would mean and the tactics by which it should be achieved. A number of supporters and leaders agreed with Brazauskas and the Supreme Soviet. To strengthen themselves and heal the developing schism that was immediately exploited in the official press, the leadership council adopted a declaration of unity. They also began to formalize the movement by first clarifying membership criteria and electing Vytautas Landsbergis president. A mild-mannered and diplomatic professor of musicology, Landsbergis inspired consensus and won handily over the passionately pro-Communist writer Vytautas Petkevičius.

Landsbergis came from a traditionally patriotic non-Communist background. His great-grandfather had fought the Russians in the insurrection of 1863. His grandfather was an influential writer and his father, a well-known architect in independent Lithuania, had been appointed a minister in the Provisional Government of the anti-Soviet rebels in 1941. He had left Lithuania in 1944 hoping to free his elder teenage son imprisoned by the Nazis in Germany for anti-Nazi resistance activities, then returned to Soviet Lithuania from Australia in Khrushchev's years. The new leader of Sąjūdis had never joined the Communist party or directly participated in its propaganda operations.

The council agreed that every council member was completely free as a private person but that council decisions were unconditionally binding. This in effect meant that obligations of membership in the Communist party or any other institution could not override the goals and decisions of the Restructuring Movement.[42] Thus, from its first real political crisis Sąjūdis emerged as a stronger organization of clarified loyalties, ready to struggle with the Communist party by all available constitutional and peaceful means, persuaded that moral strength could generate legitimate political power.

THE STRUGGLE INTENSIFIES:
THE ELECTORAL BATTLEFIELD

On November 18 the Communist old guard won a decision but little else. While winning in the Supreme Soviet, it lost among the populace. It proved impossible to please both Moscow and the Lithuanians, and the party's unpopularity increased. It could not rely for support on its membership or on veterans and other traditionally obedient orthodox Soviet groups; nor could it look to Yedinstvo. The Russian movement, too, was upset, because the party sponsored Lithuanian as the official language of the republic.

The party badly needed help. The Supreme Soviet in Moscow had approved the proposed constitutional changes and had set new parliamentary elections to the Congress of Deputies. The party needed to win these elections, but with Sąjūdis now in clear opposition, this would be a gargantuan task. To strengthen the party's starting position in the forthcoming electoral competition, First Secretary Brazauskas chose to pursue a two-pronged tactic. On the one hand, he continued the party's reconciliation with religious and nationalist forces. On the other, he tried to curtail the influence of Sąjūdis.

By then, virtually all political prisoners had been released. Christmas was declared a legal holiday. At the end of December, Commissioner for Religious Affairs Petras Anilionis informed Bishop Julijonas Steponavičius that he would be allowed to return to Vilnius and the diocese from which he was banished in 1961. After an audience with Pope John Paul, Steponavičius was met by a great and joyous crowd when he returned to his cathedral on February 5, 1989.[43] On the same day, the first issue of an independent Catholic magazine was allowed to appear. In early January, the government replaced the hardliner Anilionis with a moderate Communist lawyer, Kazimieras Valančius, an official in the Central Committee apparatus who promised to correct past mistakes made in church-state relations. From now on, he suggested, these relations would be characterized by "constructive dialogue rather than confrontation, as in the past."[44]

The restoration of patriotic Lithuanian traditions was also supported. The Ministry of Education endorsed a project of reorganizing education into a "national school" system that would be philosophically different from the old ideologically oriented Communist institution. This project, courageously explained at an orthodox all-union conference on education in Moscow, won supporters among non-Russian republic educators but incurred the wrath of Moscow ministry officials. In December, Brazauskas rehabilitated the "bourgeois" declaration of Lithuanian independence made on February 16, 1918. Contrary to a half century of propaganda, he explained that Lithuanian statehood was a progressive event because of the progress achieved in education, culture, and the economy.[45] Thus, the anniversary of independence, just a year ago brutally suppressed by police, became an officially celebrated holiday.[46]

Ironically, the party again did not receive much credit, if any, for these concessions. The effort to contain the strength of Sąjūdis was also fruitless. While Brazauskas spoke of peace between the party and Sąjūdis, his colleagues in the party resisted cooperation with their new rival and reverted to their old methods. The Sąjūdis newspaper *Atgimimas* was once again threatened with censorship.[47] The state television network curtailed its coverage, while the government temporarily blocked the movement's bank deposits. There were signs that the party might decide to screen nominations for Gorbachev's parliament at the regional level, as provided by law. The newly appointed second party secretary, Vladimir Beryozov, publicly labeled Sąjūdis an "opponent" and "critic." Although he considered the movement a "positive" factor keeping the party and the government on the ball, Beryozov said that Sąjūdis lacked the very qualities that it claimed were absent from the party, namely, glasnost', democracy, and tolerance of the opinions of others.[48]

In this climate the two groups prepared for the campaign and scheduled elections to the newly created All-Union Congress of Deputies in Moscow. Lithuania was to elect ten deputies from territorial-population districts, thirty-two from national-territorial districts, and sixteen from societal organizations. Popular electoral competition would decide the fate of forty-two deputies.

There was little doubt that the party's candidates would be contested by Sąjūdis nominees. The nonparty forces, however, were not united on the question of participation in elections. The Lithuanian Freedom League, the Christian Democratic party, and the Helsinki Watch Committee attempted to persuade Sąjūdis to stay out of the electoral process. The league regarded the elections as illegal because Lithuania was an occupied country, and furthermore, the league did not trust the integrity of the process. In the view of its leaders, it was not possible to win against Communists because the Communists would not allow a victory. Sąjūdis rightly considered such a policy a mistake.

In the electoral campaign, Sąjūdis candidates were at a disadvantage. For the most part, the state-controlled media did not cover their activities or speeches. Sąjūdis candidates compensated for this deficiency, however, by hard work and direct contact with the voters—they traveled, held meetings in every town and hamlet, got acquainted with the people, and carried their message to them.

At first, Sąjūdis nominated candidates in all electoral districts against all party candidates, including the top leaders, namely, Brazauskas and Beryozov. After the campaign heated up, however, Sąjūdis withdrew its candidates against the two party men. Both were considered valuable for their views and for their personal as well as their leadership qualities. Sąjūdis apparently did not want to embarrass them at home or to lose their main spokesmen for the republic in the Moscow parliament. A victory for Sąjūdis, in this case, would have meant a weakening of prestige for Lithuania in its dealings with Moscow's rulers.

The party published its electoral platform on January 25, 1989. Sąjūdis prepared its draft in February. The party's program, set in an appropriately Soviet context, expressed support for perestroika and opposed "anti-Socialist" goals and "conservative forces."[49] The platform embraced the plan for economic self-government, starting in 1990; favored a "national" system of education; promised respect in church-state relations; and supported a "pluralism" of opinions based on democracy, glasnost', and "shared values of mankind," not on "class consciousness" or a class division of society. Much of what the party advocated Sąjūdis could and would accept. There were differences between the platforms, of course. The party was less open, for example, to Sąjūdis's views on private farming and local military service. The biggest difference concerned the meaning of "sovereignty," even though both sides used the term in their slogans.

In contrast, Sąjūdis defined sovereignty in broader terms. "The Lithuanian nation," Sąjūdis said, "has an old and strong tradition of statehood that it has never renounced of its own free will; it therefore has the natural and inalienable right to reestablish independent Lithuania." Movement leaders argued that Russia and other Soviet republics must respect the peace treaty that Lenin signed with Lithuania on July 12, 1920, by which Lithuania was recognized as an independent state. Further, they wanted the government of the USSR to publish and declare null and void the Soviet-Nazi agreements of 1939 and 1940, which had opened the way "for the occupation and annexation of the Lithuanian republic." For them, sovereignty meant that current legal relations with the USSR should be regulated by treaties and that Lithuanian laws would be supreme over all-union laws on republic territory.

Sąjūdis represented the "nation's will by peaceful means to reestablish our right to live independently of any dictates." The movement stated that its goal was "to reestablish state sovereignty, not limiting progress toward it by partial achievements." The organization based this demand on Gorbachev's speech at the United Nations on December 7, 1988, in which the Soviet leader had stressed the right of self-determination of nations. Sąjūdis further advocated social justice, humanism, democracy, and the cultural autonomy of Lithuania's ethnic minorities. It favored "traditional neutrality in a demilitarized zone of Europe." It supported "universally recognized human and citizenship rights that give the general right to Lithuania's citizens independently to choose and foster our own forms of state system." There is little doubt that Sąjūdis strove for complete independence from the Soviet Union.

Pressured by the Kremlin to restrain independence demands, Brazauskas quickly convened the Central Committee plenum of February 21, 1989, and raised the question of setting limits for Sąjūdis. Brazauskas accused the movement of gradually approaching the policy line advocated by the dissident Lithuanian Freedom League and the Lithuanian Democratic party. Sąjūdis had changed since June 1988, he said, and now spoke only of independence. This leaning raised questions, he warned, about "perspectives for further cooperation." Brazauskas cautioned that only common goals could assure cooperation and only unity would help Lithuania. Currently, "Sąjūdis is pushing Lithuania into ruin."[50]

The first secretary then revealed the degree to which the party had lost control. Printing houses and the media, he said, behaved as if they were not owned by the state or the party. They should stop blackening and defaming the reputations of party leaders and the party itself on television and on the radio. It was also time, Brazauskas continued, to stop excessive criticisms of the past. Laws should be passed punishing those who violated rules on meetings and demonstrations. Brazauskas was also concerned with Yedinstvo. There had occurred, he said, a polarization of forces. Sąjūdis was largely responsible because it did not provide room for non-Lithuanians and seemed unable to refrain from extremism.

Brazauskas's speech at the plenum was followed by others demanding similar or stronger measures to reestablish control.[51] But if Brazauskas and his apparatchiks were trying to frighten Sąjūdis by widely publishing criticism and threats, they were to be disappointed. Instead, three top Communist officials paid the price for obstructing the party's restraining influence on Sąjūdis. Party Secretary for Ideology and Propaganda Lionginas Šepetys, Chairman of Television and Radio Committee Juozas Kuolelis, and Minister of Culture Jonas Bielinis quietly lost their positions, presumably for not exercising sufficient control over their fields. Sąjūdis had clearly begun to infuriate the party leadership and shock the Kremlin. But instead of restraining the reform movement, the plenum's discussions further incensed the Sąjūdis leadership and angered its numerous supporters.

Elections to the Congress of People's Deputies were held on Easter Sunday, March 26, 1989, a bad time for such an event in a Catholic country. Despite the holy day and the boycott by the Lithuanian Freedom League, the Lithuanian Democratic party, and the Helsinki Watch Committee, 82.5 percent of the total voting population cast their ballots. The participation level was a little lower than in Latvia and Estonia, but still quite extensive.

For the Communist party the election proved disastrous. Of the forty-two deputies to be elected, Sąjūdis won thirty-six. It had nominated thirty-nine.[52] The Movement for Restructuring had decided to withdraw its candidate against Brazauskas, who was reportedly having difficulties in his district. Beryozov also ran unopposed. The party thus won only four contested electoral seats. Sąjūdis's majority further increased by the addition of some of the movement's leaders and supporters elected by "societal" organizations. Election casualties included two Central Committee secretaries, the chairman of the republic's Councilof Ministers, the chairman of the Presidium of the Supreme Soviet, some ministers, some district party secretaries, and the mayors of Kaunas and Vilnius.

Sąjūdis winners included eight writers, several economists, scientists, lawyers, and other professionals, and one worker. One of the movement's new deputies (Nikolai Medvedev), a Russian professional, had been elected in a strongly Lithuanian district in Kaunas by a comfortable margin. Another, a Jewish writer (Yakov Kanovich), was elected in the run-off in Vilnius. Two Yedinstvo-supported candidates won also, the Russian nominee of the party (Genadii Konoplev) and a Polish professor (Ivan Tikhonovich) of Vilnius Pedagogical Institute. Immediately after the election, Second Party Secretary Beryozov explained that the party had lost simply because the voters "categorically voted against the old times and the old order."[53] The party could not shake off responsibility for "old mistakes." Beryozov further blamed the failure on the fact that local party organizations were not used to taking the initiative and working hard in such events, whereas the opposition campaigned hard. The secretary's conclusion was that the elections were won by "those who went to the people." Beryozov was not pessimistic about the future prospects of the party, however. The electoral campaign, he said, drew the party and Sąjūdis together, since the movement's candidates had not propagandized "maximalist" demands.

THE ELECTORAL LESSON: THE PARTY COOPERATES

Some of the newly elected deputies immediately asked for an appointment with Mikhail Gorbachev. They received a session with Anatoli Lukyanov, who sought to impress the Lithuanians with his knowledge of Lithuanian culture and the republic's situation. They discussed problems of disinformation by the central press on Lithuanian events, the slow reform action in Moscow, the Molotov-Ribbentrop pact, and the model of Soviet socialism. Lukyanov was anxious to know whether Sąjūdis recognized the party's leadership role and advised the Lithuanians to concentrate on economic problems, which were the Kremlin's prime concern. He suggested Moscow's principles for economic self-management as a guide for action and rejected their model as too radical. His prime concern was that Sąjūdis might fight the party or socialism, institutions that were presented as untouchables for the Lithuanian reform movement.[54]

Probably the first public indication that a new wind had begun to blow was an announcement by the Lithuanian party's historical commission that Moscow already acknowledged the existence of the secret protocols of the Molotov-Ribbentrop pact of 1939 and that it felt the time had come for these protocols to be publicly "denounced."[55] Shortly afterward, the public's curiosity was aroused by an article published by Lionginas Šepetys, the dismissed party secretary for propaganda, who was still chairman of the Supreme Soviet. In it, he spoke of a new type of Communist party and even of "party pluralism."[56] A week later, on May 11, 1989, First Secretary Brazauskas, together with his colleagues from Estonia and Latvia, took part in the Politburo meeting in Moscow.[57] This probably was the first time since September 1940 that republic leaders of that level were invited to visit the top decision-making group in the Kremlin. Brazauskas revealed that the Politburo discussed the question of economic self-management and evaluated the "events of 1939–1940." The next day the Presidium of the Supreme Soviet of the Lithuanian SSR decided to call the meeting of the eleventh session of the legislature for May 18 to consider, in the main, the same amendments to the constitution that had been

Sąjūdis rally: Sending off the delegates to the Congress of People's Deputies in Moscow, Kalnu Park, March 1989. (Photo by R. Urbakavičius. Used by permission.)

rejected half a year earlier.[58] Representatives of Sąjūdis actively participated in the preparation for this session.[59] It seems reasonable to assume
that Brazauskas discussed this matter at the Politburo meeting.

Thus, the party and Sąjūdis finally reached a consensus to do what
could have been accomplished on November 18, 1989. Indeed, when the
Supreme Soviet met on May 18, 1990, exactly six months after rejecting
the concept of sovereignty then advocated by Sąjūdis, the mood was
solemn, happy, and expectant. The legislature approved revisions of the
necessary constitutional articles with ease,[60] declaring that all land and
resources in the republic's territory belonged to the republic, not to the
USSR (Article 11); that Lithuania would have its own citizenship and
would control its own immigration (Article 31); and most important, that
only laws adopted by the Supreme Soviet of the Lithuanian SSR or by a
referendum would be valid in Lithuania. Laws and "legal acts" adopted
by the USSR would be valid only if confirmed and duly registered by the
Lithuanian Supreme Soviet.

During the same session, the legislature proved that it was serious by
declaring invalid a decree passed on March 21, 1989, by the USSR
Supreme Soviet. It dealt with taxation of private cars and means of transport.[61] The Supreme Soviet snubbed Moscow in still another less conspicuous way, namely, by electing Jonas Sabutis, a former high official of the
republic's Procurator's Office, to the post of secretary of the Presidium of
the Supreme Soviet. Only three months earlier, he had been fired by his
Moscow superiors because of his nationalist sympathies.[62] The Supreme
Soviet also addressed a special request to the newly elected USSR Congress of People's Deputies and Gorbachev's government in Moscow. In
the appeal, it demanded that the secret agreements the Soviet government had made with Germany in 1939 and 1941 be condemned and declared null and void from the day they were signed.[63] Finally, it also approved a law to adopt a new model for economic independence, to be
effective January 1, 1990.

All the documents were adopted by a "majority vote."[64] Constitutional
revisions were apparently agreed upon unanimously. Only two deputies,
the chief of the Lithuanian KGB and the editor of the party journal *Komunistas*, voted against the declaration of sovereignty. The session lasted
long into the night and was occasionally stormy and emotional. The
crowds outside the Supreme Soviet building waited for fourteen hours
for the deputies to come out. This time there were flowers, cheers, and a
new feeling of euphoria.

Why did the Lithuanian authorities change their minds after harping
the entire winter that such actions could bring nothing but disaster to Lithuania? First, the party finally made peace with the fact that the movement

for perestroika had grown into a movement of "national rebirth."[65] Sovereignty was the goal of this rebirth and thus had to be pursued. Second, the vote was a reaction to Moscow's indifference concerning Lithuania's economic autonomy. Neither the central authorities nor Soviet economists wanted to hear about the Lithuanian plan, nor did the central press want to open its pages for Lithuanian scholars to argue the republic's case.[66] Four times in the past six months the Lithuanian government had addressed Moscow's government on this question, and four times it was rebuffed. As one journal reported, "Lithuania was forced to take the steering wheel into its own hands."[67] It also was noted that the Estonian declaration of independence on November 18 did not cause the repercussions threatened by Politburo member Victor Chebrikov; nor did it endanger the Estonian leadership. Instead, the declaration had earned Estonia respect throughout the world. Finally, there was also an important political reason, namely, the discovery that only strong support for the republic's independence could redeem the party's credibility and political life.[68] According to Raimundas Kašauskas, a well-known Communist writer and journalist,

> In 1989 the Lithuanian Communist party will accept responsibility for mistakes made in the past. But how will it restore its prestige, how will its decent members be able to face the nation, when they hear the echoes from Siberia [and various localities where heinous crimes were committed by party activists and by the Red Army] and when they know that "executioners of direct repression" are still accepted in the party ranks?[69]

THE DIALECTICS OF
DECLARING INDEPENDENCE

After the opening of the newly elected All-Union Congress on May 28, 1989, the action largely shifted to Moscow. The group of fifty-six deputies from Lithuania was dominated by Sąjūdis's leaders, who saw in the Kremlin's Congress not only an opportunity to advance democratic reform but also a chance to promote Baltic independence. The Lithuanians, together with most of the Estonian and Latvian representatives, joined the Interregional Group of legislators headed by Boris Yeltsin and others on July 2–9. The group supported Gorbachev's early perestroika reforms and challenged the overwhelmingly conservative congressional majority. Its existence allowed Gorbachev to balance the conservative influence and advance perestroika without becoming formally aligned with the generally radical Interregional Group. The Baltic group of deputies formed one of the key pillars of this democratic faction of legislators.

The Lithuanians in Moscow

Lithuanian deputy headquarters in Moscow quickly developed into a hub of feverish activity where plans were hatched and tactics discussed on how to fight the conservatives. It is small wonder that Russian leaders of the Interregional Group were angered one year later when the Lithuanians decided to withdraw from the Congress and the Supreme Soviet altogether. They were accused of hurting the struggle for democracy in the Soviet Union.

At the Congress, the Lithuanians supported the election of Gorbachev as presiding officer but quickly began to create problems for him by their disobedient behavior—something to which the Kremlin's leader had not been exposed in the past. The first confrontation came when the Congress got ready to approve the creation of a constitutional commission with vaguely defined powers that presumably would decide whether the laws passed by republic legislatures complied with the union constitution. The Balts feared that such a commission would nullify all the sovereignty achievements of May 18. In an attempt to force reconsideration of the proposal, the Lithuanians, accompanied by many of the other Baltic deputies, stormed out of the hall. Furor ensued. The Balts were denounced as "secessionists" and "agitators of disturbance."[70] Gorbachev reacted by requesting Brazauskas to ask the deputies to return.[71] Some did. Gorbachev's quick thinking saved not only embarrassment but also political face for Brazauskas, who otherwise would have needed to make a choice between Gorbachev and his own people. The next morning, Gorbachev met with protesting deputies but could not win their support. To the Balts' surprise, the consideration of the proposed commission was thrown back into committee for a new draft and the congressional vote was postponed. The incident persuaded the Lithuanians that their legislative action made a difference and that radical proposals and tactics could attract helpful international attention to the Baltic cause.

Gorbachev's early support for Baltic autonomist stirrings won still another concession from the Congress, namely, the creation of a commission to examine the legality of the Molotov-Ribbentrop pact. On June 1, 1989, Estonian deputy Endel Lippmaa introduced a resolution to establish the commission.[72] Gorbachev approved the initiative, but he was known to have doubts that the original secret texts of the protocols to the pact really existed. To guarantee the integrity of the enterprise, he proposed the appointment of Alexander Yakovlev to the commission as its chairman.

Since the Balts used the protocols as evidence proving their illegal annexation in 1940, Baltic deputies pressed for a quick decision. Soviet historian and deputy Yuri Afanasyev and the Baltic deputies wanted to have the preliminary report published before the August 23 anniversary, but the Communist party's Politburo did not allow this. Publication of the findings was later opposed by some members of the commission, among them Valentin Falin, chief of the International Department of the Central Committee of the party, who knew the truth; and by Chinghiz Aitmatov, the prize-winning writer, and Georgii Arbatov, director of the American-Canadian Studies Institute, both of whom feared Russian chauvinist backlash, as did Yakovlev himself.[73] On August 18, the hard-pressed Yakovlev in a press interview defended the pact and revealed the existence of the additional protocols. Very likely to please the party leadership, in the same breath he insisted that the Baltic "joining" of the Soviet Union was a separate and legal act. According to Yakovlev, "The legal and political status of Lithuania, Latvia, and Estonia was determined by neither the pact nor the protocols."[74] Nevertheless, on December 23, the commission's report was rejected by the Congress.

The next day Yakovlev struck back. He revealed the texts of secret documents and won, by a vote of 1,432 to 252, the annulment of secret protocols between Stalin and Hitler from the time they were signed in 1939. Underplaying their political and legal implications, he denounced the secret protocols as "mirroring the inside nature of Stalinism."[75] They should be condemned, he said, for the purpose of "restoring the honor of socialism, which was trampled upon by Stalinism." Relations with the Baltic states, according to the commission's report, were conducted by the Soviet Union on the basis of treaties that respected their sovereignty and territorial integrity. Yakovlev earned the hatred of Moscow's reactionaries, who derailed his career in the Kremlin. Paradoxically, for his historical achievement he did not win new friends among the Balts, who were disappointed that he had separated the issue of the Stalin-Hitler conspiracy from the question of the Soviet Union's illegal annexation of the three countries.

Before the Congress in December condemned the Molotov-Ribbentrop pact, the Lithuanians and their Baltic neighbors won another concession from Gorbachev's government, namely, the approval, on November 27, of a law recognizing their self-declared economic autonomy.[76] The authorization of "economic self-management" won against the vigorous opposition of Prime Minister Nikolai Ryzhkov and Gosplan chairman Yurii Maslyukov. The future prime minister of Lithuania, Kazimiera Prunskienė, claimed that the law would allow the republic to control 93 percent of its industries, leaving to Moscow's management only eleven enterprises.[77] Changes that seemed dramatic at the time, however, soon paled to the even greater events that overtook the Congress.

THE COMMUNISTS DIVORCE MOSCOW

The summer and fall of 1989 were very stormy in Lithuania. By Christmas the little country had decidedly turned away from Moscow. Although the

May 18 sovereignty declaration was a consensus decision, Sąjūdis had to negotiate for the Communist party to accept it. Afterward, the Restructuring Movement continued to grow in strength, whereas the Communist party was declining. It now could not act without Sąjūdis and found itself a junior partner fighting for its political life. The fear combined with deference that earlier had sustained the authority of Communist leadership now had disappeared, and the party began hemorrhaging from a steady and conspicuous loss of membership. Brazauskas attempted to save the party by giving it a national Lithuanian identity without losing Moscow's support. He soon discovered, however, that it was impossible to serve two masters. Disturbed by repeated rebukes from Moscow, Brazauskas decided to take his party and cross the Rubicon.

In June 1989, he strengthened the government of the Lithuanian SSR by adding to it as deputy prime minister Kazimiera Prunskienė, an economist and reform Communist who was one of the leaders of Sąjūdis. At the same time, Brazauskas moved to dismantle the ideological Communist structures of society, especially in culture and even in politics. Finally, while the Baltic congressional deputies were demanding the publication of the findings of the Molotov-Ribbentrop pact, the Communist-controlled Supreme Soviet of the Lithuanian SSR sprang to action. On July 21, another special commission of the legislature declared the 1939–1941 Soviet-German agreements "null and void from the moment they were signed." The agreements legitimized forcible Soviet interference in Lithuania's affairs, the commission said, and made it possible for the Soviets to arrange for an illegal election of the People's Diet to request admission to the ranks of Soviet republics.[78] As the commission's declaration stated, the "issue of incorporation into the USSR was kept hidden from Lithuania's citizens before and during the elections." Thus, the subsequent declaration of July 21, 1940, by the People's Diet requesting admission to the USSR was illegal together with the Soviet law of August 3, 1940, which accepted Lithuania into the Soviet Union.

On September 23 the commission's declaration was accepted by the Supreme Soviet. The issue in the upcoming republican electoral battle was clearly independence, and the statement seemed to assert the Communist party's firm commitment to it.

Baltic pressure on Moscow to condemn the Soviet-German pact of 1939 reached its apogee on August 23, its fiftieth anniversary, when 1.25 million Estonians, Latvians, and Lithuanians linked hands in a human chain extending from Tallinn to Vilnius, a distance of some 470 miles. Families, individuals, and groups, with flags and without them, lined up on the main thoroughfares in a peaceful protest, called the "Baltic way," against a conspiracy that had resulted in the fifty-year Soviet occupation of their land.

Moscow's reaction to these pressures, especially the "Baltic way" demonstration, was furious. Alexander Yakovlev's insistence that Soviet rule in the Baltics was legal despite the secret protocols of the Molotov-Ribbentrop pact was tame in comparison to the outburst by the ruling Politburo following the demonstration. On August 26, *Pravda* published a full page denunciation of Baltic "separatists" by the Politburo, threatening even the physical safety and survival of the three Baltic nations.[79] This was a rare explosion, unusual in its vicious frankness.

Undaunted, the Supreme Soviet prepared for gradual statehood. It established a commission chaired by the poet Justinas Marcinkevičius and drafted laws on citizenship and popular referenda. The first was to separate Lithuanian citizenship from Soviet citizenship; the second provided a mechanism for direct decision-making by the citizens. Finally, a landmark decision was made that changed the very nature of the country's constitutional and political system. On December 7, by a vote of 237 to 1, the Supreme Soviet abrogated the Communist party's monopoly of power and legalized a multiparty system.[80] Lithuania thus became the first Soviet republic to eliminate the famous Article 6 of the 1977 Soviet constitution, which had defined the core of the Soviet political system. Thus Lithuania joined Hungary and other East European nations where the Communists had given way to public pressure to become a more radical force undermining the traditional pillars of its power.

The Lithuanian Communist party's move, moreover, did not entail just the abrogation of monopoly power but also signified a clear rejection of Moscow's leadership. The historical decision was taken without Moscow's approval even as it challenged the core principle of democratic centralism critical to the successful organization of the Communist party. In the past, centralized party control had provided an integrating and disciplining force indispensable for Moscow's control of the giant, ethnically diverse Soviet empire. The Lithuanian decision foreshadowed the apogee of the Communist rebellion. At Lithuania's 20th Party Congress on December 19–20, 1989, the Lithuanian Communist party, by a vote of 855 to 160, separated itself from the all-union organization.[81]

The minority that voted against cutting ties with Moscow refused to accept the majority's decision and maintained a separate rump party. It consisted of conservative Lithuanian, Russian, and Polish delegates. Meeting separately, the pro-Moscow group elected an ideologically orthodox leadership. The Stalinist historian Mykolas Burokevičius became the first secretary, Vladyslav Shved, an ethnic Pole and professional Communist apparatchik, was the second secretary, and the propagandist philosopher of atheism Juozas Jermalavičius was the third secretary. Jermalavičius's appointment caused a personal tragedy: His wife and children abandoned and opposed him. Moscow, which at first kept lines of communication open to both groups, quickly decided to accept the pro-Moscow minority as the legal successor to the traditional Lithuanian Communist party.

This divorce from Moscow unleashed the largest furor from the Kremlin thus far. A special meeting of the Central Committee was called for December 25 to consider the Lithuanian challenge. Gorbachev told Brazauskas that he would have to speak out against the Lithuanian leader.[82] Stunned and perplexed by the Lithuanian daring, the plenum nevertheless hesitated outright to condemn the unprecedented Lithuanian separation and decided to ask Gorbachev himself to go to Lithuania and appraise the situation.[83]

Gorbachev's visit to the rebellious republic on January 10–13, 1990, was the first in fifty years by a ruling general secretary of the CPSU.[84] He was received politely, even warmly. In frank discussions with many groups he discovered that the idea of independence was not an abstract fabrication by self-seeking politicians or arrogant professors, as he had been publicly asserting, but a deeply held goal of wide social support. The chief of the Kremlin failed to persuade the Lithuanians in factories or on collective farms that independence was a mere emotional illusion and bad rational choice. Promises of impending revisions of the federal constitution to allow for a multiparty system and a mechanism for allowing secession similarly failed to mollify the Lithuanians. They regarded the first promise as irrelevant since a multiparty system was already a reality in Lithuania and considered the second a threat, since only obstacles to separation from Moscow were expected. Gorbachev was frequently angered, and he especially objected to being treated as head of a foreign though friendly country, which was the strategy advised by Sąjūdis leader Landsbergis. Nevertheless, he left Lithuania satisfied and smiling, according to Brazauskas, who considered that this augured well for Lithuania's peaceful separation from Moscow. Brazauskas apparently hoped that the Kremlin's leader had recognized and accepted the reality of political consensus in Lithuania on independence. Events shortly proved that Brazauskas was badly mistaken.

THE DECLARATION OF INDEPENDENCE

The first multiparty election in the history of the Soviet Union and Soviet Lithuania was held on February 24, 1990. A total of 522 candidates competed for 141 seats in the new legislature.[85] Candidates were nominated by political parties or by Sąjūdis, which refused to become a party despite strong pressures to do so. The reform movement endorsed individual candidates on the strength of their personal qualifications and political views, without regard to their formal party affiliation.

The composition of the list of candidates running in territorially designed districts generally reflected the ethnic composition of Lithuania. It was dominated by the well-educated scientific and managerial elite. Almost 90 percent were Lithuanians (Lithuanians constituted 79.6 percent of the population of the republic), 6.3 percent were Russians (9.4 percent of the population), and 6.1 percent were Poles (7 percent of the population). Some Byelorussians, Jews, and others also ran. The overwhelming majority (84.7 percent) were professionals between thirty and sixty years of age. Educationally, an amazing 19.5 percent possessed doctorate or candidate of science degrees, and 92 percent of all those running had higher education diplomas, mostly in the social and technical sciences. Most of the candidates at the time were serving in managerial positions either in government, industry, agriculture, or education or served in the Communist party apparatus. Only 5 percent were employed as workers.

Politically, 61.7 percent of candidates were Communists belonging to the newly independent Lithuanian Communist party. The next largest group of candidates (28.5 percent) had no party affiliation, and the remaining candidates (9.2 percent) were split among the newly established democratic parties, namely, the Christian Democrats, the Democrats, the Social Democrats, and the Greens.

Sąjūdis and all the political parties, with the exception of Yedinstvo and the rump all-union Communist party, supported independence. The independent Communist party of Brazauskas, however, preferred a gradual pace. The contest for power was between candidates supported by Sąjūdis and those not supported by Sąjūdis.

Sąjūdis itself won ninety-one seats in the round of balloting on February 24. The results were a crushing defeat for the independent Lithuanian Communist party despite its switchover to supporting independence. On its own, the LCP won only twenty-three seats. The additional seventeen independent Communists were elected with the endorsement of Sąjūdis. Ballots were cast by 71.72 percent of the voters.[86] Party leaders were in advance reconciled to the loss of a majority but were downhearted by the depth of the defeat. The platforms of both Sąjūdis and the Communist party favored independence, but the voters chose representatives of new forces over vestiges of the old. Despite the fact that under Brazauskas the Communist party had made a political about-face and even risked Moscow's fury, its repressive legacy badly compromised its candidates. Thus, although LCP leader Brazauskas scored a huge electoral success and rode into office on an extremely high wave of popularity, the party he transformed had lost.

The gains by the newly established parties were small: The democratic political process was a new experience for the citizenry and the fledgling parties had no time to organize or to formulate specific platforms. The Social Democratic party nevertheless won nine seats, the Greens four, the Democratic party three, and the Christian Democrats two. Moscow's branch of the Communist party won five seats. The majority of the new parliament—a total of seventy—however, were nonpartisan.[87] They formed the bulk of the strength of Sąjūdis, as it ascended to the position of leadership in government.

The victory by Sąjūdis assured its leaders not only of a legislative majority but also of a quorum of two-thirds needed for constitutional action. The new Supreme Soviet set its first meeting for March 10, without waiting for the results of the run-off elections from remaining electoral districts.

Before the new parliament met, however, Brazauskas was summoned to the Kremlin for a talk with Gorbachev. This was a formal meeting between the president of the Soviet Union and the chairman of the Presidium of Lithuania's expired Supreme Soviet. Gorbachev tried again to convince him that Lithuania must stay in the union. He said that if Lithuania became independent, it would have to repay the Soviet Union $33 billion dollars for industrial and other investments.[88] He further threatened that independent Lithuania would lose territories in eastern Lithuania and also the harbor city and territory of Klaipėda. The eastern territories would be detached, he argued, because of alleged violations of the Soviet-Lithuanian treaty of October 1939 that fixed the boundaries. Klaipėda, according to Gorbachev, after World War II was ceded to the Soviet Union, not the Lithuanian SSR, and therefore belonged to Moscow, not to Vilnius.

Upon his return from this ninety-minute discussion, Brazauskas rendered an extensive report of the meeting in a long TV interview and in the press, stressing Lithuania's current economic dependence on the Soviet Union. But Gorbachev's threats did not dampen patriotic enthusiasm as much as they forced its rebellious expression.

The new legislature met in the old parliament building on March 10, 1990, as scheduled. During its first day in session it adopted radical resolutions that supported the need for reform in the Soviet Union and at the same time began the process of separation. First, the new legislature signaled its unwillingness to compromise by refusing to reelect Brazauskas to the republic's top government position. By a two-to-one vote, the Supreme Soviet chose the leader of Sąjūdis, Professor Vytautas Landsbergis, for the post of chairman of the Presidium.[89] Although a majority of the parliament membership was nominally Communist, the legislators wanted a clean break with the Communist past. They also dropped the designation of Lithuania as "Soviet" and "Socialist."

The Lithuanians had strong reason to seek an even further break. Gorbachev was decidedly cooling his enthusiasm for democratization in light of the trouble it was causing as much in the periphery of the empire as in the capital. His decision to become elected president of the USSR by the Congress was feared by most reformers as an expansion of his powers and a return to more authoritarian rule.

Landsbergis is elected chairman of the new Soviet Lithuanian Supreme Council, March 11, 1990. (Photo by M. Baranauskas. Used by permission.)

National minorities were deeply concerned that Gorbachev's request for presidential powers could block further progress toward national freedom by mandating an insurmountable legal mechanism. The Lithuanians feared that Gorbachev would immediately decree a law on secession that would make it impossible to secede from the union. Sąjūdis leaders reasoned that if they declared independence before then, the laws of the USSR Congress of Deputies would not have juridical legitimacy in Lithuania. The extraordinary session of the Congress of People's Deputies in which Gorbachev was planning to expand the president's powers was to meet March 12.

On March 11, after rejecting the symbols of their Communist heritage, the Supreme Soviet unanimously proclaimed the restoration of Lithuania as an independent democratic republic.[90] The echoes of the old national anthem resounded in the hall. Communist and Soviet symbols were replaced by the rising Lithuanian flag. Outside of the parliament the cheering crowd removed Soviet insignia. Joy and tearful emotion filled the building and the streets outside as the shocked Lithuanians witnessed the long-awaited liberation that few expected to see in their lifetime.

The first official act of the independent parliament was to put the declaration of independence in terms of "the restoration of the exercise of sovereign powers of the Lithuanian state which were annulled by a foreign power in 1940."[91] Thus the parliament established a direct link to the first modern Lithuanian republic and restored the legitimacy of the 1930 constitution by declaring that "neither the February 16, 1918, independence act nor the May 15, 1920, [legislation] passed by the founding Diet concerning the reconstructed democratic state of Lithuania had ever lost their legal force."[92] The parliament also annulled, effective immediately, the validity of the Soviet constitutions of the Lithuanian SSR and of the Soviet Union and established a working Temporary Basic Law to grant them the necessary legal framework for further action.

Kazimiera Prunskienė, an economist and member of the last Politburo, became the new prime minister of the republic. Upon her election, she immediately resigned from the Communist party. Brazauskas was stung by his loss to Landsbergis and rejected the victor's offer to become his

The Lithuanian women's movement protests the draft into the Soviet army. The posters commemorate Lithuanian youths who have died during their service—not always on the field of battle. (Photo by R. Urbakavičius. Used by permission.)

deputy. After some negotiations, however, he agreed to serve as a deputy prime minister to Prunskienė.

After the adoption of these historical decisions, the new leader of the republic, Vytautas Landsbergis, asked President Gorbachev to "start negotiations for the regulation of all questions related to the already accomplished restoration of Lithuanian statehood."[93] He also requested protection for Lithuanian youths serving in the Soviet armed forces. To Prime Minister Nikolai Ryzhkov, Landsbergis proposed that economic relations between the republic and the Soviet Union remain undisturbed until they could be newly defined by bilateral agreements.

Landsbergis further appealed to the international community for recognition of Lithuania's restored independence as well as for "brotherly solidarity and support." The Lithuanians had informed U.S. secretary of state James Baker III and U.S. ambassador Matlock of their planned action. Landsbergis suggested that Lithuania's decision was not directed against the Soviet Union "nor against nationalities which live in Lithuania" and solicited understanding and "support for our aspirations" from the nations of the Soviet Union. He invited Lithuania's national minorities to join in a "brotherly endeavor whose purpose is to return Lithuania to the family of Europe's democratic states and to secure the rights of all citizens and of all national communities in Lithuania for the fostering of their own language, culture, and customs." Finally, he invited all people of Lithuania to a life of civic harmony. "Independence is not a wrathful last judgment [on those who may have been compromised by the old system], not a triumph of victors, but a way of our historical reconciliation, love, and rebirth."[94]

NOTES

1. Petras Vaitiekūnas, *Sąjūdžio žinios,* no. 72, March 7, 1989, p. 2.

2. *Gimtasis kraštas,* June 16–22, 1988, p. 3.

3. *Atgimimas,* no. 1, September 16, 1988, p. 15.

4. Ibid., p. 14.

5. *Tiesa,* July 2, 1988, p. 2.

6. *Tiesa,* July 9, 1988, p. 3.

7. *Tiesa,* October 11, 1988, p. 2.

8. Cf. Radio Liberty Research/395, "Alexander Yakovlev and the Nationality Issue," August 31, 1988; *Radio Free Europe Research, Baltic Area 10,* September 9, 1988, "A Change of Policy in the Lithuanian Communist Party," p. 17; *Tiesa,* August 14, pp. 2–3.

9. *New York Times,* October 28, 1988.

10. *Tiesa,* August 18, 1988, p. 3.

11. *Tiesa,* August 20, 1988, p. 1.

12. *Tiesa*, August 23, 1988, p. 3.

13. *Sąjūdžio žinios*, no. 39, September 29, 1988, p. 2.

14. *Tiesa*, September 14, 1988, p. 1.

15. Ibid.

16. *Sąjūdžio žinios*, no 39, September 20, 1988, p. 2.

17. *Radio Free Europe Research, Baltic Area SR 11*, October 5, 1988, pp. 3–5; Vincent J. Schodolski, *Chicago Tribune*, September 29, 1988; *Tiesa*, October 1, 1988, p. 3.

18. *Tiesa*, October 11, 1988, p. 2; *Atgimimas*, no. 3, October 15, 1988, p. 3. For a description of attempts to depose Songaila as well as his efforts to survive see Alfred E. Senn, *Lithuania Awakening* (Berkeley: University of California Press, 1990), pp. 205–214.

19. *Tiesa*, October 22, 1989, p. 1.

20. Ibid., p. 3.

21. *Tiesa*, October 21, 1989, p. 1.

22. Rein Raud in *Sirp ja Vasar*, no. 48, November 25, 1988, translated in *Atgimimas*, no. 10, December 12, 1988, p. 7.

23. *Tiesa*, October 23, 1989, p. 4.

24. Ibid.

25. See *Atgimimas*, no. 2, October 2, 1988, p. 13.

26. See *Tiesa*, October 5, 1988, p. 3.

27. Text of the first draft in *Atgimimas*, no. 2, October 10, 1988, pp. 7–12; second draft in *Atgimimas*, no. 7, November 15, 1988, pp. 2–6.

28. See *Atgimimas*, no. 7, November 15, 1988, p. 6.

29. *Atgimimas*, no. 6, November 11, 1988, p. 6.

30. *Literatūra ir menas*, June 17, 1989, p. 2.

31. *Tiesa*, November 16, 1988, p. 2.

32. Ibid.

33. *Tiesa*, October 22, 1988, pp. 1–3.

34. *Tiesa*, November 16, 1988, p. 2.

35. *Tiesa*, November 18, 1988, p. 1; November 19, 1988, pp. 1–3; November 20, 1988, pp. 1–3.

36. See *Atgimimas*, no. 8, November 22, 1988, p. 3.

37. *Tiesa*, November 20, 1988, p. 1.

38. *Tiesa*, November 21, 1988, p. 1.

39. *Tiesa*, November 20, 1988, p. 1.

40. Ibid.

41. *Atgimimas*, no. 8, November 22, 1988, p. 5.

42. *The Lithuanian Reform Movement: Sąjūdis* (Vilnius: Sąjūdis, 1989), p. 58.

43. *Tiesa*, February 7, 1989, p. 4.

44. *Tiesa*, January 13, 1989, p. 3.

45. *Tiesa*, December 17, 1989, pp. 1–2.

46. *Tiesa*, January 25, 1989, p. 1.

47. *Atgimimas*, no. 11, December 16, 1988, p. 1.

48. *Atgimimas*, no. 13, December 30, 1988, p. 3.

49. *Tiesa*, January 25, 1989, pp. 1–2 passim. For Sąjūdis's platform, see *Atgimimas*, no. 6, February 10, 1989, p. 6.

50. *Tiesa,* February 23, 1989, pp. 2–3.

51. Ibid., p. 2.

52. Election results in *Tiesa,* March 29, 1989, pp. 1, 4; April 11, 1989, p. 11.

53. Interview in *Komjaunimo tiesa,* March 30, 1989, pp. 1–2 passim.

54. *Tiesa,* April 11, 1989, p. 4; BBC interview with Landsbergis, documentary "The Second Russian Revolution," Part 4, 1991.

55. *Tiesa,* April 21, 1989, p. 1.

56. *Tiesa,* May 3, 1989, p. 2.

57. *Tiesa,* May 13, 1989, p. 1.

58. Ibid.

59. Ibid.

60. See texts in *Tiesa,* May 19, 1989, p. 1.

61. See text in *Tiesa,* May 24, 1989, p. 1.

62. *Gimtasis kraštas,* no. 21, May 25–31, 1989, p. 3.

63. Text in *Tiesa,* May 19, 1989, p. 1.

64. Ibid. Also information from Lithuanian Information Center, Brooklyn, New York. The number of those voting against the declaration is disputed. Five were reported, but the journalists wrote down four names only.

65. See Šepetys in *Tiesa,* May 3, 1989, p. 2.

66. Ibid.

67. *Gimtasis kraštas,* May 21, May 25–31, 1989, p. 2.

68. Interview with Justas V. Paleckis, new chief of CC division on ideology, *Komjaunimo Tiesa,* May 19, 1989, p. 4.

69. *Tiesa,* February 16, 1989, p. 2.

70. Kazimiera Prunskienė, *Gintarinės ledy išpažintis* (Vilnius: Politika, 1991), p. 21.

71. Interview with Algirdas Brazauskas, BBC documentary, "The Second Russian Revolution," Part 4, 1991.

72. For the story of the commission, see Lev Bezumenski, "Niemand kann uns überführen," *Der Spiegel,* no. 3 (1991): 104–112.

73. Interview with Justinas Marcinkevičius, Lithuanian poet and deputy of the Congress, *Gimtasis kraštas,* August 24–30, 1989, p. 2.

74. *Pravda,* August 19, 1989, p. 1; also Justinas Marcinkevičius in *Gimtasis kraštas,* August 24–30, 1989, p. 2.

75. Quoted by Lev Bezumenski, "Niemand kann uns überführen," p. 112. See also the text of the congressional decision signed by Gorbachev, *Tiesa,* December 18, 1989, p. 1.

76. Prunskienė, *Gintarinės ledy išpažintis,* p. 27.

77. Lecture in Toronto, Canada, reported in *Tėviškės žiburiai* (Toronto), December 5, 1989, p. 9.

78. Text in *Tiesa,* August 22, 1989, p. 1.

79. Text in *Pravda,* August 26, 1989, p. 1.

80. *New York Times,* December 9, 1989, p. 1.

81. *Tiesa,* December 21, 1989, pp. 1–2.

82. Interview with Algirdas Brazauskas, BBC documentary, "The Second Russian Revolution," Part 4, 1991. This documentary covered the Central Committee meeting as well as Gorbachev's visit to Lithuania.

83. See *Tiesa*, January 11–16, 1992; also *New York Times*.

84. Data on candidates from the sources of Sajūdis.

85. *Tiesa*, March 12, 1990, p. 1; also see U.S. Congressional Commission on Security and Cooperation in Europe, *Report on the Supreme Soviet Elections in Lithuania*, March 6, 1990, p. 2 passim.

86. *Tiesa*, March 12, 1990, p. 2.

87. *New York Times*, March 8, 1990, pp. 1, 10; *Tiesa*, March 8, pp. 1, 4.

88. *Tiesa*, March 12, 1990, p. 2.

89. *Tiesa*, March 13, 1990, p. 1.

90. Ibid. The declaration is also found in *Lietuvos Respublikos Aukščiausios Tarybos, Lietuvos Respublikos Aukščiausios Tarybos Prezidiumo, Lietuvos Respublikos Vyriausybės Svarbiausių Dokumentų Rinkinys* (Collection of the Most Important Documents Adopted by the Supreme Council, Presidium of the Supreme Council, and the Government of the Lithuanian Republic), March 11–May 11, 1990 (Vilnius: Mintis, 1990), p. 8. Afterward cited as *Rinkinys*.

91. *Rinkinys*, p. 8.

92. Ibid., p. 34.

93. Ibid, pp. 35–36.

SIX

Between the
Kremlin and the West:
Securing Independence

Just after being elected executive president of the Soviet Union, Gorbachev, in March 1990, pushed through legislation on secession. Shortly afterward, former U.S. secretary of state George Shultz made a speech in San Francisco advising Gorbachev to accept Lithuania's separation from the Soviet Union. "Mikhail Sergeyevich," Shultz said, "take the Soviet army out of its threatening positions in Lithuania, announce your acceptance of Lithuanian independence and then—under really equal terms—negotiate the details of the separation."[1] By the vote of the Supreme Soviet, Shultz continued, the Soviet Union had decided that "the annexation of Lithuania and the other Baltic countries was illegal." Addressing Gorbachev, he said, "Knowing you as a lawyer, I thought you were laying the groundwork for the realization of that independence and also for differentiating the Baltic States from the other republics of the USSR." It is now clear, however, that if Gorbachev ever contemplated such a course of action, he had changed his position by this time.

THE KREMLIN'S RESPONSE

Gorbachev labeled the Lithuanian action "alarming" on March 12.[2] The next day he denounced the Vilnius declaration as "invalid and illegal" and rejected Landsbergis's call for negotiations. "You can carry out negotiations," he said, "[only] with a foreign country."[3] Shortly afterward, however, Algirdas Brazauskas met with Gorbachev and told foreign correspondents that Gorbachev's reaction had been "just for public consumption."[4] Estonia's president, Arnold Rüütel, confirmed this impression, saying that Gorbachev's public stand was different from his private views and that the Kremlin's leader was open to negotiations, in this case, with Estonia. Nevertheless, the Soviet military brass were violently opposed to the Lithuanian and generally Baltic independence, as was the party and government apparatus in Moscow.

Thus, on March 15 Moscow formally went on record opposing Lithuania's independence. Under Gorbachev's direction, the Soviet Congress of Deputies denounced the Lithuanian action as "contrary to Articles 74 and 75 of the constitution of the USSR" and therefore "invalid." Article 74 asserted the supremacy of Moscow's law, and Article 75 stressed the integrity of Soviet territory and the sovereignty of the USSR. The Congress, which usually could be relied upon to support Communist party interests because one-third of its deputies were party-appointed, directed Gorbachev to "protect" the lives of citizens and "the interests and sovereignty of the USSR in Lithuania." In what was to become a duel by telegraph, the Soviet president dispatched a telegram to Lithuania demanding that in three days Landsbergis tell him of "measures taken to comply with the ruling."[5] The Lithuanian leader replied, on March 18, that the edict adopted by the USSR Congress was "invalid" and had "no legal basis in Lithuania." He also explained that individual human rights and the law and order of society in Lithuania were guaranteed by Lithuanian laws. As far as protection of Soviet interests was concerned, Landsbergis proposed these first be "concretely defined through negotiations."[6]

The response to Landsbergis came not from Gorbachev but from Prime Minister Nikolai Ryzhkov, who refused an invitation to talks and forbade negotiations on the expropriation or managerial takeover of any industrial enterprises currently under Moscow's control. Ryzhkov also asked the Customs Office of Moscow's Interior Ministry "to secure customs control in Lithuania,"[7] thus rejecting Lithuania's right to establish its own customs service for controlling the movement of goods. On March 21, Gorbachev stepped up the pressure with a new decree. He ordered KGB border guards to intensify the surveillance of Soviet frontiers in Lithuania and to interdict any "illegal" activities. Thus, the work of Lithuanian customs service and border patrol personnel was being closely watched. He further demanded that the population surrender hunting rifles—a demand the Lithuanians considered insulting—and, even more ominously, ordered the departure from Lithuania of all foreigners, including journalists and diplomats. The Foreign Ministry was told to curtail the issuance of visas to foreigners for entering Lithuania.[8]

The next day Gorbachev "suggested" that Landsbergis disband "the volunteers for the so-called national defense organizations which are [intended] to replace the activities of the [KGB] border army, and in part, organs of [the ministry] of internal affairs."[9] On that same day, Soviet tanks rumbled through Vilnius. Three days later the military took over the central press building, which housed the republic's largest printing plant and the editorial offices of the republic's largest newspapers and periodicals. The troopers also took over some other buildings that had belonged to the Communist party. The military insisted that these buildings were the property of the rump Communist party that had remained loyal to Moscow.

Continuing to communicate with Landsbergis by telegraph, Gorbachev repeatedly objected to what he considered the Lithuanian parliament's unconstitutional invasion of the central government's jurisdiction. He denied the parliament's right to invalidate the Soviet military service law, and on March 27 the Soviet military removed several former soldiers, whom they considered deserters, from a hospital in Vilnius. Three days later, the military took over the republic prosecutor's office and installed a new, Moscow-appointed prosecutor to replace Landsbergis's appointee. If this move was meant to start a dual administration to eventually regain control of the republic's government for Moscow, it did not succeed. An overwhelming majority of the prosecutor's employees and lawyers refused to work for Moscow's man.

Unable to soften Lithuanian determination by military assaults, on March 31 Gorbachev directly appealed to the Supreme Council and to the Lithuanian people.[10] Speaking to the Lithuanian parliament, Gorbachev charged that the Lithuanian leadership refused "to listen to the voice of reason," continued to ignore the rulings of the USSR Congress, and had taken actions that were "openly confrontational" and insulting to the Soviet Union. In a televised address to the Lithuanian people, addressing them as "esteemed citizens of the Lithuanian SSR," Gorbachev claimed that "the resolutions of March 11" would have serious effects on the Soviet Union, on perestroika, but most of all on Lithuania itself. Gorbachev accused the parliament of taking unilateral, ultimative, and hasty action, "literally in the course of one night," and claimed that Lithuania's "demonstrative" disregard for the Soviet constitution and for all-union obligations and laws had caused "justified indignation" throughout the Soviet Union. He warned that "measures [against Lithuania] of economic, political and administrative character" were "suggested" and would include the annexation of some Lithuanian territories [of Klaipėda and eastern Lithuania] to the Kaliningrad region and Byelorussia. Gorbachev concluded that if the Lithuanian government did not listen to the "voice of reason, events may bring grave consequences for us all."

Landsbergis immediately responded with a bold statement of his own. The Lithuanian president charged that instead of listening to the "voices of the world"—which counseled negotiations—Gorbachev made threats "similar to those made last year on August 26 [by the Politburo of the Central Committee of the USSR Communist party]." With a pride that equaled Gorbachev's arrogance, the Lithuanian president curtly declared that his parliament would consider the demands along with other planned items on the agenda when it met in two days. After thorough parliamentary discussion, however, Landsbergis softened and dispatched a conciliatory and even friendly answer to Moscow. The Soviet president, Landsbergis said, deserved praise for his Afghanistan and East European policies and for his "courage to denounce the consequences of Josef Stalin's domestic and foreign policies." He sought to establish common intellectual ground with the Soviet president by suggesting that the declaration of March 11 was valid "under the terms of the USSR constitution." In the same breath, however, he repeated Lithuania's legal claim that "the basis for the reestablishment of Lithuania's independence" was "the de jure continuity of the Lithuanian state."

Gorbachev would not soften. Under the terms of the Soviet constitution, he answered, Lithuania had no right to "restore" independence or unilaterally declare it. This argument was repeated by Ryzhkov in his letter of April 6 to Prime Minister Prunskienė. "We favor," the chairman of the Soviet Council of Ministers said, "businesslike discussions of the entire complex of problems," but only "within the framework of the constitution of the USSR." The door to this discussion would be opened by an "immediate repeal of the illegal acts adopted by the Supreme Soviet of the Republic."[11] Unperturbed by this rejection, the optimistic and flexible "amber lady" of Lithuanian politics proposed "dialogue" as a middle road between Ryzhkov's "discussions" and Landsbergis's "negotiations," especially on questions involving the Soviet armed forces.

But Moscow did not want even a "dialogue" with an "independent" republic. It counted on a split in the Lithuanian leadership. Even Foreign Minister Eduard Shevardnadze thought that the Lithuanians would "come around."[12] Concluding that neither verbal admonition nor military intimidation would change the Lithuanian disposition, on April 13 Gorbachev and Ryzhkov jointly sent an ultimatum.[13] Lithuanian developments, their telegram announced, had reached a "political dead end." Moscow's leaders demanded that within two days the Lithuanian parliament revoke "documents and resolutions which set the Lithuanian SSR against other republics and the Soviet Union as a whole." The parliament should "reestablish the situation of the republic as of March 10, 1990." Otherwise, they said, Moscow would "suspend delivery . . . of production of the type sold on foreign market for hard currency." This "type" referred mainly to oil and gas, but as it developed, included various metals, parts, and raw materials as well, without which Lithuania's industries would stay idle. In other words, Moscow threatened economic blockade.

The Lithuanian Supreme Soviet attempted to stave off the calamity on April 18 by promising Moscow that it would not adopt any new laws "during the period of preliminary consultations between Lithuania and the USSR, if these consultations began sometime before May 1."[14] The legislature also appointed a delegation to be sent to Moscow to discuss the "conditions of negotiations." Moscow, however, disregarded the suggested compromise and immediately, on the same day, turned off the supply of oil and of 84 percent of the natural gas consumed by the republic.[15] The blockade was on.

The Kremlin's action did not apply only to supplies from the Soviet Union. Moscow sealed off the republic's borders to prevent deliveries from other countries as well. The Lithuanian government appointed a commission under Deputy Prime Minister Brazauskas to deal with the blockade. Energy supplies and some food products were rationed. Tens of thousands of workers who stood idle in factories that could not operate were taken care of by payments of "vacation" salaries that drained the republic's budget. Lithuanian managers signed contracts with enterprises in Leningrad and elsewhere to get needed materials, but the railroads did not always deliver them. Car and truck transportation stopped, public transportation thinned, and people were forced to bicycle or walk. The blockade cost the republic tens of millions of rubles in damages and lost production.[16] According to Lithuanian data, 35,000 industrial and construction workers lost their jobs, 435 enterprises could operate only part time, 6 large industrial enterprises were completely closed down, and the republic lost 415.5 million rubles worth of production and 125 million rubles for the state budget up to July 1.[17] Nonetheless, Lithuania sold almost the same tonnage of meat as in previous years.

Moscow also suffered from the blockade: Many Lithuanian products could not easily and immediately be replaced. Lithuania produced 95 percent of the compressors used in pneumatic brakes for Soviet trucks and cars; all tank and tractor carburetors, TV remote control devices, and household electricity meters; and a very large percentage of all bathtub and bathroom fixtures.[18] Moreover, the closure of the oil refinery in Mažeikiai cost Moscow additional losses of foreign currency for contracted exports of oil products. Finally, the blockade contributed to further havoc in the Soviet economy. The hard-pressed Lithuanians bartered with enterprises in Russia, Uzbekistan, and Kazakhstan, thereby diverting supplies from their originally intended destinations.

For Lithuania the blockade also had costly political consequences. The unexpected economic crackdown killed the euphoria of independence and caused disagreements in the parliament, as well as in the country, about the nature of Lithuania's relations with the Soviet Union. Brazauskas, first secretary of the independent Lithuanian Communist party, counseled compromise, arguing that critical shortages of oil and gas would occur quickly and put a stop to Lithuanian industry.[19] He had support among Communist and some former Communist deputies. He also drew strength from the vigorous Communist showing in local elections. In early April, the independent Communist party of Brazauskas scored a major victory by winning 34.8 percent of the total seats on local government councils while the pro-Moscow Communists elected 461 deputies, or 5.87 percent of the total.[20] The pro-Moscow party made gains only in Polish- and Russian-dominated districts, such as Šalčininkai, which has a very large Polish majority, and Ignalina, which includes the city of Sniečkus, where the Russian workers from the nearby power plant live.[21]

Communist support for a compromising attitude toward Moscow raised new doubts about the party's commitment to full independence and incited intense anti-Communist reaction, especially in the parliament. In addition, these suspicions polarized the parliament between Left and Right. The split did not immediately become confrontational, but it fueled the emergence of a radically nationalist and intensely anti-Communist group of deputies largely from the city of Kaunas. In late May 1990, differences in public policy, especially on negotiations with Moscow, surfaced between Landsbergis, who had never belonged to the Communist party, and Prime Minister Prunskienė, a former Communist who had several Communists in her cabinet. The parliament sought supremacy, goaded by a strident right wing that was suspicious of Prunskienė's every move. The press took a highly critical attitude toward the parliamentary right wing, and the parliament's reputation generally was not enhanced by the TV exposure of its daily sessions.

Sąjūdis and Landsbergis experienced a loss of popularity. A poll showed that Landsbergis's popularity rating dropped from 45 percent approval in April to only 28 percent approval in June.[22] The popularity of the now dominant Sąjūdis sank below that of the independent Communist party for the first time. Only 21 percent of those polled expressed confidence in Sąjūdis; 39 percent preferred Brazauskas's party. The pro-Moscow group did not receive any votes. Brazauskas, however, had to concede the first place in popularity to Kazimiera Prunskienė, the prime minister. Her government also proved to be more popular than the parliament. It received only 12 percent of the negative votes, whereas 21 percent of respondents negatively evaluated the work of the parliament.

Interestingly enough, these changes in public opinion did not break the public's support for resistance to Moscow. Of the Lithuanian respondents, 48 percent said they were determined unconditionally to endure the blockade. Another 43 percent were willing to suffer but wanted to know the limits. Only 9 percent said they had already had enough. Of the other nationalities, 12 percent were determined unconditionally to survive the blockade, 53 percent wanted to know the limits, and 45 percent were unwilling to suffer and disapproved of resistance to Moscow.

Moscow and its supporters in Lithuania were encouraged by the growing divisions, squabbles, and difficulties experienced by the fledgling democracy, and destabilization became the main goal of Soviet policy in Lithuania.

WESTERN POWERS
BETWEEN GORBACHEV AND LITHUANIA

Despite the blockade, destructive in economic and destabilizing in political terms, the struggle between Moscow and Vilnius did not degenerate into violence. Three reasons seem to account for the Kremlin's uncharacteristic restraint. First, the Lithuanians were committed to peaceful, parliamentary tactics and did not resist the Red Army by any force of arms. Their two-year drive for independence did not demand a single civilian or military casualty. Second, there had been an enormous public outcry in the Soviet Union against the earlier deadly use of force and poison gas in Azerbaijan and Georgia. Finally, Gorbachev's wrath and personal anger at the Lithuanians was mitigated by his need for good relations with the West, which would be threatened if Moscow used force for settling this unprecedented dispute. The world later learned that, in December 1989, Gorbachev had even pledged to President Bush in Malta that he would not use force in the Baltic republics; in exchange, he obtained Bush's promise not to create "big problems" for Gorbachev on the question of Baltic independence.[23]

Western powers were known for their support of the perestroika reformer who allowed the unification of Germany. Lithuania's aspiration to assert its independence the way Eastern Europeans had caught the Western leaders in a bind. The first Western nation to react to Lithuania's declaration of independence was the United States. On March 11, possibly hours before Gorbachev publicly decried the Lithuanian decision as "alarming," the White House issued a statement urging Moscow "to respect the will of the citizens of Lithuania."[24] President Bush urged the Soviets to negotiate: "We have consistently supported the Baltic people's inalienable right to self-determination and we call upon the Soviet government to address its concerns and interests through immediate constructive negotiations with the government of Lithuania. We hope that all parties will continue to avoid any initiation or encouragement of violence." The United States refused to extend formal recognition of Lithuania's restored statehood or of the newly formed government, however. A spokesperson for the Department of State rationalized that recognition of independent statehood was not even necessary because the United States had "recognized the independent state of Lithuania already in 1922" and had never withdrawn that recognition. The question therefore was not of recognition but of establishing diplomatic relations. Diplomatic relations with any country, the department's spokesperson explained, can be established only if "a government is in effective control of its territory and capable of entering into and fulfilling international obligations. When we are satisfied that the Lithuanian government can meet these requirements, we will establish formal diplomatic relations."

This verbal support was much less than the Lithuanians expected. Rumor had it that the State Department had a stronger statement prepared but that the White House had toned it down for fear of hurting Gorbachev, on whom alone the Bush administration now relied for reform of Soviet domestic and international relations. Nevertheless, as lukewarm as the U.S. statement was, it reaffirmed the right of self-determination, reminded everyone of the U.S. policy of nonrecognition of Baltic annexation, and preached the virtue of nonviolence, a decisively important factor in the political change in Eastern Europe. There is little reason to doubt that the U.S. policy at the time helped to prod the Kremlin into a war of telegrams and economic pressure instead of military action.

Western Europeans generally followed the lead of the United States. The newly freed East European nations demonstrated the most empathy for Lithuania's situation. The Polish government, after a long cabinet meeting, issued a statement supporting "self-determination of nations, including self-determination leading to separate statehood," and stressed that the "Poles are interested in good relations with the nation [state] of Lithuania."[25] Solidarity leader Lech Wałesa sent Landsbergis a telegram expressing "my delight that Lithuanian independence has been restored." These statements by the erstwhile partner and one-time antagonist country were very gratifying to the Lithuanians, especially because they indicated much greater support for independence than was shown by groups of Lithuania's Polish minority, large segments of which in 1990 had sided with the Russian anti-independence Yedinstvo organization.

No nation would recognize Lithuania's restored statehood, however. For the large and strong powers, Lithuania's decision was inconvenient since it disturbed their presumably promising future relations with Gorbachev. The smaller powers simply did not dare or, like the East Europeans or West Germany, had too much at risk because of the remaining Soviet troops on their territory.

While denying recognition to Lithuania, Western powers continued nonetheless to warn the Soviets against the use of force or intimidation. On March 22, 1990, after the Soviets had brought additional troops into Lithuania and raised fears of a military crackdown, President Bush appealed to Gorbachev to refrain from using force in order to avoid "a serious setback" in U.S.-Soviet relations.[26] Three weeks later, on April 14,

Bush and Prime Minister Margaret Thatcher of Great Britain, meeting in Bermuda, again urged Gorbachev to negotiate with the Lithuanians instead of erecting an economic blockade.[27] After the Soviets cut off gas and oil pipelines, however, the strongest action Bush took was to consult with the visiting President François Mitterrand of France and call Chancellor Helmut Kohl of West Germany.[28] On April 20 the White House politely characterized Gorbachev's economic crackdown as "another unfortunate step."[29] On the other side of the Atlantic, in Dublin, on April 21 foreign ministers of the European Community echoed the U.S. president, expressing "serious concern" with the embargo. Two days later, the White House publicly threatened to curtail promised financial investment and trade assistance to the Soviet Union. Yet again no action was taken. This time the White House feared for the summit meeting with Gorbachev scheduled for May 30 in Washington.[30]

President Bush's action conformed to the views of some influential public figures and to public opinion in the United States generally. The American Committee on U.S.-Soviet Relations, an important public policy group, supported by former defense secretary Robert McNamara and the industrialist Armand Hammer, labeled Lithuanian independence a "parochial" interest and strongly endorsed the president's "policy of moderation" aimed at bolstering Gorbachev's position in the Soviet Union. In an NBC News–*Wall Street Journal* poll taken in April 1990, 61 percent of respondents said that if they had to choose between friendly ties with Gorbachev or support for Lithuania, they would pick the Soviet president. The U.S. Congress generally acquiesced to the administration, and many feared that the Lithuanian "emotion and nationalist fervor" would spread elsewhere and undermine the Soviet Union and Gorbachev's reforms. A U.S. journalist mused at how unusual it was that U.S. opinion sided with the Soviets against an underdog. Indeed, although several commentators and newspapers supported U.S. recognition of the Lithuanian independence declaration, on April 21 an editorial of the *New York Times* demanded that Bush "lean on the Lithuanians." The president was soon to oblige.

Instead of risking the success of the far-sighted Soviet leader and his radical reforms, Western powers decided to downplay the Lithuanian attempt for freedom. President Bush himself stayed in the background but asked France's Mitterrand and Germany's Kohl to approach Lithuania's President Landsbergis. In a letter dated April 26, 1990, they proposed "immediate" discussions between Lithuania and the Soviet Union to unravel "a complex situation" created by many interwoven "political, legal and economic ties."[31] To make such discussions easier, the two West European leaders suggested, Lithuania should "temporarily delay the results of your parliament's decisions." This letter, one commentator insisted, did "not implicate any demands to renounce Lithuanian independence."[32]

While the Lithuanian parliament began to debate the issue, Prime Minister Prunskienė made a tour of Western capitals to appraise the situation. She saw, among others, Mahoney, Bush, Thatcher, Mitterrand, and Kohl, but she was always received as a merely private person. The White House subjected her to the indignity of walking through the White House tourist entrance, where she had to show her Soviet passport and have her purse rifled through.[33] In Europe, Prunskienė received the coldest shoulder from Mitterrand, who, like Bush, was anxious not to offend Gorbachev. In Washington, responding to the president's prodding to negotiate with Moscow, Prunskienė asked for international guarantees recognizing Lithuanian sovereignty, government, and borders if Lithuania suspended laws adopted for the implementation of the declaration of independence. She also suggested a mediator's role for President Bush. In a hastily summoned press conference, however, the president disavowed any "constructive role" in mediation and lavished praise on Gorbachev. Bush saluted "the man for what he has done [in relations with the West]."[34] In the forty-five-minute conference, he advised Prunskienė that the Lithuanians should "talk, talk, talk" to the Soviets.

The Lithuanian prime minister was much more sympathetically received by the U.S. Congress, which had passed a nonbinding resolution suggesting the president deny the Soviets trade concessions for their oppressive treatment of Lithuania.[35] In Europe, Thatcher urged compromise; Mitterrand and Kohl, like Bush, refused the role of mediator. Nonetheless, it turned out that the United States had secretly been an active intermediary. First of all, the idea of "suspension" of the declaration of independence was suggested by U.S. officials after the State Department had checked with Gorbachev to see whether its acceptance by the Lithuanians would lead to negotiations. After receiving a positive reply, Secretary of State Jim Baker informed Landsbergis of the option. The Lithuanian president was gratified by the prospect of a possible break in the stalemate but made clear that he would consider only a "temporary" suspension.[36]

Finally, the uncompromising Landsbergis gave in to Prime Minister Prunskienė's more flexible attitude toward Moscow. On May 17 she went to see Gorbachev and reached an accommodation that would ostensibly lead to further negotiations and the lifting of the blockade. Moscow also endorsed the initiative of European leaders because it was interested in ending the internationally embarrassing and economically damaging blockade without losing prestige but without committing itself to Lithuanian independence. For Vilnius, the demanded price was very high. It took two months to work out a formula for the moratorium that was both acceptable to Moscow and agreeable to the parliamentary majority in Lithuania.

Prunskienė saw Lithuania's chances as heavily determined by Gorbachev and the West. She remembered Chancellor Kohl telling her that even West Germany, which, he said, very likely was not weaker than Lithuania, could not get all it wanted from the Soviets. He advised her not to ask for complete compliance with Lithuania's demands, but to be willing to negotiate. Kohl, however, was sure that Lithuania would eventually get 90 percent of its demands met.[37]

Landsbergis's views were rather opposite from Prunskienė's. As a non-Communist he did not feel deference to Gorbachev; nor was he charmed by Gorbachev's personality. Instead of accepting Western views on how Lithuania should behave, he berated and angered Bush and the West by comparing their policies to those of Arthur Neville Chamberlain and Munich, when he had hoped to appease Hitler by acquiescing to his claims on Czechoslovakia. Boris Yeltsin was shunned not only by President Bush and his administration but also by Brazauskas, Prunskienė, and other Lithuanian Communist leaders. Landsbergis, however, consulted with Yeltsin and knew that Russia would soon follow the Baltic states in declaring its sovereignty, which it did on June 8. On a May 30 visit to President Vaclav Havel of Czechoslovakia, Landsbergis said he believed the Soviet Union would disintegrate:

> If the processes there are peaceful, as we have seen in Lithuania, Latvia and Estonia, then in place of the USSR there could arise a free association of free states and then, the question of whether the central monopolies and the all-encompassing military-industrial complex will be necessary, the states themselves will decide this. I'm sure that then the old Soviet Union will not be needed by anyone.[38]

This prediction became a reality a year and a half later. In the early summer of 1990, however, it split Lithuanian opinion and the parliament. Most of the press supported Prunskienė's and Brazauskas's gradualistic approach. The parliamentary majority, however, endorsed Landsbergis and the determined view that "time was on our side."

Moscow endorsed the initiative of European leaders at the end of April,[39] but it took the Lithuanian parliament until June 29, 1990, to declare "a moratorium of 100 days" from the start of negotiations "on the Re-establishment of an Independent state of Lithuania."[40] This meant that Lithuania agreed to suspend the legal actions taken after March 11, as Moscow had desired, although only for a "temporary" period of time. If negotiations were broken off, the parliament said, the moratorium would lose force.

The Kremlin responded eagerly and produced immediate economic results. A day after the passage of the moratorium resolution, central authorities resumed shipments of oil, and shortly afterward, they gradually lifted the blockade. The Soviets did not restore all economic ties with Lithuania, however; nor did negotiations begin. Prunskienė and her political allies accused Landsbergis of spoiling the possibility of accommodation. As for Gorbachev, he had just come back from a triumphant trip to Canada and the United States where he had made passionate speeches denouncing Lithuania. More important, he faced a crucial meeting of the Communist party Congress coming up in July. A schism between the reformers and the conservatives threatened to emerge at that event. Although the expected split did not occur, the disagreements helped eventually to push Gorbachev in a conservative direction and to harden his position on economic reform generally as well as on Lithuania specifically.

The Soviet president appointed a commission to negotiate with Vilnius on July 9. It was headed by Prime Minister Nikolai Ryzhkov. The Lithuanian parliament chose Landsbergis rather than Prunskienė as chairman of its delegation and specified that first a protocol "on the commencement and conditions of negotiations" be signed by both delegations before the negotiations began.[41] The parliament's action indicated that the president no longer fully trusted the prime minister. Agreement on the newly required protocol, furthermore, dragged out the preparations with Moscow until August 7.

Two long consultative sessions of the Ryzhkov-Landsbergis groups were held on October 2 and 20, 1990, but they did not lead to official negotiations. Such negotiations, indeed, never started. Instead, on November 10 Prime Minister Ryzhkov and Gosplan chairman Maslyukov told Prunskienė and the prime ministers of Estonia and Latvia that unless the Baltic republics retained union republic status and refrained from independent economic reforms, the Soviet Union would consider severing all economic relations with them.[42] Upset as the Balts were by this threat of a new economic blockade, they were even more perturbed by the threats of the conservative Soyuz faction. Led by Colonel Viktor Alksnis, this angry group of Congress deputies said that the democratically elected Baltic governments should be removed by force and that all laws passed by these governments should be rescinded.[43] If Gorbachev would not do so, Alksnis said, his own position would be in question. The Lithuanians recognized that their hopes of negotiations for independence had turned to ashes. Even more, they now suspected a real danger to the very survival of their independent government.

Through his own channels Landsbergis learned that the Kremlin was contemplating military action against Lithuania.[44] On November 24, 1990, he warned the population in a TV and radio speech and suggested that Gorbachev had become an ally of the reactionaries. In a clever move, he said, Gorbachev had decided to support the United States and other

Western nations against Iraq and expected to receive for it the West's acquiescence for Moscow's use of military violence against the Baltic states. Preparations for such action, according to the Lithuanian president, had already begun.

At the same time, Deputy Prime Minister Romualdas Ozolas declared that "the time for diplomatic games" was "over"; in case of suppression, "armed resistance remains the most extreme means of self-defense."[45] There would be no repetition of the events of 1940, Ozolas said, so that "my children will not be able to accuse me that nobody shot back, as in 1940." Lithuania's government disowned this statement, reiterating its commitment to nonviolent and passive resistance and feverishly beginning to marshal its diplomatic forces against the expected Soviet crackdown.

Moscow's threats gained additional credibility against the background of Gorbachev's open shift toward reaction beginning in October 1991 in alliance with the Interior Ministry, the KGB, the army, and the Communist party apparatus. A number of events in Moscow reinforced the perception of a foreboding future. On November 27 Defense Minister Dmitri Yazov, in Gorbachev's name, warned against the "attacks" on the armed forces. He declared that insults would not be tolerated and that the honor of Soviet soldiers and the army would be protected by "all necessary means provided for in the valid constitution, the laws of the USSR, and those adopted by the president of the USSR."[46] Three days later, on November 30, the Politburo of the Communist party of the USSR spoke of the "antidemocratic actions and violations of human rights in the Lithuanian SSR."[47] In Moscow, the Communist and KGB hardliner Boris Pugo replaced the relatively liberal Vladimir Bakatin as minister of the interior; censorship was reestablished over TV and radio; and on December 20 Foreign Minister Shevardnadze warned of an impending dictatorship and resigned.[48] Two days later, delegates to the Congress from the Army Society of the Baltic States and delegates from Kaliningrad announced in Riga that they were ready to use any means for "the defense of the integrity of the USSR" and the protection of the "life, honor, and rights" of the Soviet military in the Baltic and Kaliningrad regions.[49]

The Baltic leaders declared that their countries would defend themselves against force.[50] To stress unity and raise alarm, all three Baltic parliaments, on December 1, held a joint session in Vilnius, issuing "an appeal to the parliaments of the countries of the world." Prunskienė traveled to Australia and Japan seeking support. Landsbergis went to Canada, the United States, and Norway. In Washington he saw President Bush. On December 10 the White House said the United States "hoped the Soviet government would work constructively with Baltic leaders, without resorting to threats, intimidation, or the use of force."[51] In the meantime, from Moscow came another ominous message: Deputy Prime

Minister Doguzhyev curtly told the Lithuanian government that a consultative meeting on negotiations scheduled for December 14 could not take place.[52] At Christmas, the Soviet post office stopped Lithuanian newspaper and mail delivery to the West.

Deeply disturbed by the increasing signs of a gathering storm, Lithuania's parliament on December 28 indicated its willingness to compromise and removed both conditions for negotiations, namely, the insistence on the initial protocol stating the purpose of negotiations and the 100-day moratorium.[53] The Soviets did not respond. Instead, on January 7, 1991, the Kremlin sent additional troops to Lithuania.[54] According to the Soviet Ministry of Defense, in 1990 only 12.5 percent of draft-age youth had reported for service in the republic and the Soviet troops were brought in to apprehend draft-dodgers. At the same time, troops were dispatched to Latvia, Estonia, Georgia, Moldavia, and western Ukraine. It soon became clear, however, that the military forces were sent to Lithuania not to search for recruits but to overthrow the Lithuanian government and to disperse the parliament.[55]

The military's arrival coincided with the first serious crisis in the Lithuanian government. As part of the economic reforms agreed upon among the Baltic republics, on January 7 Prunskienė's government raised the retail prices for food products.[56] The next day, even before she left for Moscow to discuss the increased Soviet military presence with Gorbachev, crowds were gathering in the parliament square to protest the price increases. The move was seized upon by Yedinstvo to demand the government's resignation. Yedinstvo's demonstrators physically forced their way into the parliament building and had to be repelled by a water cannon. The Lithuanian Freedom League of Antanas Terleckas also demonstrated the same day against the price increases, demanding Prunskienė's resignation. The league withdrew, however, after realizing that the real purpose of the Russian crowds was to take over the parliament building. Landsbergis immediately reacted to the crowd's demands for rescinding the increases, which the parliament did within hours. It also changed Article 95 of the temporary basic law to allow a dismissal of government by a simple majority, and immediately ousted Prunskienė.[57] Her opponents in the parliamentary Right, for months searching for reasons for her removal, had won the day. Prunskienė returned from Moscow to face her dismissal. She resigned without consulting her cabinet and was replaced by another economist, Albertas Šimėnas.

Outside the parliament, the Soviet military seized the railroad station and stopped train service; Russian workers struck at the airport, stopping civil transport but not the arrival from Moscow of Deputy Defense Minister Vladyslav Achalov and his load of paratroopers. The pro-Moscow Communist party also organized strikes in some of the factories in Vilnius.

Yedinstvo began another demonstration, but it now faced a large crowd of Lithuanians who had come to defend the parliament. In Moscow, Gorbachev met with the pro-Moscow Lithuanian Communist party and other leaders who demanded that he introduce presidential rule. On January 10, Gorbachev presented the Lithuanian parliament with an ultimatum "immediately to restore the validity of the USSR and Lithuanian SSR constitutions."[58] This demand was almost a year old, but it now was embellished by the charge that the parliament "under the slogans of democracy is pursuing a policy whose goal is to restore a bourgeois system and order against the interests of the people."

In the meantime, on January 11, the first blood was spilled as Soviet troops began to take over individual buildings in Vilnius, first the multistory press building, which houses the editorial offices and publishing presses, then the Police Academy. The buildings were occupied on grounds that they belonged to the pro-Moscow Communist party. The parliament building itself was now barricaded and guarded by thousands of unarmed civilians called to defend the legislature by Landsbergis. A mysterious National Salvation Committee made its first appearance that same day, claiming that it had assumed responsibility for the fate of the Lithuanian people.[59] The group never revealed its membership, however. Its spokesman was Juozas Jermalavičius, formerly a professor and propagandist of atheism and now a leader of the pro-Moscow Communist party.

The night of January 12–13, the National Salvation Committee claimed to have seized power in Lithuania. At the same time, Soviet tanks and paratroopers were storming the television transmission tower. The tanks drove through crowds of unarmed civilians who had gathered to guard the tower. Thirteen were killed that night by tanks or paratrooper fire and two additional casualties died of wounds later. Altogether, fifteen people were killed and over 500 were wounded. The new prime minister, Albertas Šimėnas, mysteriously disappeared. Fearing he had been kidnapped, the parliament replaced him with still another economist, Gediminas Vagnorius, a leader of the parliamentary Right.[60]

Moscow had timed the military crackdown to coincide with the start of the Western coalition's war against Iraq, apparently hoping that neither Western governments nor the media would shift attention from Saddam Hussein to tiny Lithuania. They were wrong. The shooting of innocents by black berets competed with the headlines on the Gulf War on the pages of newspapers in the United States and other Western countries. Democracies were appalled to discover that Gorbachev, a Nobel Peace Prize winner, would unleash the military and use tear gas, rifles, and tanks against unarmed people. There was also a loud protest registered in the Soviet Union itself as well as in Eastern Europe. Tens and hundreds of

Soviet troops take over buildings in Vilnius, January 11, 1991. (Photo by M. Baranauskas. Used by permission.)

Crowds defiantly sing the national anthem, January 11, 1991. (Photo by M. Baranauskas. Used by permission.)

Angry citizens throng the streets of the capital, protesting the Soviet aggression, January 13, 1991. (Photo by M. Baranauskas. Used by permission.)

thousands held sympathy demonstrations in Leningrad, Moscow, Lviv, Riga, Tbilisi, Kuzbass, and other cities.

The attack in Lithuania was taken by democratic movements in Russia as a sign of the coming dictatorship predicted by Eduard Shevardnadze. Stanislav Shatalin, once Gorbachev's economic adviser and author of the 500-day conversion plan to a free-market economy, exclaimed that the attack in Vilnius signaled not merely a warning but "a proclamation of dictatorship."[61] Russian leaders feared that the Russian Federation, now run by Yeltsin's democrats, would be the next victim. The Lithuanian tragedy inspired the democrats to organize a defense of the freedoms already achieved. Additional demonstrations in Moscow followed shortly afterward. Demonstration leaders demanded Gorbachev's resignation. On January 13, immediately after learning of the murders in Vilnius, Boris Yeltsin, chairman of the parliament of the Russian Federation and Gorbachev's antagonist, flew to Tallinn (he was prevented from landing in Vilnius by the pro-Moscow Salvation Committee). There, he signed a declaration, together with Baltic leaders, confirming mutual recognition of their republics' "state sovereignty." The four leaders also denounced as illegal actions by "parallel structures which pretend to have authorization to rule" and pledged mutual aid.[62] They invited governments around the world to condemn "the actions by armed force against the autonomy of peaceful inhabitants of the Baltic states as a threat to the democracy and stability of the Soviet Union and the international community." Demonstrations in front of Soviet embassies, attended by thousands, took place in the newly liberated Warsaw, Prague, and Sophia.

The West was shocked. It found Soviet reprisal with tanks, tear gas, and rifle fire repulsive and unacceptable on moral and philosophical grounds. In Washington, President Bush said on January 13 that he found "the turn of events deeply disturbing" and asked the Soviets to withdraw troops. On January 14, Chancellor Kohl of Germany "deplored" the deaths and injuries and sent a confidential message to Gorbachev. The Bundestag passed a resolution similar to one passed by the U.S. Senate, asking the Soviet president to refrain from using force and to withdraw the military from Lithuania.[63] Similar reactions came from most Western governments from Sweden to Australia. An exception was Finland, which, under President Mauno Koivisto, refused to condemn the Soviet repression. Iceland's foreign minister, J. Baldwin-Hannibalsson, visited Lithuania on January 20 and in a press conference at the parliament building declared "solidarity with small nations."[64] On February 12, Iceland informed the Lithuanians that its recognition of the Lithuanian state of 1922 was still valid and that it intended to restore diplomatic relations with Lithuania.[65] Not long afterward, Danish and Lithuanian foreign ministers signed an agreement of a similar nature.

The European Parliament temporarily blocked a $1 billion European Community food aid package to the Soviet Union on January 22;[66] Japan withheld the delivery of $100 million in food supplies. The U.S. Congress, which had earlier rejected sending humanitarian aid to the Baltic countries, sent $5 million in medical supplies to the Baltic. Although Mitterrand of France refused Landsbergis's request to raise the Baltic question in the Security Council of the United Nations, he offered condolences, support for Lithuania's goals, and hope that "the trial of the Baltic states [was] ending."[67] The morning after the bloody night in Vilnius, U.S. secretary of state James Baker said, "The use of force by the Soviet government in the Baltics fundamentally and tragically contradicts the basic principles of perestroika, glasnost and democratization."[68] Baker, in Turkey at the time because of the war against Iraq, felt that U.S.-Soviet relations were in danger because "partnership is impossible in the absence of shared values."

Western reaction stopped further bloodshed in Lithuania. The expected attack on the parliament never materialized, although sporadic violence

Folk art and candles commemorate the victims killed at the television tower, January 14, 1991. (Photo by M. Baranauskas. Used by permission.)

continued for weeks. In his State of the Union address January 29, President Bush revealed that the Soviets had promised to withdraw troops and to reopen the dialogue with the Baltic republics.

The democratic media in Vilnius would not be silenced. Although, the day after the massacre, troops had taken over radio and TV studios and newspaper warehouses in the city, thus gaining control of the mass media and access to central newsprint supplies, soon makeshift television transmitters and printing presses were in operation.

The damage to Gorbachev's reputation, however, and to the credibility of his official reform, was irreparable. Many intellectuals, including some Nobel Prize winners such as Czeslaw Milosz and Josef Brodsky, raised questions or even suggested that Gorbachev's prize be revoked. The Norwegians, by public appeal to Norwegian society, collected about half a million dollars for a peace prize for Landsbergis instead. Gorbachev, the shining hero of historic reforms, now was looked upon with anger, disappointment, and sadness. His reputation was further deflated by his response to the killings in Vilnius. No one assumed responsibility for the military's actions. Both Dmitri Yazov, the defense minister, and Boris Pugo, the minister of the interior, said they did not order the troops to shoot and falsely accused the unarmed civilians of provocation. According to Pugo, the troops were provoked by Lithuanian behavior. Lithuanians flashed "real bayonets" at supporters of the National Committee of Salvation, he said.[69] Gorbachev claimed that he learned of the massacre only the next morning; Landsbergis, however, had called him immediately after the attack began. Although the president did not accept responsibility for the attack, documents show that he was personally involved in a plan to overthrow Lithuania's government.

Gorbachev's deputy first secretary of the Communist party, V. Ivashko, approved plans to arrest leaders of Lithuania's "nationalist" groups and recommended that military formations be put at the disposal of the pro-Moscow Communist party led by First Secretary Mykolas Burokevičius.[70] After the massacre, Burokevičius confirmed that "strikes, activities of the Soviet army, attempts to introduce into Lithuania direct presidential rule were all organized and planned in advance."[71] Creation of salvation committees to save Communist rule in the Soviet Union had been proposed on November 1 by the Russian Federation's Communist party leader, Polotskov. In Lithuania, the National Salvation Committee was to implement the Communist party's goal of achieving direct presidential rule as the only means of preserving the Communist system and keeping Lithuania in the empire. Leaders of the pro-Moscow Lithuanian Communist party consulted with Gorbachev on the details of taking over television and the press, including their need for a "few" soldiers for the operation.[72] In the end, a commission of independent military experts from the Soviet national military organization "Shchit" (Shield), concluded,

> A coup d'état was attempted in Lithuania with the help of the army, the internal forces of the Interior Ministry, and the KGB of the Soviet Union for the purpose of restoring political rule of the Communist party of the Soviet Union [to be exercised] by its constituent part, the Lithuanian Communist party. The president of the USSR had to know about the planned concomitant actions of the Soviet army, the internal forces of the Ministry of the Interior, and the KGB. Such actions could not be taken without his personal permission.[73]

Instead of acknowledging his responsibility, Gorbachev blamed the local military commander for choosing the wrong type of response "to requests for protection by workers and intellectuals" of Lithuania.[74] He offered condolences to the relatives of those murdered.

The plan for the coup d'état was reminiscent of Stalinist tactics in Eastern Europe, such as the repression of Czechoslovakia in 1968. It brought little more than grief and further loss of prestige for Gorbachev at home

Caricature of Gorbachev, Nobel laureate, in light of
the January bloodshed. (Photo by M. Baranauskas.
Used by permission.)

and abroad, however, while threatening normal relations with the West.
In contrast, Lithuania emerged from the ordeal with greater unity of purpose and determination than before. Moreover, the West finally became
aware that Baltic independence was an international problem and not just
an internal domestic affair of the Soviet Union.

REAFFIRMATION OF THE
GOALS OF INDEPENDENCE AND DEMOCRACY

After the attempted coup, the parliament embarked on drafting legislation on economic reform. The republic's leadership also searched for a response to the referendum planned by Gorbachev on the question of a new
union treaty. It was the policy of the Lithuanian government not to sign
this treaty or participate in Moscow's referendum. Instead, on January 16

Funeral for the fourteen Lithuanians killed by
Soviet troops on January 13, 1991. (Photo by R.
Urbakavičius. Used by permission.)

the parliament scheduled a poll for February 9 of all eligible voters on the
question of Lithuanian independence. The question to be asked in the
poll was, "Do you favor [the idea] that the Lithuanian state should be an
independent democratic republic?" In this way, the Lithuanian leadership
sought to demonstrate popular support for its position and neutralize
proposals for "flexible" ties with the Soviet Union.

The poll's results overwhelmed even the independence optimists. Of
the total of 2,652,738 voters in Lithuania, 2,247,810, or 84.7 percent, cast
their ballots. Of those, 90.5 percent voted yes, supporting the proposition
of independence and democracy.[75] President Gorbachev denounced the
vote even before it took place and held his own all-union referendum on
March 17 on the territorial integrity of the USSR. According to a pro-
Moscow Communist party spokesman, 666,222 voters participated in
Lithuania, of whom 98 percent voted in favor of Gorbachev's proposal to
keep the union.[76]

This battle of referenda did not decide the big issues, such as the start of negotiations between Vilnius and Moscow. Eight days before the independence poll, on February 1, Gorbachev announced the membership of a new negotiating team. The meeting between the Russians and the Lithuanians did not take place until April 4, however. Both sides were satisfied with the outcome of the discussion, which covered mostly the principles, goals, and procedures for future work. A compromise formula characterized the goal of negotiations as the "regulation of relations between the republic of Lithuania and the USSR"; this language avoided the term "independence" and avoided calling Lithuania the "Soviet Socialist Republic of Lithuania."[77] The Soviets, however, refused to include in the protocol a statement denouncing the use of force for settling disputes.

Despite the new opening for consultations, the situation in Lithuania remained very tense. Pskov division paratroopers were replaced by other troops. Contrary to Gorbachev's assurances, the military continued taking over buildings and property that allegedly belonged to the pro-Moscow Communist party or paramilitary organizations. In April Soviet paratroopers seized twelve buildings, two airports, an airplane factory, schools, and a hotel, stripping them of equipment.[78] It seemed that virtually in every district and city the military was securing a base of operations for the pro-Moscow Communist party. The small country, furthermore, was terrorized by OMON troops, the notorious Soviet black berets.

OMON, or special police units, were established in Leningrad in 1987 and were used in the January 1991 coup attempts against the Lithuanian and Latvian governments and earlier in Ukraine, Caucasus, and Russia.[79] Their commander was General Major Boris Gromov, former commander of Soviet forces in Afghanistan and now deputy to Minister of the Interior Boris Pugo. OMON troops helped the military to hunt draft resisters and seize commercial or other facilities, such as banks or the Vilnius center of telecommunications, which was taken in July. It also harassed, arrested, and even killed guards and officials of the Lithuanian Defense Department and intimidated the parliament by blocking access to its building. Their most provocative attack gained international attention after six Lithuanian customs officials were killed and one left for dead at the Medininkai customs office on the Byelorussian border in Lithuania.[80] The sneak attack occurred in the middle of the night. Customs officials and guards were all laid on the floor and killed execution style, shot in the head with silencing guns. TASS and Gorbachev, at a joint press conference with Bush, had characterized the killings as the regrettable result of an armed border incident similar to those between Armenia and Azerbaijan.[81] The suggestion was self-serving and misleading: There never was violence between ethnic groups in Lithuania or on its borders. Gorbachev expressed regrets and condolences, saying that KGB chief Kryuchkov had offered Lithuanian president Landsbergis cooperation in finding the criminals. Kryuchkov, however, had never approached Landsbergis.[82] Later investigation pointed to an OMON unit from Riga as perpetrating the massacre—though local OMON leaders and authorities of the Interior Ministry in Moscow denied any responsibility.

Intimidation and terrorism perpetrated by OMON and military troops characterized Moscow's relations with Lithuania throughout 1991 until the Moscow putsch on August 19. The struggle between conservatives and democrats in the Soviet Union had sharply intensified, and by spring 1991 Gorbachev, even if he wanted to, was most likely no longer capable of peacefully resolving the issue of Lithuanian independence. The time for negotiations had passed, to the extent they were ever really possible.

Instead, Lithuania broke free in the historically most common way: The great power that had dominated was no longer able or willing to exert control. With republics from all sides clamoring for more freedom, Gorbachev called for a meeting to decide on a new union treaty that would fundamentally shift power to the republics and away from the center. The meeting never took place. On August 19 the coalition of KGB, Interior Ministry, military, and party apparatus forces staged a coup d'état. Gorbachev was detained in the Crimea.

At the same time, General Fyodor Kuzmin, the commander of the Baltic military district, announced that he was taking control of Lithuania, Latvia, and Estonia and threatened to arrest those who disobeyed his orders. The three Baltic leaders, however, did not give way. In Lithuania, Landsbergis denounced the coup, the parliament was called into special session,[83] and Prime Minister Vagnorius issued a proclamation stating that the government would continue in office unless deposed by force. Furthermore, Baltic governments called for a general strike in support of Boris Yeltsin, who was dramatically defending the Russian parliament in Moscow. In Lithuania, crowds of civilians ringed the parliament building as on January 13. Soviet troops took over TV facilities in Kaunas, a radio station in Sitkūnai, near Kaunas, and TV and radio facilities in the industrial city of Šiauliai and also in Juragiai, Marijampolė, Alytus, Panevėžys, and Viešintos. In Vilnius the putschists announced that they would censor the press and decide what newspapers would be allowed to continue.

Not all military officers were, however, willing subordinates of General Kuzmin. A number of local commanders said they would not move without direct orders from Moscow. Moscow's conspirators were also incompetent organizers. They failed, among other matters, to take control of telecommunications. This gave Yeltsin an opportunity to call Landsbergis. At 11:30 a.m. August 19, Yeltsin informed him of planned work stoppages and secured Baltic cooperation against the putschists.[84] On August 20, the Lithuanian parliament urged Soviet troops to oppose the coup.[85]

Estonia and Latvia gave up a policy of gradual transition and declared full independence on August 20 and 21, respectively. Yeltsin and Landsbergis immediately extended recognition to the two republics. Furthermore, on August 20 Lithuania's parliament ratified a treaty with the Russian Federation that had been signed by Yeltsin and Landsbergis in Moscow at the end of July.[86] The treaty unequivocally recognized Lithuania's independence.

The Soviet military units were back in their barracks by August 22. There were some Lithuanian casualties, but the Soviets had retreated. They returned the occupied TV and radio facilities and buildings taken even during the January 11–13, 1991, attacks. Symbolically, the statue of Lenin in the park adjacent to KGB headquarters was removed by a crane. The KGB surrendered the building. The parliament outlawed not only the KGB but also the pro-Moscow Communist party, which had helped Moscow's coup plotters. Mykolas Burokevičius, the party's first secretary, and his cohorts, however, were able to escape arrest under the protection of the Soviet military. The commander of OMON troops, Wladyslaw Makutinowicz, at first sought political asylum in the West for himself and his troops[87] but eventually left for Russia, fully armed.

What happened next was almost anticlimactic. Yeltsin accepted the empire's demise, first by recognizing Baltic independence and later that of the other republics. And Yeltsin was in control in Moscow. The Europeans who had vacillated on the Baltic question now resolved their doubts. They eagerly seized the opportunity to follow Yeltsin's example. Lithuania had already been recognized by Iceland. Denmark and Norway followed suit on August 23.[88] The day Ukraine declared independence, August 24, the enemy of Baltic freedom Marshall Sergei Akhromeyev committed suicide in Moscow. The next day, Germany, Italy, Austria, Japan, France, and others declared their intention to recognize the Baltic states, and on August 27 the nations of the European Community followed suit. Sweden was the first actually to establish an embassy in Vilnius.

Canada recognized the new states on August 27, but President Bush, vacationing at Kennebunkport, still waited. He explained his tardiness by saying that the United States had "special responsibilities" not to make "hasty" decisions.[89] He said he would "like to see a little bit more, a few more cards on the table before we take another step."

Bush's speech earlier in the Ukraine, in which he had identified nationalism with extremism and counseled the Ukrainians against independence, indicated his administration's disorientation. It was difficult for the president of the United States to accept a total breakup of the Soviet empire, which, despite the Cold War, was easier to deal with than several small new nations, some of which would possess nuclear arms. The president had hoped that Gorbachev would make the first move and either reassert Soviet control or admit defeat. Finally, on September 2, 1991, the United States became the thirty-seventh nation to accept not only the legal theory but also the political fact of Lithuania's separation from the Soviet Union.[90] The State Council of the Soviet Union finally closed the chapter on September 6.[91] The Lithuanians were not very happy with the laconic statement the State Council had issued, but the deed was done. The Soviets even promised to help Lithuania and the other Baltic states rejoin international organizations.

The three Baltic states were admitted to the United Nations on September 17. At the admission session, Lithuania's president said that Lithuania's choice of nonviolent tactics in the struggle for rights and justice had prevailed against violence and tanks.[92] Exit to freedom thus came through the collapse of the Soviet empire, a historically inescapable but difficult and often tragic process.

NOTES

1. Text in the *Wall Street Journal*, April 9, 1990.
2. *New York Times*, March 13, 1990, p. 1.
3. *Dallas Morning News*, March 14, 1990, p. 14.
4. *New York Times*, March 14, 1990, pp. 1ff.
5. Texts in *Tiesa*, March 17, 1990, p. 1.
6. Text in Supreme Council of the Republic of Lithuania, *The Road to Negotiations with the USSR* (Vilnius: Supreme Council of the Republic of Lithuania, 1990), pp. 24–25.
7. *Tiesa*, March 12, 1990, p. 1.
8. *Tiesa*, March 22, 1990, p. 1.
9. Texts in Supreme Council, *Road to Negotiations*, pp. 32–24.
10. *Documents Pertaining to Relations Between the Republic of Lithuania and the Union of Soviet Socialist Republics*. Translated and compiled by the Information Bureau of the Supreme Council of the Republic of Lithuania (Vilnius: Information Bureau of the Supreme Council of the Republic of Lithuania, 1990), p. 32. Afterward cited as *Documents*. Gorbachev's and Landsbergis's texts.
11. *Documents*, pp. 37–38.
12. Michael R. Beschloss and Strobe Talbott, *At the Highest Levels: The Inside Story of the End of the Cold War* (Boston: Little, Brown, 1993), p. 202. This book, based on interviews with involved policy makers, contains many details relating to Lithuania from 1989 to 1991. It may be noted that private revelations contained in this volume do not detract in any way from the analysis of events and policies presented in this chapter.
13. Ibid., pp. 40–41.
14. *Lietuvos Respublikos Aukščiausios Tarybos, Lietuvos Respublikos Aukščiausios Tarybos Prezidiumo, Lietuvos Respublikos Vyriausybės Svarbiausių Dokumentų Rinkinys* (Collection of the Most Important Documents Adopted by the Supreme

Council, Presidium of the Supreme Council, and the Government of the Lithuanian Republic), March 11–May 11, 1990 (Vilnius: Mintis, 1990), p. 85.

15. *Tiesa*, April 21, 1990, p. 1.

16. See, among others, *Chicago Tribune*, April 21, 1990.

17. See *Lietuvos rytas*, June 6, 1990, p. 1; July 25, 1990, p. 1; also *Tiesa*, May 18, 1990, p. 4; July 14, 1990, p. 3.

18. Cf. *Time*, April 30, 1990, pp. 44–45.

19. *New York Times*, April 22, 1990, p. 11.

20. *Tiesa*, May 12, 1990, p. 3.

21. Ibid.

22. For popularity rating figures and responses to the blockade, see *Lietuvos rytas*, June 27, 1990, pp. 1–2, and *Politika*, no. 10 (1990): 20–23.

23. Beschloss and Talbott, *At the Highest Levels*, p. 164.

24. *New York Times*, March 12, 1990, pp. 8ff.

25. *New York Times*, March 13, 1990, p. A6.

26. *New York Times*, March 23, 1990, p. 1.

27. *Tulsa World*, April 14, 1990, p. A5.

28. Associated Press, *Norman Transcript*, April 19, 1990, p. 3.

29. *New York Times*, April 21, 1990, p. 1.

30. American Committee on U.S.-Soviet Relations, *Policy Bulletin* (Spring 1990); "White House Notebook: Bush Succeeds in Hushing Lithuania," *National Journal*, May 12, 1990, p. 1176; also Rochelle L. Stanfield, "Lithuania's a Challenge to the West, Too," *National Journal*, May 5, 1990, p. 1094; *New York Times*, April 21, 1990, p. 15.

31. Text in Supreme Council, *Road to Negotiations*, pp. 50–51.

32. Ibid., p. 51.

33. *New York Times*, May 4, 1990, pp. 1ff.

34. Ibid., p. A7.

35. *Wall Street Journal*, May 4, 1990, p. A12.

36. Beschloss and Talbott, *At the Highest Levels*, p. 202.

37. Kazimiera Prunskienė, *Gintarinės ledi išpažintis* (Vilnius: Politika, 1991), p. 77.

38. Voice of America, June 1, 1990.

39. *New York Times*, April 29, 1990, pp. 1ff.

40. Supreme Council, *Road to Negotiations*, Document no. 49, pp. 72–73.

41. Ibid., Document no. 55, pp. 78–79.

42. See *Tiesa*, November 13, 1990, p. 1; *Lietuvos rytas*, November 16, 1990, p. 1.

43. *Lietuvos aidas*, November 22, 1990, p. 1.

44. Algirdas Kumža, "Vytautas Landsbergis," in *Jie valdo pasaulį*, ed. Algimantas Semaška (Vilnius: Politika, 1991), p. 66.

45. *Gimtasis kraštas*, November 22–28, 1990, pp. 1–2.

46. See text in Ernst Benz, "Der Blutsonntag in Vilnius," *Acta Baltica* 28 (1990): 289ff.

47. Ibid.

48. The text of Shevardnadze's speech appears in Edward Shevardnadze, *The Future Belongs to Freedom* (New York: The Free Press, 1991), pp. 223–226.

49. See note 46.

50. *Lietuvos aidas*, November 22, 1991, p. 1.

51. White House press release, December 10, 1990.

52. Lithuanian Information Center, Brooklyn, New York, press release.

53. *Lietuvos Respublikos Aukščiausios Tarybos nutarimas*, signed by Vytautas Landsbergis.

54. *Tiesa*, January 8, 1991, p. 5.

55. For a detailed eyewitness account of the events of January 7–14, see Alfred Erich Senn, "The Crisis in Lithuania, January 1991: A Visitor's Account," *AABS Newsletter* 15, no. 1 (March 1991): 1, 2, 4–12. Among the works that depict the massacre of "bloody Sunday," Beschloss and Talbott, *At the Highest Levels*, pp. 303–310, discusses the event and its policy implications.

56. *Tiesa*, January 8, 1991, pp. 1ff.

57. *Tiesa*, January 9, 1991, p. 7.

58. *Tiesa*, January 11, 1991, p. 1.

59. Quoted in *Tiesa*, January 26, 1991, p. 4.

60. Report of January 23, 1991, by the Lithuanian Health Ministry; also *Tiesa*, January 15, 1991, p. 1.

61. Quoted in *New York Times*, January 19, 1991, p. 3.

62. Text in *Lietuvos aidas*, January 15, 1991, p. 1.

63. *This Week in Germany*, January 18, 1991, p. 2.

64. Iceland's foreign minister, J. Baldwin-Hannibalsson, excerpts of press conference in *Lietuvos aidas*, January 22, 1991, p. 1.

65. *Lietuvos aidas*, February 13, 1991, p. 1.

66. *New York Times*, January 23, 1991, p. 1.

67. Text in *Lietuvos aidas*, February 8, 1991, p. 1.

68. Full text in *BATUN News* (Baltic Appeal to the United Nations), January 21, 1991, p. 9.

69. *New York Times*, January 16, 1991, p. 4.

70. *Nezavisimaya gazeta*, January 29, 1991; documents published in *Acta Baltica* (1990): 296–326.

71. See *Tiesa*, January 17, 1991, p. 4.

72. Former Lithuanian deputies in the federal Supreme Soviet describing what Gorbachev told them in a private meeting of January 21, 1991. See *Tiesa*, January 26, 1991, pp. 1–2.

73. "Zaklyuchenie nezavisimykh voennykh ekspertov obshchestvenoi organizatsii 'Shchit' na sobytiya v Vilnyuse 11–13 yanvarya 1991 goda," p. 15.

74. Associated Press, *Norman Transcript*, January 14, 1991, p. 1.

75. Results of the vote by district and city in *Lietuvos aidas*, February 14, 1991, p. 4.

76. Voice of America, March 19, 1991.

77. Release no. 189 of the Information Bureau of the Lithuanian parliament.

78. For details see "Baltic Chronology," in *BATUN News*, esp. April 1991, pp. 4–5.

79. Brief history of OMON in *Lietuvos aidas*, August 23, 1991, p. 2.

80. See *Lietuvos aidas*, August 2, 1991, p. 2, and other Lithuanian press of the time.

81. *Lietuvos aidas*, August 2, 1991, p. 1.

82. Ibid.

83. See *Lietuvos aidas,* August 19, 1991, pp. 1–2; August 20, 1991, p. 1; *Tiesa,* August 22, 1991, p. 3.

84. *Lietuvos aidas,* August 20, 1991, p. 1.

85. *New York Times,* August 22, 1991, p. 7.

86. *Lietuvos aidas,* August 20, 1991, p. 1.

87. *New York Times,* August 30, 1991, p. 6.

88. For the sequence of nations that recognized Lithuania's independence, see "The Soviet Coup: August 19–22, 1991," *BATUN News,* September 1991. See also *New York Times,* August 26, 1991, pp. 1ff.

89. *New York Times,* August 27, 1991, p. 1.

90. *New York Times,* September 2, 1991, p. 1.

91. See, e.g., *Tiesa,* September 7, 1991, p. 1.

92. United Nations, press release, September 17, 1991, p. 7.

SEVEN

New Beginnings:
The Politics of Transition

Lithuania had broken with the Soviet empire and embarked upon a new era as an independent nation. The rebel republic had to make the transition from communism to democracy and take its place in a reshaped geopolitical map with Russia as its neighbor. At the turn of 1989–1990 there was no model, precedent, or experience for the former Soviet bloc from which to draw lessons on shifting from totalitarianism to liberal democracy. At the same time, the transition to a new system did not take place in a vacuum but was based on the institutional heritage and political culture of the Soviet regime. In its initial stages, therefore, there were many parallels between the Baltic shift to democracy and a market economy and the experience of other Soviet republics.

POLITICS:
THE LITHUANIAN SYNDROME

In the hastily drawn provisional constitution adopted after the March 1991 declaration of independence, the Lithuanians followed the Soviet state structure by merging the legislative and executive branches of government. The legislature, which was still called the Supreme Soviet, was led by a chairman who had powers, however, superior to those of the prime minister and the cabinet. In Lithuania this arrangement very quickly developed into a dual government under Chairman Vytautas Landsbergis on the one hand and Prime Minister Kazimiera Prunskienė on the other. These leaders competed for supremacy, especially in the conduct of relations with Moscow. The legislature insisted on micromanaging government operations, as the constitution gave it the power to do, and it interfered with the government on a daily basis. The obvious difficulties of operating such a system were overcome in the Soviet regime by the hegemony of the Communist party. In the absence of dictatorial control, the structure of Soviet-era governance led to anarchy in policy making and government.

The fledgling state had also inherited the Soviet interpretation of the concept of a constitution. In the Soviet system, the constitution was a political instrument. Although it defined presumably uniform principles or rules, these could be easily changed according to the needs of daily politics. Although the Lithuanians now sought to establish the rule of law, they had little real experience of a lawful state and the law remained subjected to political expedience. The Left, or the former Communists, and the Right, the supporters of Landsbergis, accused each other of breaking the rule of law, but both treated the constitution in a cavalier fashion. For example, when on January 8, 1991, the Right majority finally decided to remove Prunskienė from the position of chair of the Council of Ministers, it found itself thwarted by a constitutional provision requiring a two-thirds majority for the action. Without blinking an eye, the majority changed Article 95 to require merely a 51 percent majority, and within an hour or so Prunskienė was voted out of office.[1]

This mentality did not change after the adoption of a permanent constitution in October 1992. A new parliamentary majority, dominated by the Democratic Labor party (Lietuvos Demokratinė Darbo Partija, or LDDP), considered that politically they needed two deputy speakers, but the constitution specified only one. The majority simply disregarded the constitutional provision and elected two deputies. Although the constitution provides for only one electoral commission for national elections, the parliament's Democratic Labor party authorized a special commission for the presidential election. Its chairman, furthermore, decreed that five days before the election day the media would have no right to publish any compromising information about competing presidential candidates.[2] He thus single-handedly overruled the constitution's provisions and the legislature's decisions on the freedom of the press without, most likely, thinking he was doing anything wrong, illegal, or undemocratic. Similarly, although the constitution assures the inviolability of private property, the new Council of Ministers formed by Brazauskas's party decreed that industrial enterprises surrender to the government one-quarter of all their hard currency earnings, just as in Soviet times.[3]

Another inherited characteristic that was not conducive to the development of democracy was the parliament's refusal to accept the majority's verdict. Thus, three months after the first competitive elections in Soviet Lithuania, a group of leftist deputies published an open letter deploring the "low" quality of the winners and demanding a new election.[4] After half a century of denunciation, demagoguery, and disdain for public accountability, the new political groups in parliament were no more equitable than the Communists had been. Inexperienced in democratic parliamentary procedures, the Lithuanians adopted rules on quorums and voting to engage in group abuse, dilatory tactics, and individual obstruction of due process. When the leftist Democratic Labor party was in the minority, for example, its deputies would quietly boycott parliamentary sessions to deny quorums for decision making, and then accuse the parliamentary majority of inaction. After Sąjūdis was reduced to a minority at the end of 1992, its members tried the same tactics.

In addition to these legacies from Soviet rule, Lithuania's new nationalist parties and rulers immediately faced challenges that did not afflict most other Eastern Europeans. First, the government in Vilnius had to reorganize its new institutions under Soviet military occupation. The military sought to destabilize the country and, ultimately, in January 1991, to overthrow the Lithuanian government itself. Second, Moscow severely punished Lithuania with the economic blockade of April–June 1990. This setback made systemic reform and reorganization extremely expensive. Finally, the difficulties of the Lithuanian transition were compounded by the peculiar political situation, namely, the existence of a well-organized, disciplined, pro-independence Communist party that nonetheless played a key role in helping to dismantle the Soviet system.

The Communists lost heavily in the March 1990 election, the first after independence. Their membership had dwindled to 15,000. They remained the only disciplined and experienced political force in the country, however, and had many properties, buildings, newspapers, and seasoned government administrators. Although they lost in the first national elections, they won about 40 percent of the votes in the local elections of April 1990 and thereby kept power in the provinces.

In addition, party leaders wisely chose to reorganize the party and change its image. In December 1990, some months after the declaration of independence, the Lithuanian Communist party became the Lithuanian Democratic Labor party under the leadership of the old Communist party secretary, Algirdas Brazauskas. Gediminas Kirkilas, a young Central Committee clerk, was chosen as his deputy. The party's organization became territorial, as required by law. Many old members quit, but the organizers retained a Socialist platform and attracted many new people who had not been in the Communist party before.

The new party's relative advantage in the parliament, though the number of its deputies was not large, was enhanced by the absence of countervailing forces. Sąjūdis refused to reorganize itself into a political party. The Social Democrats, Greens, Christian Democrats, and other new parties that emerged were small, inarticulate, and lacked the political cohesion needed for effective action. In the legislature, these groups organized themselves into "fractions" formed independently of their electoral strength by deputies who shared compatible views. Sąjūdis deputies were not subject to institutional partisan restraints, and soon their large bloc began to split and splinter. This process left many deputies without political constituencies outside or inside the parliament. It also reduced Sąjūdis to a potentially weak, unstable political force. Furthermore, the squabbling and immaturity of individual deputies that was supported and even promoted by parliamentary rules and the Soviet political legacy was exposed to the voters by daily telecasts of parliamentary sessions and helped to further undermine the parliament's reputation and effectiveness.

Under the pressure of Moscow's blockade, a palpable tension developed between the nationalist supporters of Landsbergis and those largely leftist deputies who advocated flexibility toward Moscow. The conflict was cast in terms of the "patriots" who defended independence at any cost and the "Communists" who were suspected of supporting a confederation with Russia. Further tensions were incited by the conflict between the press, which was in the hands of former or current Communists, and the Sąjūdis majority in the parliament. Almost within hours after Landsbergis's victory in the first free election in more than fifty years, many newspapers denounced him. Some took the side of Brazauskas against Landsbergis, advocating gradualism and immediate negotiations with Moscow while questioning the parliament's political realism and ability. Landsbergis felt that his views could not reach the public through TV and radio. His newly established "state newspaper" was named *Lietuvos aidas* (Echo of Lithuania), a distinguished title from the days of World War I that was later blackened by President Smetona, who used the newspaper as the official organ of his authoritarian regime in the 1930s. Thus, Landsbergis was accused of pulling the country into Smetona's authoritarian past. A further storm over Landsbergis's alleged authoritarianism arose after his parliamentary leadership outlawed an allegedly pornographic sheet entitled *Dvidešimt kapeikų* (Twenty Kopecks). The publication was judged harmful to society, especially the youth, but its suspension interfered with the freedom of the press, in violation of a law passed by the parliament itself and against the spirit of earlier openness that had brought Landsbergis himself to power.

Concern with Landsbergis's alleged inflexibility and moral stridency excited several leftist intellectuals, together with a dozen parliamentary deputies, to publish "an appeal to the people of Lithuania."[5] The signers charged that Landsbergis and the new parliament sought personal power at the cost of justice and democracy by usurping executive powers and frustrating the efforts of Prunskienė's government to arrange negotiations with the Soviet Union. The parliament, they added, failed to work on legislation Lithuania really needed and therefore a new legislature, or "founding Diet," was needed to establish the "democratic foundations" of the republic.

Such rejection of a sitting parliament was unprecedented. Recriminations flew in all directions. Chairman Landsbergis accused the signers of actually hurting Lithuania's chances in the forthcoming negotiations with Moscow by inciting hostility between the parliament and the government. He suggested that the leftists were tools of Moscow, saying, "There exists very interested and very strong political power which attempts to undermine [our mutual] confidence on an international scale."[6] A month later he was more specific. It was "the conservative forces of the USSR"[7] that were instigating social and political strife in Lithuania and the other Baltic states.

The opening of KGB archives in Lithuania after the failed Moscow coup d'état of August 1991 further inflamed the conflict between the "patriots" and the "Communists." A parliamentary commission, established to examine whether any deputies had "consciously" collaborated with the KGB, found reams of documents implicating a number of parliamentarians. Ironically, the first alleged agent cited was not a leftist politician but the founder of the Independence party, a leader of the national Sąjūdis organization, and to top it all, a close collaborator of President Landsbergis. The accused informant, a well-known writer and translator, Virgilijus Čepaitis, was summarily removed from his position in Sąjūdis. The exposure was a serious blow to Landsbergis. Landsbergis's supporters, in turn, retaliated by accusing former prime minister Prunskienė of having been a "conscious" agent of the KGB. She appealed to the Supreme Court, but because her file included official reports on people and conversations, she did not succeed in repudiating the charges.

Collaboration with secret police has been an inflammatory and sensitive political issue across the former Communist countries. Czechoslovakia faced it squarely by adopting a law temporarily banning some 140,000 Czechoslovaks from holding government positions because they were named as agents or collaborators in secret police files.[8] The issue was difficult because the concept of "collaboration" is difficult to define and can include writing innocuous travel reports, something many intellectuals were guilty of doing. Yet the issue of collaboration, as of 1996, is neither dead nor innocent. Some of those accused of ties with the KGB maintain that the agency networks still exist. U.S. sources also report that though "dismantled after the failed Soviet coup, the KGB is flourishing in Boris Yeltsin's Russia."[9] Although the name of the agency has changed, its networks and operatives remain in Lithuania and elsewhere to take part in politics by subterfuge.

In Lithuanian politics in the 1990s, the question of collaboration became not just a factual but a poisonous political issue used by both sides.

The warring sides were briefly united to face Soviet tanks on January 13, 1991, and again during the attempted coup d'état in August of the same year. The new government of young economist Gediminas Vagnorius was installed during the January crisis and vigorously proceeded with measures to return private property and nationalize former Communist party property. But the takeover of two newspapers that formerly belonged to the party scared other opposition papers and a press strike was organized as Brazauskas's Democratic Labor party protested the seizures. The party's relations with Vagnorius were worsened further by the government's efforts to pass a law on desovietization and collaboration.

Brazauskas's party formally declared its opposition to the government in November 1991. Legislative exchanges and legislative-executive disagreements reached crisis proportions, and in January 1992 supporters of Landsbergis and their opponents met separately to discuss the situation.[10] Of the nine party fractions in the legislature, four supported Landsbergis, but his majority, marginal already in the summer of 1991, continued to slip away and the coalition that kept Vagnorius's government in power began to dissolve.[11] By the end of 1991, most of the original Sąjūdis participants had left to join political parties and the movement shifted further to the nationalist right. This "third" Sąjūdis repelled the more moderate deputies, who unsuccessfully sought to forge a "centrist" force between the "patriots" and the "Communists." The chance for a middle ground to emerge looked bleak.

To get a firm hold of the situation and strengthen his position, Landsbergis decided to create an executive presidency independent from the legislature, such as Boris Yeltsin had won in 1990 in Russia. A referendum was held on the question on May 23, 1992, but by that time confidence in Landsbergis was already shaken. Amid opposition charges that he wanted to introduce a dictatorship, the voters turned down the proposal. Fifty percent of eligible voters needed to support the measure for it to pass, but only 40 percent voted.[12] The opposition called for Landsbergis's resignation, but he called for new parliamentary elections instead.

About one month later, on June 14, a referendum was held on the question of immediate withdrawal of Russian troops from Lithuania plus compensation for the damages they had inflicted.[13] Seventy-six percent of all registered voters cast their ballots, with 69 percent of those voting supporting the proposition. Landsbergis's forces had made efforts to hold both referenda on the same day on the theory that the anti-army referendum would help the president, but the idea was rejected by the legislature. Although the populace supported the demand for Russian troop withdrawal, the road to political independence was no longer dominated by a unified movement or led by its original leader.

The legislature agreed to new elections to be held on October 25 and passed a no-confidence vote that terminated Vagnorius's government. The parliamentary election astounded the new politicians and shocked the world. As the *Wall Street Journal* put it, "Lithuania, the first republic to break away from the Soviet Union, also became the first in which former Communists have scored a political comeback in a popular parliamentary vote."[14] In Eastern Europe, the phenomenon became known as the "Lithuanian syndrome" and was soon repeated in Poland, Hungary, and elsewhere.

The Democratic Labor party won a landslide victory in the new 141-seat Seimas (Diet). "The results were better than we hoped," said its leader, Brazauskas.[15] His party won a total of seventy-seven seats. The coalition of Sąjūdis won only sixteen, to be later reduced to thirteen because three seats contested by Brazauskas's party were assigned to it by the Supreme Court. Social Democrats landed eight seats; Christian Democrats, ten; Citizens Charter, ten; Political Prisoners and Exiles, twelve; the Polish minority, under special consideration, four; the Democratic party, four; the Center, two; the Christian Democratic Association, one; and the Independence party, one.[16] A total of seventeen groups or coalitions ran candidates. The elections were held under new rules drafted on the West German model. The new electoral law provided for the election of seventy deputies on the basis of proportional representation and

Inexplicable Lithuania. (From *Suddeutsche Zeitung.* Used by permission.)

seventy-one from single-member districts. To win a seat, every party, except for the Polish, had to receive a minimum of 4 percent of the vote.

The victorious former Communists hastened to assure their own people and the world that their party was not Communist and that they did not desire to return to Soviet-style governance either politically or economically; nor, indeed, did they wish to accept the embrace of Moscow.[17] They claimed to be a party of "Social Democratic profile" and said they would not seek to join the Commonwealth of Independent States but instead would continue policies to strengthen Lithuania's full independence. The withdrawal of Russian troops from Lithuania would be pushed, as agreed between Landsbergis and Yeltsin. The party would concentrate on the "economic situation, especially the critical condition of agriculture," and would not reverse Lithuania's free-market reforms.[18] Democracy was not endangered either. Although Landsbergis warned that the new Seimas would lead the country back "toward the one party rule we saw before 1988," Brazauskas's party reiterated its commitment to democratic order and invited "all political forces represented in the Seimas to a grand coalition in the name of civil concord and welfare of the Lithuanian state." At the same time party leaders claimed that closer relations with Russia were needed for economic reasons and that economic reform should not override social concerns.

Doubts existed as to whether the Democratic Labor party was really a new Social Democratic party of independence, but the voters trusted its leader Brazauskas. Indeed the electoral contest was not just between political parties or even their programs as much as it was between the two leaders, Landsbergis and Brazauskas. The first was perceived as calm, moral, authoritarian, and skilled in foreign policy but inexperienced and inept in domestic affairs. The second was appreciated for his populist views by the rural population and was seen by supporters as politically sober and administratively experienced. Vytautas Landsbergis, like his archenemy Mikhail Gorbachev in Moscow, gained respect abroad but became disliked at home.[19]

Thus, the pendulum's swing from support for nationalists to support for former Communists did not signify return to communism but disappointment in Sąjūdis for unfulfilled hopes and expectations. The *New York Times* put it sagaciously, saying, "Making even relatively enlightened former Communists look attractive is a difficult task, but the inexperienced leaders of Lithuania accomplished it."[20]

Indeed, Sąjūdis lost not only because of Brazauskas's popularity but also because Sąjūdis's members made many political mistakes. The more politically astute members left to join and create political parties. The inability of the little-known new parties to unify the country left a vacuum in the political center. Thus, the voters had to make a choice between two extremes. In turn, the remaining Sąjūdis leaders were ill-advised to cast their competition with Brazauskas's party in terms of patriotism versus communism. Their romantic nationalism and nostalgia for the days of prewar independence held little meaning for a populace suffering real hardship in economically trying times. Given the uncharted waters of market transition and the Moscow blockade, however, no one group could really have stopped the downward slide of the economy in 1991–1992. On one level, Sąjūdis simply paid the price for governing during trying times.

THE NEW PRESIDENT:
BRAZAUSKAS RETURNS AS CHIEF EXECUTIVE

The adoption of a new constitution in October 1992 opened the doors for the choice of a new president. An election was set for February 14, 1993. The victorious Democratic Labor party had a superb candidate, Algirdas Brazauskas. Because his personal popularity had helped to carry the day in the parliamentary contest, a presidential victory seemed to be assured. The eyes of the nation were also on Vytautas Landsbergis, the hero of the movement for independence whose political movement had suffered a deep and unexpected defeat. Upon reflection, he decided not to run. His prospects were not auspicious, even if all the small parties in the center of the political spectrum could unite with him against Brazauskas. Landsbergis's popularity in Lithuania had dropped to the level of Gorbachev's in Russia. On January 5, several candidates declared their intention to run, but by January 21 only two were able to gather the required 20,000 signatures each. Those were LDDP leader Algirdas Brazauskas and Lithuania's ambassador to the United States, Stasys Lozoraitis.

Brazauskas came from a middle-class Lithuanian family. Young Algirdas graduated from an engineering school and went to climb the Communist party career ladder to ultimately become the party boss. Like most apparatchiks, he liked hunting and drinking. He also enjoyed sailing. His ruddy complexion exuded health and sociability. It was only after the election that it was revealed Brazauskas suffered from a mild condition of diabetes that was treated by oral medicine.

Lozoraitis came from a well-known professional family. He was the son of Lithuania's former foreign minister and envoy in Rome and had spent his youth and the most productive years of his life there. He had worked in the exile diplomatic service, first in the Vatican during the Cold War and from the mid-1980s in Washington. Unlike Brazauskas, who was married to a native Lithuanian physician, Lozoraitis's wife came from a distinguished Italian family. Although she was dedicated to the Lithuanian cause and spoke Lithuanian, however, indigenous Lithuanians would not accept her as more than a foreigner and were often troubled by the fact that Lozoraitis himself was raised and lived abroad.

Lozoraitis ran as an independent candidate and was supported by all smaller parties except the LDDP and the Polish minority fraction in parliament. Even the candidate of the Social Democrats withdrew in his favor. Brazauskas, by then the acting president, had to face a united front as his political competition no longer seemed divided. The electoral campaign was short, only three weeks. With a U.S. Lithuanian as his campaign chairman, Lozoraitis brought high standards and graceful behavior to the electioneering. He steadily began to gain name recognition, and his standing rose in the polls. The amount of time allotted for campaigning, however, was too short for him to catch up to his formidable adversary.

Programmatically, the candidates were not as disparate as their backgrounds suggest. Both swore to develop Lithuania's full independence, both insisted upon the schedule for the withdrawal of Russian troops that had already been worked out, both criticized the economic reforms of the previous government, and both pledged to develop a free-market economy. Their differences, however, were also clear. Although both candidates professed to seek balanced relations with Russia and the West, Brazauskas prioritized ties with Russia. The old party secretary, too, had an advantage over Lozoraitis in that he was able to present the voters with a "comprehensive" program of administration and to outline his future cabinet. Lozoraitis had neither the time nor the experience for such preparation. The two were furthermore conspicuously different in their style of expression and behavior. Brazauskas was pragmatically and cautiously articulate in familiar surroundings with familiar clichés. Lozoraitis brought to the campaign intellectual sophistication and a challenging, broader European perspective. Journalists noted that even their use of the Lithuanian language differed.

The self-confident LDDP leader, who at first did not even think about extensive campaigning, nevertheless had to face Lozoraitis as a serious candidate. Their lively contest stayed generally at a high ethical level and increased voting participation to almost 80 percent, of whom 60.1 percent cast their ballots for Brazauskas and 38.2 percent for Lozoraitis.[21] Brazauskas won majorities everywhere except in the old capital city of Kaunas. The former Communist leader scored especially well in districts inhabited by Russian and Polish majorities. As in the October parliamentary elections, his victory was secured by the rural vote.

The election was more of a personal victory for Brazauskas than a partisan triumph for the LDDP. Brazauskas won generally because his personality and experience inspired trust; there was nostalgia for past economic security; and rural voters believed he could bring back prosperity. Finally,

Brazauskas heavily benefited from the voters' disappointment with Sąjūdis and Landsbergis, particularly because Landsbergis had publicly endorsed the former ambassador. Such an embrace raised fears, however unjustified, that Lozoraitis would be politically dependent on Landsbergis. Most of all, Lozoraitis was deeply hurt by a successful LDDP effort to tag him as a "foreigner" who had not shared the nation's tragic fate in the past and did not understand its present crisis. The Lithuanians denied their trust to the expatriate, just as the Serbs had done to Panich, despite the fact that the "expatriate" Lozoraitis had spent his entire life in the struggle for his native land's independence.

After his election, Brazauskas took on a statesman quality that surprised even his most ardent critics. He tried to distance himself from the role of LDDP party leader and was able to rise above the fray of partisan politics. He even excoriated the members of his own party in parliament for their seemingly obstructionist and extreme behaviors.

PROSPECTS FOR THE FUTURE: THE ECONOMY

In the fall of 1992, the Lithuanian economy was in deep crisis. Different explanations were offered to account for the country's ruinous condition. The leadership of the former independent Communist party loudly claimed that the economy had been destroyed by the "big jump" or "shock treatment" reform Vagnorius had instituted. Individual economists as well as liberal deputies blamed the mess on Vagnorius's "Socialist" policies: His government had insisted that reform would not be pushed at the price of destroying social support networks and full employment. Vagnorius promoted "egalitarianism," his critics charged, and shied away from the austerity required by free-market reform.

The economic difficulties had begun, however, before Landsbergis and his government had come to power. The decline started in 1990, when industrial productivity dropped as a consequence of Gorbachev's economic blockade. It declined further the next year because the Soviet military had created instability, especially in January through August 1991. In 1992, severe drought damaged agricultural harvests. Overall, productivity and the standard of living were hurt across the Soviet Union by several factors: diminution of cheap energy supplies from Russia; dislocations caused by the political reorganization of the Soviet Union; and inflationary pressures created by the faltering economic policies of Russia, especially after the coup d'état of August.

Yeltsin increased the price of Russian oil, coal, and natural gas from fifteen to thirty times during 1992. Russia also demanded payment in hard currency, which the Lithuanians could not earn in the West or from Russia. The Russians did not pay in hard currency for industrial and agricultural products they bought from Lithuania. Energy shortages caused long interruptions in production and reduced factory work schedules. Homes were cold, and warm water was usually not available, making life generally miserable. The government of the caretaker prime minister, Aleksandras Abišala, negotiated with Moscow but could not reach a lasting agreement.

Industry suffered great difficulties because of disrupted economic links among enterprises now separated by political boundaries. Lithuania's large factories had been a part of the Soviet military-industrial complex and suffered a lack of access to raw materials and supplies. In addition, most factories could be kept afloat only by infusion of state subsidies, as in Russia and across the USSR. Despite its commitment to free-market reform, Sąjūdis continued the subsidies in order to prevent worker layoffs. Unemployment, full- and part-time, began to grow nonetheless, from 9,000 in 1991 to tens of thousands a year later.[22] Industrial production shrank by 45 percent from 1989 to 1991 and the national product went down almost 48 percent. The decline was experienced across Russia and Eastern Europe. Poland fared better than the rest; in Lithuania the drop was much bigger than in Hungary but similar to declines in Estonia (a 40 percent decline) and Latvia (42 percent). If in industry the Lithuanian government had many less choices for the resolution of difficulties, it possessed many more alternatives in agriculture but failed miserably in exploiting them.

Agricultural production dropped 39 percent in 1992. The Lithuanian countryside fell victim to uncharted and, in the end, unsuccessful experimentation with the transition from a collective farming system to private family farming. The Landsbergis parliament had resolutely sought to reverse immediately the system of collectivized agriculture.

To achieve decollectivization, in 1991 the parliament passed three laws: on agricultural corporations, on land reform, and on privatization of the property of agricultural communities and enterprises.[23] The intent of these measures was to dissolve collective farms, to return land to its pre-1941 owners, and to spur the growth of private farming. But the provisions of these laws were confusing, contradictory,[24] and easily obstructed in their implementation. The rapid pace of privatization created havoc. Those who managed the land took advantage of the new rules. Collective farm managers stole the best equipment and livestock; herds of cattle and pigs were slaughtered because the government no longer provided cheap fodder; and fields were abandoned for lack of certainty of ownership.[25] Many former land owners or their descendants had no current interest in farming. They reclaimed the land but left it fallow. Families intending to farm could not properly cultivate their land for lack of equipment, fertilizer, and credit for supplies. Since legislation did not make adequate arrangements for displaced collective farm members, grievous social problems also arose: Social reformers organized to fight the government and proposed that land should belong only to those who actually worked it. The result of the radical land reform was disastrous. According to a leading Lithuanian economist and strong critic of Landsbergis, the decision to dismantle collective farms "set agriculture in this country back by at least a century."[26]

Since agriculture still employs almost a fifth of the total workforce and accounts for almost a quarter of the total national product, the economic consequences of this failed reform experiment were enormous. The reform legislation destroyed collectivism but did not replace it with a viable system. The reformers relied on small farm ownership as a substitute for huge farms, but the new farms were too small, inefficient, and insufficiently supplied.

Agricultural reorganization was just one, albeit a substantive, element of a program of privatization of a state-owned economy. The basic privatization law was passed on February 28, 1991, and covered diverse property with the exception of housing, agriculture, and communications. To start privatization, this law provided for "investment checks" of 10,000 rubles to each thirty-five-year-old citizen. Younger citizens received checks of lesser value. State property was to be acquired in public auctions and through public signing of acquired stock.[27] A law on privatization of housing that was passed four months later allowed the investment checks to be used toward the purchase of apartments.[28] Half a million apartments and houses were sold to private owners by the end of 1992. As in the case of agriculture, here, too, the more substantive citizens with means had an initial advantage to acquire better housing. Inflation ate up investment checks for those who could not quickly accumulate additional funds. Nevertheless, this part of the privatization program proved to be the most successful.

Privatization of industrial objects affected only 30 percent of intended capital investment value until the end of 1992[29] and quickly became controversial. Auctions offered opportunities for criminal elements to acquire industrial and commercial holdings. They colluded in bidding, threatened competitors, and bribed officials. Partially for this reason, the Democratic Labor party's majority postponed the privatization process for a month after coming to power.

Still another element of Lithuanian reform in 1991 was the liberalization of prices. Prunskienė's efforts had failed in January, but they were resumed by the Vagnorius government at the end of the year. The higher inflation that followed could not be successfully handled because Lithuania was still in the ruble zone. The Baltic states intended to protect themselves by introducing their own convertible currencies. Estonia succeeded in doing so in 1992. Lithuania's government planned to introduce the *litas*, but a conflict arose between the Vagnorius government and the Bank of Lithuania that hampered this effort in part because the actual physical printing of litas did not meet designated standards. To be effective for inflation control, Vagnorius wanted the litas introduced when Lithuanian price controls were lifted and before Yeltsin in Russia liberalized prices in early 1992. The president of the Bank of Lithuania, however, an appointee of Prunskienė's government and supported by Brazauskas's party, was inclined to separate gradually from the Commonwealth of Independent States rather than to aid the politically antagonistic Vagnorius. A "coupon" (*kuponas*), instead of the litas, was finally introduced half a year later. On October 1, 1992, the kuponas was replaced by the "talon" (*talonas*).

The ruble had finally disappeared, but the tide of inflation by then could not be stemmed or even slowed. The bank fueled further inflation by printing additional billions of talonas. The new government of Bronislovas Lubys, who took over from Abišala with Brazauskas's blessing in November 1992, blamed the Sąjūdis government for not taking action on the currency at the end of 1991 when Vagnorius freed the prices. In 1992 prices rose over 900 percent while wages and salaries increased by only 400 percent.[30] In his report on the state of the economy, given in January 1993, Brazauskas noted that in three years the value of money had decreased by sixty-five times, indicating inflation of 6,500 percent.[31] A representative of the International Monetary Fund, however, maintained that the postponed introduction of convertible currency was not the first order of business because of the talonas.[32] Inflation continued to soar but at a slower pace than in Moscow. Estonia and Latvia experienced a much lower inflation: three and two times lower, respectively, than in Lithuania.

As elsewhere across the region, the high inflation rate, continued economic shortages, and inability of government to discipline its own bureaucracy conspicuously intensified various forms of state corruption. Alexander Yakovlev, the philosophical father of perestroika and former ally of Gorbachev, denounced organized crime as "the No. 1 threat to Russia's strategic interests and national security."[33] Similarly, the state comptroller under Sąjūdis, labor leader Kazimieras Uoka, confessed, "The managers of economic government structures and the operators of the shadow economy have accumulated such enormous funds and acquired such influence in the past two and a half years of business dealings that I can no longer assert myself or cope with them."[34] Economic crime became rampant; for example, thieves stole precious metals by dismantling copper installations, bridges, or gravestones and selling them in Poland or farther away. Street crime increased by 80 percent over the 1989 rate.[35] There is little consolation in the fact that the Lithuanian crime rate did not rise to Estonian or Latvian levels. "Is this what the 15 people at the TV tower died for?"[36] asked a young Lithuanian who defended the parliament against Soviet tanks on the bloody Sunday of January 13, 1991.

Despite the falling living standards and rising crime rates, real progress on the road to a market economy was made in the first four years of the new Lithuanian republic. The dramatic fall in production characteristic of all post-Soviet economies stabilized in 1993, and gross domestic production rose by 0.6 percent in 1994. Most economic activity in post-Soviet Lithuania took place in the service sectors, including retail and wholesale trade; agriculture, historically Lithuania's strength, accounted for only 8 percent of total production. As in Latvia, Estonia, and other border countries to Russia, most economic wealth was initially generated in the sale and transport of natural resources from elsewhere in the former Soviet Union. Actual domestic consumer production suffered in the competition from imported and better-made Western goods and is only now beginning the long process of adjusting to new market conditions. Like most other East European countries, Lithuania has followed the problematic rationale of privatizing ownership first and expecting effective restructuring to follow.

Privatization of large enterprises generally stayed on the fast track established by the government under Landsbergis. By the end of 1994, over 50 percent of those large industrial sites able to privatize had done so and small businesses were not far behind. At the same time, Lithuania had the lowest unemployment rate in the region. Perhaps most impressively, however, over 93 percent of all housing was also privately owned by the end of 1994. Although the shift to a market economy had extracted costs from the average citizen, and especially from those living on fixed incomes, such as pensions, the benefits of free enterprise were also within reach.

A NEW CONSTITUTION AND AN EMERGING GOVERNMENT STRUCTURE

Boisterous political infighting by parliamentary factions overshadowed the fact that they were capable of consensus and compromise on crucial matters, such as the constitution of 1992, which took two years to complete. Two constitutional models competed for adoption. One advocated a presidential system with a strong executive branch, which was in some ways similar to the U.S. and the French constitutions. The other advocated a parliamentary model of legislative supremacy that called for a much weaker executive branch and only a figurehead president. Confident of electoral approval, Landsbergis's group favored the strong presidential system on grounds that only a strong executive could propel the country toward domestic progress. Brazauskas's party and sundry deputies opposed this proposal out of fear that it would lead, especially with a Landsbergis victory, to some type of authoritarian regime.

Landsbergis's political opponents had been accusing him of authoritarian behavior since the spring of 1990, and rumors of an impending Landsbergian coup d'état were widespread. At a Democratic Labor party conference in January 1992, Brazauskas declared, "In the absence of democratic traditions, there exists a high probability of the rise of an authoritarian regime, and in an extreme case—even of the establishment of Lithuanian national [ethnic] socialism."[37] With great energy, his party argued for a system of legislative supremacy. The question of a strong presidency was decided by popular referendum on May 23, 1992. Landsbergis lost.

The defeat and the end of Vagnorius's government clearly signaled the political decline of Sąjūdis. They also motivated Landsbergis's forces to compromise on the constitution before the upcoming parliamentary elections. In the end, a document was produced that excited nobody but created a system all parties could accept. Consensus was reached quickly, almost hurriedly, at the beginning of October 1992 so the document could be submitted to a referendum on the day of the parliamentary elections, October 25.

The constitution was approved by 75.4 percent of the votes, or by 56.8 percent of the electorate.[38] The compromise model drew from the French, U.S., German, and earlier Lithuanian constitutions and was in compliance with international agreements on human rights, including the rights of minorities. It attempts to combine modern democratic principles with Lithuania's national traditions as well as with the more recent inheritance of the Socialist welfare state.

Defining Lithuania as an "independent democratic republic," the constitution specifically condemns any seizure of power by violent means. It lists the usual personal rights, including the inviolability of private property and workers' right to strike in an economy "founded on the right of private property, personal freedom and initiative."[39] At the same time, the document provides for social rights such as free medical care for all citizens, free higher education, old age pensions, unemployment benefits, and other hardship support, including a guarantee of paid maternity leave.

The attempt to reconcile modern democratic principles with national traditions is best seen in provisions concerning freedom of religion. Thus, on the one hand the constitution declares that "freedom of thought, religion and conscience shall not be restrained," but on the other it specifies that the state "shall recognize those churches and religious organizations which are traditional in Lithuania while other churches and religious organizations [shall be recognized] if they have support in society and if their teaching as well as their rituals do not contradict law and morality" (Article 43). In Lithuania, "traditional" denominations are old churches, such as Catholic, Lutheran, Calvinist, Orthodox, and Jewish (synagogues). The constitution, furthermore, allows the teaching of religion in public schools "according to the wishes of the parents." Education, however, is declared to be "secular." Moreover, a cryptic Article 19, which may be interpreted as giving grounds for opposing either abortion or capital punishment, insists that "a person's right to life is protected by law."

In contrast to the old Soviet system, the new constitution establishes separation of powers almost on a U.S. model. The legislature, now known by the traditional name of Seimas, is to be composed of 141 members elected to four-year terms by all citizens above eighteen years of age. The Seimas is to meet twice a year for a total of seven months and three days, thus setting the stage for the executive branch to dominate for the other half of the year. Members of the parliament, just as the president and state ministers, may not simultaneously serve in the other branches of government; nor may they occupy positions in financial, commercial, or other private enterprises.

In addition to the usual legislative jurisdiction, the Lithuanian parliament has the power to establish state institutions provided by law and to appoint their administrators. It also appoints justices of the Constitutional and Supreme courts, as well as the director of the Bank of Lithuania, who is equivalent to the chairman of the Federal Reserve System in the United States. Finally, the Seimas approves the budget proposed by the government, but it has a maximum of only seventy-five days for doing so. In this way, the legislature is not allowed to stop the government from functioning for lack of budget; state expenditures in case of the legislature's tardiness are limited to those of the previous year on the basis of a monthly average. More important, the Seimas cannot reduce proposed budgetary expenditures without changing the original laws authorizing these expenditures, and, like the French Assembly, it cannot increase proposed expenditures without indicating the sources for funding them.

For their executive branch, the Lithuanians adopted the French rather than the U.S. model. The president, elected directly by the people for a five-year term, is "the leader of the state" and is specifically designated as chief foreign policy maker and chief of national defense. In peacetime, he confers top military ranks without legislative approval, though with a signature of the prime minister. He also appoints, with the Seimas's consent, the chiefs of the armed forces and of internal security.

Following the French model, the president's most important power in running the government is the appointment and dismissal of the prime minister and of individual ministers. These appointments, however, require the legislature's approval. The president can also issue decrees, though in most cases these need to be countersigned by appropriate ministers. Similarly, the president can greatly influence the court system because he has the power to nominate three justices of the Constitutional Court and to choose the justices of the Supreme Court. With the approval of Seimas, he also appoints the judges of the appellate courts as well as district and local judges and has the power to transfer and even to dismiss them. The president's influence extends also to finances because he nominates the director of the Bank of Lithuania for the parliament's approval. Thus, his powers extend from the executive to the legislative and even judicial branches of government.

In relations with the legislature, the president's hands are further strengthened by a limited veto power and the right to dissolve the parliament. A law returned by the president must be readopted by over 50 percent of the total membership of the legislature or, in the case of "constitutional" legislation, by three-fifths of the entire legislative body. Finally, the president can dissolve the parliament if within sixty days the legislators twice fail to approve the government's program submitted by the prime minister. The balance of powers between the two branches is neatly calibrated, however: If the president dissolves the parliament, the newly elected parliament, by a three-fifths majority, may in effect remove the president by declaring a presidential election before the expiration of the incumbent's term in office.

The experience of the post-Communist years persuaded the Lithuanians that their political system needed an arbiter between the legislative and executives branches. Eager to restore the severely disturbed balance between these branches of government, they in effect established not one but two such arbiters. One is the presidency, as the constitution denies the president not only any other institutional membership but also demands that upon election he abandon any participation in partisan activities or in political parties. He is supposed to be a nonpolitical, nonpartisan actor. In democratic systems, there is no precedent for denying a partisan role to the leader of a political constituency. The requirement reflects the level of mistrust of partisan politics in the management of the Lithuanian state.

The other nonpolitical arbiter in the Lithuanian system is the Constitutional Court. The Lithuanians borrowed the principle of constitutional review from the United States, the name of the institution from the West Germans, and the French method of appointing justices. The Lithuanians themselves detailed the rest of this key element. One-third of the justices are to be nominated by the president, the other third by the speaker, and the remaining third by the chief justice of the Supreme Court, which tops the pyramid of the regular court system. Thus, all three branches of government participate in choosing the justices who decide the constitutionality of legislative and executive actions. The court also has the duty of deciding whether election laws have been violated during presidential or parliamentary elections and whether the president's health condition allows him to remain in office. Access to this court is not open to the public but only to a qualified number of legislators and the government. Thus, in some ways the Constitutional Court is most similar to the operation of the French Constitutional Council.

Extremely anxious about the inviolability of their hard-won independent sovereignty, the Lithuanians have specified that the declaration of independence of March 11, 1990, constitutes an integral part of the constitution, as does the parliamentary decision of June 8, 1992, not to join "post-Soviet Eastern associations." The latter was supposed to give assurances to the supporters of Sąjūdis that Brazauskas's party would not lead Lithuania back to the Commonwealth of Independent States after the demise of the Soviet Union. Similarly, the provision of Article 1, which says that Lithuania is an "independent democratic republic," virtually cannot be altered except by a referendum approved by three-fourths of the eligible voters. Nor can the constitution be changed during legal emergency or war. With all these measures, Lithuanians hoped to close off any openings that could be used to seemingly legalize an unlawful occupation, as the Bolsheviks did in 1940.

Although new ministries were formed as others were consolidated at the republic level, the state administration at this level was strengthened by new laws putting constraints on local government passed in spring 1995. In the past, local and regional governments were able to control their own administration under the rubric of locally elected councils that controlled their own budgets, collected local (commercial) taxes, and set their own prices for municipal services. Seen as a vestige of the Communist order by many, the councils were abolished in favor of individual district representatives appointed by and responsible to the Seimas.

In the years since independence from the USSR, deficiencies in two fundamental respects have handicapped the effectiveness of democratic government: lack of technical/managerial skill and underdevelopment of political platforms and party ideologies. A centrist political ground is only beginning to emerge, with the clearest political choice still polarized between Brazauskas and the LDDP on one side and Landsbergis with his supporters on the other. Voters seem to swing between the two. Just as in 1993, when Brazauskas and his party ousted Landsbergis, the 1995 local elections shifted power once again from the incumbents to the challengers. The LDDP lost soundly to center-right parties and Tėvynės Sąjunga (National Union), the new party created by Landsbergis, took the lead in the countryside by capturing about 30 percent of the local vote.

As in Russia and across the former Soviet Union, most Lithuanian political and industrial leaders have been able to flourish financially while the majority of the population has suffered a deep initial loss in their standard of living. This disparity has led to a great distrust of public institutions and elites that ultimately hinders the democratic process by replacing political involvement with apathy. At the same time, the political middle ground is solidifying gradually. Parties such as the Christian Democrats and others made a respectable showing in the 1995 elections and hold out the promise of offering the kind of real political alternatives upon which the future of the democratic system rests. Thus far, therefore, the strong presidential system has not been a harbinger of a return to dictatorial rule but offers instead a solid point of policy and decision-making. With this as a basis, other governing institutions, such as parties and the parliament, will likely find a conducive environment in which to mature and develop.

CIVIL SOCIETY TAKES SHAPE

The energy and excitement of the early days of Sąjūdis did not completely dissipate with the formalization of independence. Instead, independence helped to inspire the formation of many different and active social groups like those constituting the backbone of civil society in any democracy. Indeed, before political apathy set in, opposition members tended to take their issues straight to the populace, since a legislative majority of one extreme or another tended to dominate in the Seimas. A particularly popular form of political expression between 1988 and 1993 was the hunger strike. Lacking a sufficient voting majority, conservative opposition Seimas members have encouraged a politically involved electorate by promoting referendums as well, and two were voted on in August 1994.

By mid-summer 1994, there were more than 700 social groups registered in Lithuania. These included 74 charitable funds, 65 professional associations, and 31 political organizations. About 300 of the groups have substantial memberships and are active on a continuous basis. Among the most active are women's organizations, known for their international links and for the effectiveness of their charitable organizations, and the organizations for national minorities, of which there are 12 Jewish organizations, 11 Polish, and 10 Russian.

Active social groups exist in almost all sectors of the economy as well, where the general pattern mirrors the polarization of official politics. Some of these groups are descendants of official Communist organizations active during the Soviet era; other, newer groups have formed in reaction to these and often operate under the auspices and leadership of early Sąjūdis activists. The newer groups were more popular early in the transition, but the descendants of Soviet-era groups have more organizational savvy and resources. Their larger memberships generally reflect their successful efforts to represent member interests in the new, post-Soviet era. For instance, the descendant of the Lithuanian branch of the USSR's All-Union Central Council of Trade Unions lost much of its wealth and power under the Landsbergis chairmanship, when it renamed itself the Confederation of Free Trade Unions (CFTU). Since the return to power of the former Communist administration, it has reinherited most of the facilities that once belonged to the former Communist group and began to regain membership. In March 1993, it was joined by eight other unions to become the Lithuanian Trade Union Center. In contrast, the opposition Lithuanian Workers Union (LWU) was formed in 1990 as an outgrowth of Sąjūdis and as a competitor to the CFTU. It distinguishes itself by more aggressively seeking contact with Western labor groups and claims to have 50,000 dues-paying members.

Farmers also have several social groups, although only a minority of interested farmers or potential farmers are actively involved in farming organizations. Those who first started private farming efforts in 1990 were strongly supported by the Landsbergis administration and created the Farmers' Union. Two groups organized in opposition: the relatively small Land Owners Union demanded that land redistribution be completed before new owners were allowed to farm. The larger Peasants' Union is based on the Soviet-era organization of the same name and is made up of collective farm chairmen and some workers. It largely represents those in support of collective farming and until recently provided the backbone of support to the LDDP. The government's continued nonpayment for the produce it took since coming to power and its lack of promised subsidies soured the relationship and resulted in heavy losses in the countryside for the LDDP in the 1995 local elections.

The Minorities: A New Deal

Conventional wisdom has it that the collapse of communism unleashed nationalist passions and caused political instability that endangered the nascent democracies of the former Communist realm. Most successor states, indeed, have experienced ethnic conflict, but not because the prior Communist regime had eased tension; it simply repressed hostilities and laid the foundation for future conflict. With the demise of communism, the new states inherited a legacy of unsolved problems and even new ethnic issues.[40] The democratically organized successor states thus had to rewrite their charters to address ethnic minority issues fairly. But this task posed several difficult problems.

What standards should a group meet to be entitled to self-determination and how far should this privilege go?[41] Should not only Lithuania but also the internal Russian areas of Tataria, Chechnya, or Yakutiya have the right to become independent? Should self-determination be recognized for a district in Lithuania or Latvia inhabited by Poles or Russians? How should successor nations liquidate the consequences of institutionalized hostility between nations and ethnic groups? This question is particularly pressing in areas such as the Caucasus and Central Asia, where Communist rulers purposefully maintained the conflicts. The third problem concerns ethnic Russian diasporas planted and nurtured by Moscow throughout the Soviet empire. Kazakhstan, Ukraine, and Moldova have substantial Russian populations, but nowhere is this issue as controversial as in Estonia and Latvia. There, demographic development has produced a hitherto internationally unexplored conflict between two valid principles that generally govern social and political life elsewhere in the Western world: human rights and the right to national self-determination.

In Lithuania, the same level of conflict with the local ethnic minorities does not exist—not because the Lithuanians are less nationalistic than their northern neighbors but because they feel more secure as a national community.[42] The laws that laid the foundation for Lithuania's minority policies were adopted as early as November 3, 1989, when Lithuania was still a Soviet republic but on the road to democratization. One law dealt with citizenship, the other with the rights of national minorities.[43]

The first law automatically extended Lithuanian citizenship to all post–World War II immigrants and their descendants, which is not the case in Estonia and Latvia. All persons who had permanent residence of at least ten years and employment or another legal source of income in Lithuania at the time the law was passed were declared to be citizens. Immigrants, in addition, were given two years to decide whether they wanted to accept Lithuanian citizenship. Thus, citizenship requirements in Lithuania were more strict than in the United States but easier than in Germany.[44] This legislation was amended after the declaration of independence on December 5, 1991, to exclude active Soviet military but to liberalize some other provisions. Although the law eased much tension, minorities were still concerned with possible discrimination and the use of native languages in public institutions.

The second law, on minorities, passed on November 23, 1989, sought to alleviate fears surrounding the preservation of ethnic identity, culture, and development. The law assured public education in minority languages; professional training of teachers and other specialists; the right of publication, association, and employment; the use of minority languages alongside Lithuanian in areas with "substantial" minority populations; and a guarantee of functioning minority communities. A Department of Nationalities and a Center for Research on Nationalities and Their Socioeconomic Problems were established in 1990.

Lithuania has representatives of more than one hundred nationalities living within its borders. Of these, however, three—Russians, Poles, and

Jews—are historically and politically important. Together they constitute 17 percent of the 20 percent of the population of other than Lithuanian ethnicity.

The Russians

The Russian minority is dispersed throughout Lithuania's cities. The population of Vilnius is 20.2 percent Russian; Klaipėda, 28.2 percent; Šiauliai, 10.5 percent; and Visaginas (formerly Sniečkus), the nuclear plant town, 64.2 percent.[45] Moscow beams two Russian TV programs on the Ostankino channels, and Lithuanian TV and radio also provide some Russian programming. The government runs a total of eighty-three primary and secondary schools with Russian as the language of instruction and also maintains more than 200 Russian-language groups in preschool institutions.

Russians run minority candidates in elections, but more often than not they participate in the political process through established groups. Russian members of parliament were elected as members of major political parties rather than by the use of minority privilege. One of the reasons for their lack of interest in separate political self-assertion is that they believe the development of national culture, not participation in politics, is of primary importance for the survival of the Russian community.[46]

Are the Russians comfortable in the new Lithuania? A poll of Russian respondents in 1992 indicated that one-fifth of Russians want to return to Russia.[47] Another fifth are undecided. Reasons for wanting to leave include a perceived lack of guarantees and freedoms, problems with occupational and professional education, and personal family situations. However, 56 percent of the Russian population regard Lithuania as their homeland. About the same percentage know the Lithuanian language, though often not very well. Although 50 percent of respondents felt insulted at least once because of their nationality, 77 percent were generally satisfied.

The Russian minority has a problem of adjustment. According to Russia's ambassador to Lithuania, it is often very difficult for the Russians to reconcile themselves to the fact that they live in a foreign country. "Some simply can't understand it."[48] In their own eyes and in the eyes of Russian authorities, their position is different from, say, the Russian-speaking minorities in France or Germany. The ambassador, however, repeated a view expressed more than once by Russia's Foreign Ministry and by President Yeltsin during the Vancouver summit on April 9, 1993, that Lithuania's treatment of the Russian minority has been fair, conforms "to international norms," and even may serve as an example for others.

The Poles

Accommodation of the Polish minority has been a politically more important and complicated process than relations with the Russians and has a long history of both alliance and animosity. The majority of Poles live compactly in three contiguous rural districts of eastern Lithuania. In two of these, Vilnius and Šalčininkai, they constitute strong majorities (63.5 and 79.6 percent, respectively). In the third, Trakai, the Poles make up one-fourth of the total population (28.8 percent). Compared to Poles in former Soviet Byelorussia or Ukraine, Soviet Lithuania's Poles enjoyed clear material advantages. Moscow kept control over Lithuanians by manipulating and improving the conditions of the Poles. Communist authorities supported some 250 Polish schools or educational programs, a republic-wide Polish daily, and several local publications as well as Polish TV and radio programs. They also monitored the appointment of Polish personnel in party and government structures.

The atmosphere for the Lithuanian-Polish dialogue generally was inhibited by historical memories. Traditionally, the Poles of the Vilnius region felt slighted by Lithuanian control over the area. They looked not only to the glorious past of the medieval Polish-Lithuanian Union but also the more recent interwar period when eastern Lithuania was a part of Poland. It was difficult for many to accept minority status under the Lithuanians. In the Soviet system, those Poles who did not send their children to Polish schools enrolled them in Russian rather than Lithuanian classes. Lithuanians, in turn, feared that a strong Polish minority could mean the loss of Vilnius to Poland once again. A U.S. analyst correctly noted, "Ethnic Polish distrust of the Lithuanians and Vilnius government will not be easily overcome."[49] The same can be said about the Lithuanian distrust of the endogenous Poles. In 1994, the Warsaw government went far in alleviating Lithuanian fears by signing a treaty accepting the status of current boundaries with its neighbors. Especially during the early transition period, however, the relationship of Lithuanian statesmen with various representatives of local Polish communities was rife with debate and negotiation over political rights.[50]

Sensitivity to Polish concerns evaporated when most local government functionaries and citizens of Polish and Russian districts supported Moscow's conspirators in the coup d'état of August 19, 1991. Following Boris Yeltsin's example in Russia, the Lithuanian government appointed governors to Polish and Russian districts, suspended local government soviets, and established a direct rule. New elections to local government councils were scheduled for September 1992 but actually took place in January and February 1993.

The imposition of direct rule over the Poles made waves in both Lithuania and Poland. President Lech Wałesa condemned the action.

High-level consultations between the two countries resumed only in fall 1992 when Prime Minister Abišala met with Polish prime minister Hanna Suchocka in Warsaw. In defense of Lithuanian policy, Abišala asked about Poland's treatment of the Lithuanian minority in Poland, which does not provide native-language education at the upper levels, has native-language instruction only as a "complementary" subject in some schools, and does not recognize the Lithuanian language even in the Lithuanian district of Punsk. Later, both sides agreed to the establishment of a common free-trade area and cooperation in transportation and some other economic matters and determined to "seek the establishment of possibilities for the Lithuanian minority in Poland and the Polish minority in Lithuania fully to satisfy their linguistic, cultural, religious and educational requirements."[51]

The greatest progress for Poles in Lithuania has been in the field of education. Since 1990, the Polish school network has been expanded. In 1991, Polish professors at Vilnius University and others established a private Polish university that aims primarily to prepare teachers for Polish schools.[52] In 1992–1993, the university had 100 students, that is, less than the number of Lithuanian Poles studying in Poland under various other auspices. It is supported by donations from Polish compatriots in Europe and North America but has not been accredited. Instead, the Lithuanians have suggested establishing a Polish studies center at Vilnius. The Pedagogical University of Vilnius already trains teachers for Polish and Russian schools. Some Polish intellectuals, however, want their own institution.

Changes in parliament and the election of Brazauskas as president very likely assure Polish minority leaders of greater attention to their concerns in the future. In the past, the Democratic Labor party has shown more sympathy than Sąjūdis to Polish demands. In turn, it received the overwhelming support of Polish districts during the 1992 campaign. (About 90 percent of the Polish vote was cast for Brazauskas in Šalčininkai district.) This may move the new president to reward his supporters.

The Jews

A Soviet census conducted in 1989 found that 12,400 Jews live in Lithuania. Emancipation of the Jewish minority began before the establishment of Sąjūdis. In 1987, at the dawn of perestroika in Lithuania, Jewish and Lithuanian intellectuals persuaded the republic's Communist leadership to accept the establishment of a Jewish cultural center.[53] Under the Soviets, Jewish cultural life was generally suppressed. Lithuania's Jewish museum and theater were closed down, and the Hebrew language was outlawed.

Several leaders of the Jewish community from the beginning took a very active part in the national resurgence movement and in the leadership of Sąjūdis. After the declaration of independence, the parliament made special efforts to secure and restore the position of the oldest Lithuanian minority.

Under the leadership of Landsbergis, whose parents had saved a Jewish family during the Hitler occupation period, the parliament addressed concerns deemed important to the Jewish community and to the restoration of Lithuanian-Jewish relations. It based this move on the recognition of the ugly truth about the Lithuanian role in the Jewish tragedy. On May 8, 1990, the legislature adopted a statement "on behalf of the Lithuanian nation" in which it acknowledged "with deep, heart-felt sorrow that among the executioners who served the Nazi occupants citizens of Lithuania also were to be found. There is no excuse or possible justification nor can there be for this crime, nor can there be any statute of limitations for crimes committed against the Jewish nation either in Lithuania or beyond its borders"[54]

The statement condemned "without reservations the genocide of the Jewish nation during the years of Hitlerite occupation of Lithuania" and urged governmental and societal agencies to help create "the most favorable conditions for Lithuania's Jews similar to those of other national communities, [and] to reestablish and develop educational, scientific, religious and other institutions." The Republic of Lithuania, the statement concluded, "shall secure eternal memory of the Jewish victims of genocide." The parliament then ended with the statement that "Lithuania will not tolerate any manifestations of anti-semitism."

A number of concrete measures also were approved by the legislature. On May 2, 1990, a law was passed to legally rehabilitate the deportees of 1940–1953 and the resisters to Soviet or Nazi occupation but not persons who had "participated in the genocide crimes as well as in the massacres and tortures of unarmed people."[55] Another law, adopted in April 1992, provided for prosecution of people charged with such crimes.[56] An agreement was signed with the United States establishing cooperation in this matter. Finally, the law on citizenship, originally passed November 3, 1989, and revised December 5, 1991, excluded from eligibility for citizenship all "persons who had committed crimes against humanity or acts of genocide" (Article 13[1]).[57]

To preserve the memory of Jewish communal life in Lithuania, by an ordinance of November 27, 1991, the Presidium of the parliament requested local government agencies to restore Jewish cemetery grounds, desecrated both under Nazi and Soviet rule. In addition, the parliament established September 23, the day of the liquidation of the ghetto in Vilnius in 1943, as the annual day for official commemoration of the Jewish

Holocaust in Lithuania. In 1992, the solemn commemoration also included recognition by the government of Israel of Lithuanians who had saved the Jews during the Nazi occupation.

The implementation of the rehabilitation law of 1990, however, created a controversy that damaged Lithuania's international reputation. On September 5, 1991, in a front-page article, the *New York Times* charged, on the basis of information provided by the Simon Wiesenthal Center, that Lithuanian agencies had been issuing documents of rehabilitation to persons who had taken part in mass murders of the Jews during World War II. Five cases were cited. Similar articles distrustful of Lithuanian actions and explanations appeared in North America and Europe. TASS, the news agency of the Russian Federation, on September 6 claimed that the Lithuanians had rehabilitated 35,000 people previously "sentenced by the Soviets as Nazi war criminals." Lithuanian authorities denied any intentional violation of the law and decried as utterly false the charge of wholesale exoneration of war criminals. The Presidium of the Lithuanian parliament declared statements such as those released by TASS to be "disinformation." Both Lithuanian authorities and Western correspondents found that KGB documents, some tampered with by the Soviet security agency, were the primary source of the criticism against Lithuania.[58] According to the *New York Times*, Lithuanian institutions had processed more than 50,000 cases before September 1992 and mistakes could have been made.[59] A Jewish Lithuanian leader implied that the KGB's "Jewish section" aimed at creating conflict between Lithuanians and Jews.[60] In November 1991, President Landsbergis, meeting with U.S. Jewish leaders in New York, labeled the accusations made by the Western press "unjust," adding that 500 applications for rehabilitation had been turned down.[61] He allowed that there might nonetheless have been oversights and promised cooperation with foreign governments and Jewish organizations to avoid future mistakes. According to the Lithuanian Central Prosecutor's Office, in three and a half years approximately 30,000 applications for rehabilitation were examined and approximately 27,000 certificates of rehabilitation issued.[62]

In early December, Acting President Brazauskas announced that five mistakenly issued rehabilitation decisions were revoked. The Wiesenthal Center in Jerusalem had repeatedly asked for the list of rehabilitated persons, claiming, "We have thousands and thousands of names of Lithuanians involved in killing Jews. We need to know which of them have been pardoned so we can ask that those pardons be revoked."[63] Brazauskas's election, in the view of the center, opened "a new day" in the investigation.

The outgoing Lithuanian officials explained that they did not publish lists of rehabilitated persons because the law did not provide for publication and because publication would implicate that the persons listed had once been considered or suspected of a crime. They suggested that they would check the Wiesenthal Center's list, if it could be supplied, against that of rehabilitated persons to assure that no mistakes had been made. An Israeli commission was invited to come to Lithuania to discuss problems related to rehabilitation. The press in Lithuania did not show much interest in the controversy in conformity with a widely held view that "the entire matter [was] being blown out of proportion as a result of foreign pressures."[64]

In the meantime, the Jewish cultural center in Vilnius came alive with professional and cultural activities. A synagogue was also opened, although at first it did not draw much attendance. A rabbi from England was appointed the chief rabbi of Vilnius to organize religious life as well as rabbinical training for the western region of the former Soviet Union. A Jewish museum, preschool, and elementary school have been established and two Jewish-oriented newspapers are being published, one in Yiddish and the other in English. On March 22, 1993, a center for Judaic studies was opened at the University of Vilnius. The community is active in politics through several civic groups, and a leader of the Vilnius community has been elected to the new parliament from Landsbergis's coalition.

Yet despite improvement of the minority's condition, Jews continue to emigrate, usually to Israel. Although emigration has decreased, in 1992 only 5,000 Jews were left in Lithuania. Jewish community leaders have said that "state-sponsored anti-semitism, prevalent in Soviet state policy," no longer exists but that occasional anti-Semitic expressions are heard or appear in print.[65] Some of these have related to alleged Jewish collaboration with the Communists in 1940–1941. In a Times-Mirror poll conducted in 1991, the Lithuanians scored relatively low on hostility to the Jews. Ten percent said their opinion of the Jews was unfavorable, as compared to 6 percent in the United States and 26 percent in Russia.[66]

GEOPOLITICS AND THE POST-COMMUNIST FUTURE

The collapse of the Soviet empire and of the Communist regime was an event of historical proportions, but for the Baltic peoples it only partially diminished the perceived threat to their national survival. Communism was gone, but Russia remained. Would the new Russian Federation, successor to the Communist as well as to the Tsarist empire, pursue similar strategic goals in the Baltic region? Would it retreat or seek once again to control the area? Ultimately, Baltic independence hinges on the capacity of the Russian Federation to become a mature democracy that is able to contain expansionist claims.

To facilitate this process, Lithuania is committed to developing a working relationship with Russia, but it has also sought to secure its independent position by turning to the West. Landsbergis and the Sąjūdis government began the process and rushed to anchor Lithuania in the Western international network. Lithuania thus joined the World Bank, the International Monetary Fund, the European Bank for Reconstruction and Development, the Organization on Security and Cooperation in Europe, and the European Council. Under Brazauskas, the trend has continued. Lithuania became an associate member of the European Community (EU) and of NATO's Partnership for Peace. Economic and diplomatic help, too, came from these organizations and their powerful sponsors, such as the United States, which helped with agricultural loans and humanitarian aid. Visits by former president Richard Nixon, Vice President Dan Quayle, and many other public figures drew attention to Lithuania's needs. Initiatives by U.S. Lithuanian businesses brought large companies, such as Phillip Morris, to invest in Lithuanian industry. Technical expertise and cooperation in economics, education, defense, and management were also extended by governmental and private agencies. The crucial issue concerning Baltic security and independence was reflected, however, in the policies of NATO.

The Baltic association with NATO began shortly after the international recognition of Lithuania, Latvia, and Estonia in August–September 1991. In October, the Baltic states were admitted to "associate" affiliation, and in November the organization established diplomatic links with Lithuania. NATO naval vessels, including some from the United States, visited Klaipėda and other Baltic ports, and security conferences were held in Baltic capitals. Some Lithuanian officers were trained in military schools of NATO members. Visitors from the Baltic states, beginning with ministers of defense and ending with parliament members and journalists, were invited to Brussels. NATO officers, both military and diplomatic, also visited the region, including the Russian Federation. Nonetheless, the Western powers have been divided on extending NATO membership to successor states of the USSR. Such a move would antagonize Russia and, it is feared, could undermine the strength of prodemocratic forces there. But where does such policy leave the Baltic states?

On a visit to Lithuania, the commander of NATO forces in northern Europe, General G. Johnson, explained that NATO looks at the Baltic region as a bridge of stability and security between Western Europe and Russia.[67] NATO is interested in the stability of this Baltic bridge, he suggested, but at the same time the Baltic states should maintain closer diplomatic relations with Russia.

Thus, the Baltic region is again perceived as a transitional land, an intermediary, between Russia and Europe. In the past the region has been too small and too weak—even with Scandinavian help—to assert itself between the East and West. It has another chance now, however, to find a stronger political niche as part of a larger "Nordic bloc."[68]

Scandinavia's Nordic Council cautiously took the initiative to strengthen Lithuania's chances. Sweden was the first Western country to establish an embassy in Vilnius in the fall of 1991. The conservative Swedish premier, Carl Bildt, said that Swedish policy toward the Baltics would be different from that of 1939–1940, when Soviet Russia moved in to occupy the region without any comment from neighboring Scandinavia. One of the reasons for the rise of Scandinavian interest in the Baltic states is to provide security against the possible rebirth of a new Russian empire. More important, the driving goal is to protect the ecological system of the polluted Baltic Sea, which these small coastal nations share. That effort involves not only the Swedes, the Danes, the Finns, the Germans, and the Balts, but also the Russians.

Political, economic, and military cooperation among the three Baltic countries has been growing as well, since they share the same problems and desire to become more integrated among Western countries. Their independence movements focused on temporary Baltic unity against a common enemy but have taken diverse paths of development, especially in terms of economic policies. The most significant international developments, after the pull-out of Russian troops, were the treaties with Poland and Belarus in which the countries pledged mutual respect for each others' territorial sovereignty.

Finally, Lithuania has established a small security force, an army consisting of some 10,000 troops to help with peacetime stability and to provide at least a symbolic element of deterrence to outside powers.[69] Formally, the army was established on November 19, 1991, and military service was made compulsory for young males. A fraction of the national budget is spent to support this psychologically valuable symbol of national sovereignty and the willingness to defend it.

WHICH WAY: DEMOCRACY OR ITS FACADE?

After centuries of oppression and violence, the little country of Lithuania again finds itself between East and West, between authoritarian traditions and a democratic future. Today's new leaders have to make choices often as difficult as those that Lithuania's first statesmen had to make over fifty years ago. President Algirdas Brazauskas saw Lithuania's "future in Europe," built on "the historically proven model of Western democracy, economy, and culture."[70] Indeed, since the demise of the Soviet Union, the Republic of Lithuania has made great strides in shaking the administrative legacies of totalitarian rule and creating a modern, democratic state based on the rule of law. A series of far-reaching and comprehensive legislation was passed in the ensuing five years of transition that aimed at strengthening the traditional cornerstones of any democratic system. New laws established the rights of the free press, reorganized the judiciary, strengthened the mechanisms for fair representation, and revamped the civil code.

New treaties and institutions have also helped to secure Lithuania's place in the international world order. Treaties with Poland, Latvia, and Belarus were signed that formally established the legitimacy of current borders between the signatories and strengthened the position of Lithuania as a new and unitary state. At the same time, Lithuania's new leaders actively sought integration with international institutions of the Western world. Lithuania was accepted unanimously into the Council of Europe, joined the Organization for Security and Cooperation in Europe, the United Nations, and other international organizations. In spring 1995, Lithuania was also accepted as an associate member of the European Community and within roughly one year complied with the most worrisome requirement for eventual full membership by extending the right to own land in Lithuania to all EU members. Finally, after much hesitation about the possibility of alienating Russia, the three Baltic states were also admitted into the Partnership for Peace, the NATO plan of cooperation with Eastern Europe.

While significant achievements have been made in the shift from authoritarianism and the East, transitions of such magnitude take time. In Lithuania, they are hindered as much as from within as from economic and political pressures from without. Corruption and the flagrant abuse of power threatened to undercut society's faith in its elected and appointed officials and evidence of malfeasance abounded. Throughout the first five years after independence, cases were made of alleged "softness" of the courts toward organized crime wherein judges dismissed or lowered charges against alleged racketeers that prompted public fears of corruption. Despite a functioning and active parliament, there were still rightful concerns that the most important political decisions were being made behind closed doors, especially concerning privatization and economic issues. The most celebrated instance cost the prime minister, Adolfas Sleževičius, his job.[71]

In December 1995, two of the largest new commercial banks were stopped in their attempts to merge by accusations of insolvency. Their top executives were temporarily arrested and funds were eventually frozen while hundreds of investors decried the loss of their funds. In February 1996, it was discovered that the prime minister was also an investor but had transferred his own account before closing the bank down. This flagrant use of insider knowledge by public officials for their personal gain was endemic throughout the former Soviet Union. It has encumbered the process of cultural reorientation in Lithuania that is critical to development of a genuine respect for the rule of law on which every successful and democratically capitalist nation is based.

With each passing generation, the old patronage culture of the Soviet era will fade, but in the meantime, many in Russia would see Lithuania reintegrated by then. Talk of regaining the former Soviet republics and recovering the former empire is still common among officials in the Russian military establishment.[72] As Lithuanians train their sights westward, they hope never again to face the loss of their freedom. But if they do, most are sure to rebel once again.

NOTES

1. See Kazimiera Prunskienė, *Užkulisiai* (Vilnius: Politika, 1992), p. 27.

2. See report in *Atgimimas,* February 17, 1993, p. 3.

3. *Lietuvos rytas,* January 27, 1993, p. 4; March 15, 1990, p. 1.

4. *Respublika,* July 31, 1990, p. 1.

5. Ibid.

6. For text see *Draugas* (Chicago), August 21, 1990; also Vytautas Landsbergis, *Laisvės byla, 1990–1991* (Vilnius: Lietuvos aidas, 1992), p. 130.

7. Text in *Darbininkas* (Brooklyn, N.Y.), October 5, 1990.

8. *New York Times,* October 18, 1992, p. 5.

9. See Jeff Trimble, "New Act, Old Tricks," *U.S. News & World Report,* February 8, 1993, pp. 42–44.

10. *Chicago Tribune,* June 28, 1992, pp. 1ff.; *Tiesa,* December 31, 1992, p. 7.

11. Cf. Terry D. Clark's study of roll call voting, "Coalition Realignment in the Supreme Council of the Republic of Lithuania and the Fall of the Vagnorius Government," *Journal of Baltic Studies* 24, no. 1 (1993): 53–63.

12. Results in *Lietuvos rytas,* May 26, 1992, p. 1.

13. *Lietuvos rytas,* June 18, 1992, p. 1; returns by district in *Lietuvos aidas,* June 16, 1992, p. 4.

14. *Wall Street Journal,* October 27, 1992, p. 1.

15. *Tiesa,* October 27, 1992, p. 1.

16. See *Atgimimas,* no. 49, December 15, 1992, p. 4. Some district results were contested and appealed to the Electoral Commission and the Supreme Court. The court disqualified three Sąjūdis victories, thus adding to the Democratic Labor party's majority three additional seats.

17. See text in *Tiesa,* October 27, 1992, p. 1.

18. Quoted in *New York Times,* November 17, 1992, p. 4.

19. Quoted in *Chicago Tribune,* December 14, 1992, p. 2.

20. *New York Times,* November 22, 1992, sec. 4, p. 2.

21. Results, by district, in *Tiesa,* February 17, 1993, p. 3.

22. Report by Acting President Algirdas Brazauskas, *Lietuvos rytas,* January 22, 1993, p. 2; *Tiesa,* December 7, 1992, pp. 39–40. More optimistic was the report of Abišala's government. See "Lithuania: Memorandum of Economic Policies," *Baltic News* 11 (1992): 5–15. Production data from Brazauskas's report.

23. For texts, see *Lietuvos Respublikos Aukščiausios Tarybos ir Lietuvos Respublikos Aukščiausios Tarybos Prezidiumo Dokumentų Rinkinys* 3 (Vilnius: Valstybinis

leidybos centras, 1991), pp. 108–117; 354–359; 370–375. Hereafter cited as *Rinkinys 3*.

24. See M. Laurinkus, parliamentary deputy and former Sąjūdis leader, *Gimtasis kraštas*, December 3–9, 1992, p. 3.

25. *Chicago Tribune*, November 23, 1992, p. 4.

26. Academician E. Vilkas, cited in ibid., p. 14.

27. *Rinkinys 3*, pp. 29–42.

28. Ibid., pp. 245–248.

29. See *Lietuvos rytas*, January 23, 1993, p. 1.

30. Government report, text in *Atgimimas*, no. 50, December 22, 1992, p. 5.

31. See footnote 22.

32. *Lietuvos aidas*, October 10, 1994, p. 3.

33. Lecture at a conference in Tulsa, Oklahoma. Quoted by Georgie Ann Geyer, "Russia Trying to Catch Up," *Tulsa World*, February 24, 1993, p. 11.

34. Quoted in *Politika* 1 (1993): 13.

35. *Lietuvos rytas*, January 26, 1993, p. 4.

36. For the impact of the economic and political crisis on Lithuania's people, see John Budris, "Is This What the 15 People at the TV Tower Died For?" *The New York Times Magazine*, August 2, 1992, pp. 34ff.

37. *Tiesa*, January 30, 1992, p. 4.

38. *Tiesa*, November 3, 1992, p. 1.

39. Lithuanian text in, among others, *Lietuvos aidas*, October 15, 1992, pp. 5–8. English translation in *Baltic News* (Vilnius) 10 (1992): 5–18.

40. For general surveys, see Bohdan Nahaylo and Victor Swoboda, *Soviet Disunion: A History of the Nationalities Problem in the USSR* (New York: The Free Press, 1989); Robert Conquest, ed., *The Last Empire* (Stanford: Hoover Institution Press, 1986).

41. Recent discussions of the standards and limitations of self-determination include Morton H. Halperin and David Scheffer with Patricia L. Small, *Self-Determination in the New World Order* (Washington, D.C.: Carnegie Endowment for International Peace, 1992), pp. 16ff.; Allen Buchanan, *Secession: The Mortality of Political Divorce from Fort Sumter to Lithuania and Quebec* (Boulder: Westview Press, 1991); also Amitai Etzioni, "The Evils of Self-Determination," *Foreign Policy* (Winter 1992).

42. Demography explains the difference. During the half century of Soviet rule, Moscow facilitated an increase of the Russian population in Estonia to 30 percent and the decline of the ethnic Estonian population from 90 to 62 percent. In Latvia, the Russian diaspora grew to 34 percent of the total population, while the ethnic Latvians sank from 75 to 52 percent. In Lithuania, the Russian percentage rose to 9.4, but of those only about 7 percent were immigrants or their Lithuanian-born descendants. As a result, the Lithuanians do not feel overwhelmed by the Russian minority or threatened as a national community. Their response to the Russian minority, therefore, has been more generous than that of the Estonians and Latvians.

43. Texts in Supreme Council of the Republic of Lithuania, *Selected Anthology of Institutional, Economic and Financial Legislation* (Vilnius: State Publishing Center, 1991), pp. 60–69; amended law on citizenship in *Parliamentary Record*, no. 1, pp. 2–12.

44. For Germany's naturalization requirements, see German Information Center, *Focus on German Citizenship and Naturalization* (New York: German Information Center, February 1993).

45. Data on minority demography, education, and so on in this section are found in Ministry of Foreign Affairs of the Republic of Lithuania, Department of Nationalities, *National Minorities in Lithuania* (Vilnius: Center of National Research of Lithuania, 1992).

46. See *Atgimimas*, no. 39, October 5, 1992, p. 11.

47. Data in ibid., April 5–12, 1992, p. 7.

48. Interview in *Lietuvos rytas*, February 6, 1993, p. 11.

49. Stephen R. Burant, "Polish-Lithuanian Relations," *Problems of Communism* (May–June 1991): 67–84.

50. See "Poles in Lithuania," in U.S. Congress, Commission on Security and Cooperation in Europe, *Minority Rights* (Washington, D.C., n.d.). Further cited as *Minority Rights*. Also Burant, "Polish-Lithuanian Relations," pp. 67–84. The conflict can be traced also through legislation, resolutions, and decrees passed by the parliament and published in *Rinkinys*. Newspapers also provided facts for the story recounted here.

51. Text in *Tiesa*, January 12, 1993, p. 2.

52. *Lietuvos rytas*, February 5, 1993, p. 15; *Narod Polski*, September 20, 1992, p. 13; *Atgimimas*, no. 45, November 16, 1992, p. 11.

53. See *Tėviškės žiburiai* (Toronto), February 12, 1992, p. 7.

54. Text in *Rinkinys 1*, p. 369.

55. Text in ibid., p. 125.

56. *Tiesa*, September 18, 1992, p. 6.

57. Text in *Parliamentary Record*, no. 1.

58. *Los Angeles Times*, September 8, 1991, p. 6. For the text of the statement by the Presidium of the Lithuanian parliament see *Rinkinys 3*, p. 467. The statement also quotes TASS.

59. *New York Times*, December 25, 1992, p. 7.

60. *Los Angeles Times*, September 8, 1991, p. 6.

61. *New York Times*, November 17, 1992.

62. U.S. Congress, 103d Congress, 1st sess., Joint Committee Print. S. Prt. 103–7, *Country Reports in Human Rights Practices for 1992*, Report submitted to the Committee on Foreign Relations, U.S. Senate, and the Committee on Foreign Affairs, U.S. House of Representatives, by the Department of State, Washington, D.C., 1993, p. 833; *Lietuvos aidas*, December 3, 1992, p. 4. Data for Lithuanian Prosecutor's Office from interview with Senior Prosecutor Vidmantas Vaicekauskas in Vilnius. See *Draugas* (Chicago), April 13, 1993, pp. 3–4.

63. *New York Times*, December 25, 1992, p. 7.

64. Ibid.

65. *Lietuvos aidas* (Elta), December 8, 1992, p. 4.

66. Times-Mirror Center for People and the Press, *The Pulse of Europe*, September 16, 1991, p. Q64; also chart of "Opinion of Jews by Country."

67. See *Lietuvos rytas*, February 12, 1993, p. 1.

68. See John Fitzmaurice, *The Baltic: A Regional Future?* (New York: St. Martin's Press, 1992), pp. 150ff.

69. On the military see *Lietuvos aidas*, February 10, 1993, p. 4; *Lietuvos rytas*, February 9 and 12, 1993, pp. 2 and 1; also March 3, 1993, pp. 16–17.

70. Presidential inaugural speech, text in *Tiesa*, February 26, 1993, p. 3.

71. See Presidential Decree in *Atgimimas*, February 1, 1996, p. 1.

72. See *Los Angeles Times*, July 13, 1994, p. 2. Also, Stephen S. Blank, "Reform and Revolution in Russian Defense Economics," *Slavic Military Studies* 8, no. 4: 691–717.

· Selected Bibliography ·

The Baltic Review (Tallin : P&S Ltd., 1993–). Periodical.

The Baltic States in Peace and War, 1917–1945 (University Park: Pennsylvania State University Press, c. 1978).

Emancipation and Interdependence (Stockholm: Centre for Baltic Studies, Stockholm University: 1994).

Kirby, David G. *Northern Europe in the Early Modern Period* (White Plains, N.Y.: Longman, 1993).

_____. *The Baltic World 1772–1993* (White Plains, N.Y.: Longman, 1995).

Lainela, Seija. *The Baltic Economies in Transition* (Helsinki: Bank of Finland, 1994).

Levin, Dov. *Baltic Jews Under the Soviets, 1940–1946* (Jerusalem: Centre for Research and Documentation of East European Jewry, Avraham Harman Institute of Contemporary Jewry, Hebrew University of Jerusalem, 1994).

Lieven, Anatol. *The Baltic Revolution.* 2nd ed. (New Haven: Yale University Press, c. 1994).

Misiunas, Romuald J. *Baltijos valstybes* (Baltic States. Lithuanian) Leid. 1. (Vilnius: Mintis, 1992).

_____. *The Baltic States: Years of Dependence, 1940–1990.* Expanded and updated ed. (Berkeley: University of California Press, c. 1993).

_____. *The Archives of the Lithuanian KGB* (Koln: Bundesinstitut fur Ostwissenschaftliche und Internationale Studien, c. 1994).

Personal Freedom and National Resurgence (Washington, D.C.: Paideia Press & Council for Research in Values and Philosophy, c. 1994).

Rowell, S. C. *Lithuania Ascending* (Cambridge: Cambridge University Press, 1994).

Sabaliunas, Leonas. *Lithuania, 1939–1940: A Nation in Crisis* (New York, 1963).

_____. *Lithuania in Crisis* (Bloomington, Ind.: Indiana University Press, c. 1972).

Senn, Alfred Erich. *The Emergence of Modern Lithuania* (New York: Columbia University Press, 1959).

_____. *The Great Powers: Lithuania and the Vilna Question, 1920–1928* (Leiden: E. J. Brill, 1966).

_____. *Lithuania Awakening* (Berkeley: University of California Press, c. 1990).

Thaden, Edward C. *Russia's Western Borderlands, 1710–1870* (Princeton, N.J.: Princeton University Press, c. 1984).

▪ About the Book ▪
and Authors

In 1990, Lithuania became the first Soviet republic to break with the Communist empire by declaring the restitution of political independence. Depicting a country at the crossroads of imperial designs, Vardys and Sedaitis trace the history, development, and ultimate triumph of the Lithuanian nation.

The late **V. Stanley Vardys** was professor of political science at the University of Oklahoma.

Judith B. Sedaitis is research associate with the Center for International Security and Arms Control at Stanford University.

· Index ·